From Backtest to Live Execution

Gateways, Safeguards, and Cutover Practices in Electronic Markets

Thomas V. Trex

Published by NobleTrex Press

For permissions and other inquiries, write to:
P.O. Box 3132, Framingham, MA 01701, USA

Contents

Introduction

Markets reward clarity, speed, and restraint in equal measure. Between a promising backtest and a profitable, well-behaved live strategy lies a corridor of engineering and governance choices that determine whether orders are merely sent or actually stewarded with precision and accountability. This book, *From Backtest to Live Execution: Gateways, Safeguards, and Cutover Practices in Electronic Markets*, is a field guide to that corridor. It treats trading not as a single algorithmic artifact but as an operational system whose success depends on determinism, instrumentation, and an ethos of safety under uncertainty.

Our organizing thesis is simple: if a result cannot be traced, reconstructed, and reversed, it is not ready for production. The path from research to live capital therefore demands three pillars. First, faithful observation of the market — understanding microstructure, time, and data with enough fidelity to replay events and reason about causality. Second, disciplined transformation of strategy intent into compliant, recoverable order flow, with guardrails that fail closed. Third, deliberate cutover practices that recognize the market's state machine and treat deployment as a sequence of reversible experiments rather than a single leap.

The journey begins with market foundations, because live execution is only as sound as the model of the venue it inhabits. We lay out order book mechanics, auction procedures, and queue dynamics that shape fill quality; survey venue fragmentation across equities, futures, options, FX, and crypto; and review the regulatory scaffolding — from SEC and FINRA to MiFID II and exchange rules — that informs market access, testing obligations, and reporting. We also encode the operational reality of trading states, halts, and price bands, and anchor all subsequent logic in the mundane but indispensable world of identifiers, tick-size tables, calendars, and corporate actions.

With the stage set, we turn to data and strategy validation. Here the emphasis is on point-in-time correctness and bias control, not just statistical elegance. We design deterministic ingestion and normalization pipelines, confront look-ahead and survivorship pitfalls, and make transaction costs, slippage, and market impact first-class citizens in forecast evaluation. Robust backtests are treated as reproducible experiments: walk-forward splits, cross-validation across regimes, latency and cancel models that reflect venue behavior, and multiple-testing controls that temper exuberance. We close the loop by decomposing returns, stress-testing sensitivities, and defining crisp exit thresholds for capital allocation.

Connectivity and market data infrastructure bridge observation to action. We treat time as a compliance surface, specifying PTP and NTP hierarchies, drift monitoring, and clock-quality budgets from colocation cross-connects to archival stores. Feed handlers reconcile snapshots with incrementals to maintain gap-free books at microsecond scales, while replay systems provide clock-accurate playback and synthetic event injections for drills and scenario analysis. Security is integral rather than afterthought: mutual TLS, hardware-backed secrets, segmentation, and least-privilege patterns protect both data and control planes. Performance work focuses on throughput and tail latency under production loads, because headroom at the median is a comforting illusion.

Order gateways and session management translate strategy intent into venue semantics. We define the order lifecycle and its invariants across gateway and exchange views, then compare FIX with native protocols such as OUCH, BOE, and iLink 3. Session recovery, sequencing, and idempotency are treated as design constraints, not patches. Throttling and flow control satisfy venue limits while preserving fairness, and drop copy paths enable real-time reconciliation and early fault detection when primary and shadow views diverge.

Risk controls and safeguards provide layered defense. Pre-trade checks enforce collars, size and notional limits, duplicate detection, and cancel-on-disconnect logic. Credit, position, and exposure controls aggregate in real time and trigger adaptive pacing or automated shutdowns when breached. Self-trade prevention reduces both regulatory and PnL risk. Firm-level kill switches define scope, mass-cancel mechanics, and post-event sanity checks, while independent verification through shadow paths confirms that controls are operating as designed.

Reliability and testing culminate in production readiness. We construct immutable, time-correlated logs, metrics, traces, and audit trails to power incident response and compliance. High availability, failover, and stateless design anchor uptime targets; disaster recovery planning turns RTO and RPO from slogans into rehearsed runbooks. Automated and performance tests catch regressions before the market does; exchange certification and conformance keep systems eligible to trade; and chaos engineering validates recovery paths when dependencies fail or clocks skew.

Finally, deployment, cutover, and governance orchestrate the move from paper to production. We align CI/CD with change control and segregation of duties; separate deployment from activation using configuration management and feature flags; and plan releases with explicit entry and backout criteria. Staged rollouts progress from shadow to canary to general availability, with volume ramping and automatic brakes on guardrail breaches. Session-aware cutovers respect auctions, halts, holidays, and freeze periods. Post-deployment validation closes the loop with dashboards, reconciliations, regulatory evidence, and periodic model and governance reviews.

This book is written for quantitative researchers, algorithmic developers, site reliability and network engineers, risk managers, and compliance officers who share custody of live trading. You can read linearly or enter at the chapter most relevant to your current bottleneck; cross-references and consistent terminology aim to keep context intact. Above all, the pages that follow treat production as a discipline. A backtest is a story we tell ourselves; live trading is a story the market tells us. Our goal is to make those stories rhyme — safely, repeatably, and with humility.

Chapter 1

Market Foundations

Before a single line of strategy code hits a live gateway, your orders must survive a far harsher environment: fragmented venues, hidden auctions, shifting market states, and rulebooks written by both regulators and matching engines. This chapter maps that terrain so that every later design choice-from symbol master files to kill-switches-rests on a precise understanding of how modern electronic markets actually work minute by minute and packet by packet.

1.1 Market Microstructure Basics

When you move from a research notebook to a live trading system, you are stepping into a mechanical world with its own rules. Prices do not change in a smooth line; they jump between discrete ticks. Orders do not magically "get filled at the mid"; they join queues, wait their turn, and sometimes never trade at all. This inner machinery is what market microstructure is about.

In this section we will build an intuitive and practical picture of that machinery, with three core goals:

- Understand how a modern electronic limit order book is organized.

- See how priority rules determine *who* trades first at a given price.
- Connect auction mechanisms and state changes to the fills your strategy actually receives.

Throughout, keep one question in mind: *If my backtest assumes frictionless execution at a given price, what has to be true in the real order book for that to happen?*

From "The Price" to a Book of Orders

Most basic finance education treats "the price" of an instrument as if there were only one number at each point in time. In reality, at any instant there is a *set* of prices: the prices at which different participants are willing to buy or sell, each with a corresponding quantity.

The standard way electronic markets organize these intentions is with a *central limit order book* (often abbreviated as LOB or just "the book"):

- A **bid** is an order to buy up to a certain quantity at a specified price or better.
- An **ask** (or **offer**) is an order to sell up to a certain quantity at a specified price or better.

The book collects all active bids and asks and groups them by price level. On one side you have bids, sorted from highest to lowest price. On the other side you have asks, sorted from lowest to highest price.

Two special prices are worth naming:

- The **best bid** is the highest price anyone is currently willing to pay.
- The **best ask** is the lowest price anyone is currently willing to sell at.

The difference between these two is the *spread*. Many naive backtests assume execution at the *midprice*, which is halfway between the best bid and best ask. In practice, unless your order is aggressively crossing the spread and there is enough liquidity, you will trade either at the best bid (to sell) or best ask (to buy), not at the mid.

The important leap is to stop thinking in terms of a single number and start seeing the full ladder of prices and quantities on both sides. Your order interacts with this ladder, not with an abstract price series.

Price–Time Priority and the Meaning of Queue Position

Within each price level, the exchange needs a rule to decide which orders trade first when an opposite-side order arrives. The most common rule in modern electronic markets is *price–time priority*:

- Better prices trade before worse prices.
- At the same price, earlier orders trade before later orders.

You can think of each price level as a queue:

- For the bid side, the first place in the queue at a given price belongs to the earliest buy order submitted at that price that is still active.
- For the ask side, the first place in the queue at a given price belongs to the earliest sell order at that price that is still active.

When a new aggressive order arrives that can trade at that price, it starts consuming the queue from the front:

- The oldest resting orders at that price fill first.
- If the aggressive order is large, it may consume several resting orders in sequence.
- If it is larger than the total resting quantity at that price, it may sweep several price levels.

Why Queue Position Matters to Your Backtest

Suppose your backtest says: "When the best bid is 100.00 and the best ask is 100.01, I send a limit buy at 100.00 and get filled on the next trade that touches 100.00." This implicitly assumes you are at the *front of the queue* at 100.00.

In live trading, that is almost never true. When your limit buy at 100.00 arrives:

- There may already be 10,000 shares of buy interest ahead of you at 100.00.
- Trades at 100.00 will first fill that 10,000 shares.
- Your order will not fill until the *cumulative* traded volume at 100.00 after your arrival exceeds the quantity ahead of you.

Two backtests that both use the same historical trade and quote data can give very different results depending on whether they model this queue effect. For any strategy that posts passive liquidity (for example, market making or spread capture), accurate modeling of queue position is often the line between realistic and meaningless results.

Visualizing the Limit Order Book and Order States

To make these ideas concrete, it helps to visualize the book as two ladders (bids and asks) and to track how an individual order moves through different states: submitted, resting in the queue, partially filled, fully filled, or cancelled.

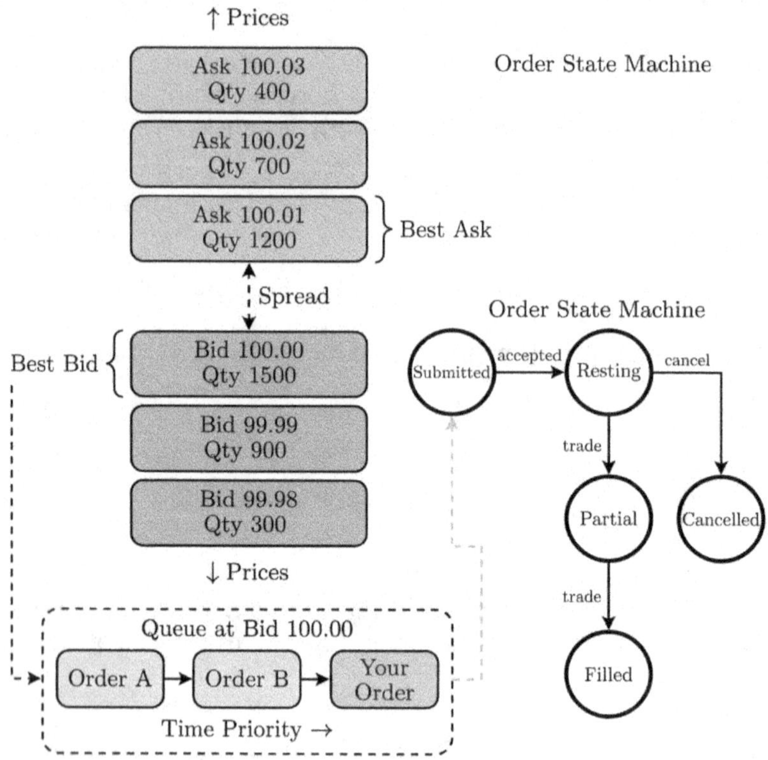

This picture captures three microstructure facts that your systems must respect:

- At each price, there is an ordered queue of resting volume.
- Your order joins that queue when accepted, at a specific position that depends on its arrival time.
- Over its life, your order moves through well-defined states, driven by events in the market and by your own cancels or modifications.

A robust backtest and a robust live gateway both need to maintain a similar state machine internally. Otherwise, your simulated fills and your real fills will diverge in non-obvious ways.

Order Types and How They Touch the Book

So far we have implicitly discussed one kind of order: a simple limit order that either joins the book or trades against it. In practice, most venues support a family of related order types. Understanding what they do *to the book* is crucial for both modeling and risk control.

Market Orders

A **market order** is an instruction to trade a specified quantity immediately at the best prices available, without specifying a price limit. A buy market order will hit the best ask, then the next best ask, and so on, until its quantity is fully filled or the book is exhausted.

- Advantage: highest chance of immediate execution.
- Cost: uncertain average execution price; can suffer from slippage, especially in thin markets.

In a backtest that assumes all market orders trade at the last midprice, you are ignoring the very mechanism that determines their cost: the actual shape of the book.

Limit Orders

A **limit order** specifies both a quantity and a price limit. A limit buy at price P will:

- Immediately trade against any resting sell orders with prices less than or equal to P, starting from the best ask and walking up.
- Any remaining quantity will rest in the book as a bid at price P, behind existing bids at that price.

The same logic applies symmetrically for a sell limit order. Limit orders can be:

- *Aggressive*: priced to cross the spread and trade immediately (for example, a buy limit above the best ask).
- *Passive*: priced to rest on your side of the book (for example, a buy limit at or below the best bid).

Many strategies rely on passive limit orders to "earn the spread." To evaluate such strategies, your backtest must account for:

- How often your passive orders are actually filled, given their queue position.
- How much adverse price movement happens before and after they fill.

Time-in-Force Variants

Most electronic venues support time-in-force instructions that modify how a limit order interacts with the book:

- **Day**: remains in the book until it is filled, cancelled, or the session ends.
- **Immediate-or-Cancel (IOC)**: any part that can trade immediately does so; the remainder is cancelled instead of resting.
- **Fill-or-Kill (FOK)**: either the entire order quantity trades immediately, or the order is cancelled without trading at all.

From a microstructure perspective, IOC and FOK orders are ways to probe or take liquidity without adding new resting volume. Backtests that assume "we always rest" but then implement IOC in production will routinely see different fill rates than expected.

Specialized Order Types

Venues often offer additional order types such as:

- **Pegged orders**, which automatically track a reference price (such as the mid or the best bid).
- **Iceberg orders**, where only a portion of the true size is visible in the book at any time.

These behave differently across venues and asset classes, and fully modeling them is beyond the scope of this introductory section. The key point is that each of these order types defines a specific behavior in the order state machine and in the way volume appears or disappears from the visible ladder. Your simulation and your gateway must agree on these rules.

Order Lifecycles as State Machines

From the perspective of your trading system, an order is not just "sent" and then "filled or not." It passes through a predictable lifecycle, driven by events:

- You submit the order to a gateway.
- The venue acknowledges or rejects it.
- The order may rest, partially fill, fully fill, or be cancelled.
- At any time, you may request a cancel or a modification, which the venue may or may not be able to honor instantly.

It is useful to think of this as a *finite state machine*. Typical states include:

- **New**: the order has been accepted by the venue but has not yet traded.
- **Partially filled**: some quantity has traded; some remains.

- **Filled**: the entire quantity has traded.
- **Cancelled**: the remaining quantity has been successfully withdrawn.
- **Rejected**: the order was not accepted (for example, due to a risk check).

Each transition between these states is triggered by a specific event in the market data or in the exchange messages your gateway receives. For example:

- A trade at your price and side moves your order from New to Partially filled, or from Partially filled to Filled, depending on quantities.
- A successful cancel acknowledgement moves your order to Cancelled.

A sound backtest engine will replicate this logic using historical order book and trade data. A sound production system will maintain it using real-time venue messages. The two should be consistent: the same simulated stream of events that drives your backtest order state machine should, in principle, be able to drive your live state machine if you were to replay it in a test environment.

Auction Mechanisms and When the Book Pauses

So far we have focused on continuous trading: at any moment, orders can arrive and, if they cross, trades happen immediately. Many markets also use auction mechanisms at key points in the trading day, most notably:

- The **opening auction**, which determines the official opening price.
- The **closing auction**, which determines the official closing price.

- **Volatility auctions** or **call auctions**, which are triggered when prices move too quickly or outside predefined bands.

During an auction:

- Orders are collected over a period of time without immediate execution.
- The trading system calculates an *indicative price* that would maximize executed volume if the auction were to end at that moment.
- At the auction end, a single price is chosen, and all compatible orders trade at that price subject to priority rules.

This has several important implications for both backtesting and live gateways:

- The usual bid/ask ladder can look strange or empty, because continuous matching is paused.
- Liquidity may *appear* and *disappear* quickly around the auction time as participants update or cancel their auction interest.
- Aggressive orders submitted just before the auction may not execute immediately; they join the auction pool instead.

A naive backtest that simply skips over auction periods, or treats reported opening and closing prices as if they were ordinary continuous-trading prices, will miss an important part of the day's liquidity. In many instruments, a large fraction of daily volume trades in the opening and closing auctions. If your strategy is active in these windows, you must model auction mechanics at least at a coarse level.

From Microstructure to Execution Realism

We can now connect these pieces back to the central theme of this book: moving strategies from backtest to live execution with appropriate safeguards.

Microstructure details—limit order books, price–time queues, auction phases—matter because they are the bridge between your high-level trading signal and the actual trades you receive. Several practical lessons follow directly:

- **The book is the environment.** Your strategy does not trade against a single "true price." It trades against the current arrangement of resting orders and the flow of new orders through the book. Backtests that ignore the depth and dynamics of the book are, in effect, simulating in a different environment than the one your live strategy will face.
- **Priority rules create hidden latency costs.** Even if you colocate and reduce network latency, your orders still arrive after others. Each microsecond can move you backward in the queue. In backtests that assume "we are always first," the impact of this latency on fill probability is invisible.
- **Order types embed risk choices.** Choosing between market, limit, IOC, FOK, or pegged orders is not just a user-interface convenience; it determines whether you are taking liquidity, making it, or probing it, and at what price uncertainty. Your backtest must use the same order logic as your intended live implementation.
- **Auctions and state changes are structural events.** Opening and closing auctions, and volatility-induced auctions, temporarily change how orders are matched. A robust system must be state-aware: it should know when continuous trading is active, when auctions are collecting interest, and how to behave safely in each phase.

All of these aspects will reappear in later chapters when we discuss gateway design, risk checks, and simulation frameworks. For now, the most important shift is conceptual: to see an order not as an instantaneous trade at "the price," but as an object that enters a complex, rule-driven machine—the limit order book and its associated auctions—and emerges, over time, as some pattern of fills and cancels.

In the next section, we will zoom out from this single order book to the broader landscape of venues and asset classes. There you will see how multiple books, different matching models, and varied contract designs create yet another layer of complexity that your backtests must approximate and your live systems must handle safely.

1.2 Venues and Asset Classes

In the previous section we treated the market as if there were a single, central limit order book where your orders meet everyone else's. That is a useful starting point, but it is not the reality your production systems will face.

In live trading, you operate in a *network* of venues spread across data centers, countries, and even regulatory regimes. The same instrument may trade in many places at once. Different asset classes adopt different matching models and contract structures. All of this directly shapes three things that matter for taking a backtested strategy live:

- **Routing**: where your orders are sent.
- **Execution quality**: what prices and fills you actually get.
- **Technical integration**: how your systems connect, monitor risk, and recover from errors.

This section surveys the main venue types and asset classes, and shows how their structural features translate into concrete design choices for gateways, smart order routers, and backtesting frameworks.

From a Single Book to a Fragmented Landscape

Modern markets are *fragmented*: the same or closely related instruments trade on multiple venues at the same time. Instead of one book, you should picture many books in parallel, plus some trading systems that are not books at all.

At a high level, venues fall into a few broad categories:

- **Primary exchanges**: the main listing venue for a security (for example, NYSE or NASDAQ for many U.S. equities), often with large volumes and strong price-discovery roles.
- **Alternative trading systems** (ATS) and **multilateral trading facilities** (MTF): secondary venues that match orders, sometimes with slightly different rules or fee structures.
- **Dark or semi-dark pools**: venues that do not display full pre-trade transparency, often used for larger or more sensitive orders.
- **Dealer and RFQ platforms**: systems where you request quotes from one or more dealers, rather than trading against a central public book.

The mix of these venue types varies by asset class. Equities are dominated by central limit order books across many exchanges and ATSs. Over-the-counter (OTC) markets, such as many corporate bonds and some FX instruments, lean more on dealer and RFQ models. Crypto assets often trade on a patchwork of centralized exchanges and, increasingly, decentralized protocols.

For a live trading system, fragmentation is not an abstract curiosity; it is a practical constraint. Every venue you connect to adds:

- Another data feed to normalize and monitor.
- Another gateway path to secure, test, and maintain.
- Another set of microstructure details your execution logic must understand.

Your backtests must keep this in mind. A strategy that assumes a single synthetic order book is implicitly assuming away venue choice, routing latency, and cross-venue differences in fees and rules.

Equities: Exchanges, ATSs, and Dark Pools

Equities are the canonical example of a fragmented electronic market. For a single liquid stock, you may have:

- One or more primary listing exchanges.
- Dozens of ATSs and dark pools.
- Internalization by brokers, where client orders may interact with one another off-exchange.

Most equity venues use the central limit order book model described earlier: price–time priority, visible depth, and continuous matching, plus opening and closing auctions.

What differs across venues?

Fee and rebate models. Many equity exchanges use a *maker–taker* model:

- If you *add* liquidity (by posting a passive order that rests), you receive a small rebate per share.
- If you *remove* liquidity (by sending a market or aggressive limit order), you pay a fee per share.

Other venues invert this model or use more complex tiered pricing. These economics affect routing because the same execution, at the same apparent price, can have a different net cost depending on which venue fills it.

Displayed vs. hidden liquidity. Dark pools and some ATSs intentionally reduce pre-trade transparency. They may:

- Not publish full order books.
- Match orders at reference prices derived from lit markets (for example, the midpoint of the national best bid and offer).
- Prioritize larger orders or specific types of flow.

For your systems, this means:

- You cannot simply look at a visible ladder to know where all potential liquidity is.

- You must track not only displayed quotes but also your own pool hits and misses over time to estimate the true liquidity profile.

Routing implications. Given this spread of venues, most active equity traders use a **smart order router** (SOR). The SOR decides, for each parent order:

- How to break the parent order into child orders.
- Which venue each child order should be sent to.
- In what sequence and with what order types (passive, marketable, dark first, lit first, and so on).

Backtests that assume a single book are implicitly assuming a trivial SOR that always routes to that one synthetic venue with zero additional latency. When you go live, a real SOR must consider:

- Different latencies to each venue's data center.
- Different fee and rebate structures.
- Different minimum trade sizes or hidden liquidity rules.

If your strategy depends on fine details of spread capture or queue position, these routing choices can make or break its performance.

Futures: Centralized Books and Contract Design

Futures markets are, in some ways, cleaner from a venue perspective. A given futures contract (for example, a specific S&P 500 index future) is typically listed and traded predominantly on a *single* exchange group. That exchange operates one central limit order book for that contract, often with global access via multiple data centers.

However, futures introduce complexity through *contract design*:

- Each contract has a specific expiry month and year.

- Some contracts have physical delivery; others cash-settle against an index.
- There are often many contracts along a maturity curve (for example, quarterly expiries several years out).

From a microstructure point of view:

- Liquidity is heavily concentrated in the "front" contracts (the nearest expiries).
- Exchanges often provide special order types for *spreads* between contracts, which internally decompose into legs across multiple books.
- Many futures have *price limits*: bands beyond which the price cannot move in a session or must pause, leading to temporary trading halts or limit states.

For your backtests and gateways:

- You must respect contract calendars and roll schedules. Treating a futures series as a continuous synthetic price without modeling rolls can be acceptable for some research questions but dangerous for execution modeling.
- You need to model exchange-specific behaviors such as price limits and how they affect order acceptance, matching, and cancellation.
- Contract standardization (fixed tick sizes, contract multipliers, and clear margin rules) simplifies certain risk calculations and pre-trade checks.

Compared with equities, futures may have fewer venues to connect to but more intricate contract and calendar logic in your reference data and risk layers.

Options: Combinatorial Explosion and Microstructure Differences

Options introduce both venue and contract complexity. A single underlying equity or future can have:

- Multiple expiries (weekly, monthly, quarterly, LEAPS).
- Many strikes per expiry.
- Both calls and puts for each strike.

This creates a grid of thousands of instruments per underlying, often traded across multiple options exchanges.

While most options exchanges use a central limit order book, key microstructure differences matter:

- **Quote-driven liquidity**: market makers are often obligated or incentivized to quote across many strikes and expiries, which shapes the visible book.
- **Complex order books**: many venues allow multi-leg orders (spreads, butterflies, condors) that are matched in a complex order book separate from the simple single-leg book.
- **Different priority rules**: some options venues use pro-rata or size-based priority at a price level, not pure price–time priority, meaning larger orders can receive a disproportionate share of incoming volume.

For your systems, this implies:

- Your router may need to choose not only between venues but also between single-leg and complex-order books.
- Modeling fill probabilities requires awareness of the priority scheme: being early in time may matter less than your displayed size.

- The risk engine must understand how fills in one leg of a spread interact with exposure and margin for the overall position.

From a backtesting standpoint, options also bring *Greeks* and implied volatility dynamics into play. Even if this section does not dive into pricing theory, remember: the microstructure of options (strike grids, expiries, multi-leg books) means that simplistic "treat each option like a stock" simulations will often misrepresent liquidity and execution risk.

FX: ECNs, Single-Bank Platforms, and Session Structure

Foreign exchange (FX) markets are historically decentralized and dealer-driven. Electronically, much FX trading occurs on:

- **ECNs** (electronic communication networks), which operate order-book-like environments for major currency pairs.
- **Single-bank platforms**, where a client connects to a specific bank's liquidity and trades directly against its quotes.
- **RFQ systems**, where a client requests quotes from multiple dealers, then trades on one of the returned prices.

Key differences from equities and futures:

- Many FX venues are not fully anonymous central books; the relationship between client and dealer matters.
- Pricing can be customized by counterparty: two clients may see different spreads for the same nominal pair and size.
- FX trades nearly 24 hours on business days, with regional liquidity waves (Asia, Europe, U.S.) rather than a single centralized session.

For routing and execution:

- A bank or broker may aggregate quotes from many liquidity providers into a synthetic book for you; your "venue" is then that aggregator rather than each underlying source.
- Latency to regional hubs (for example, London, New York, Tokyo) can have a different geography than for equities or futures.
- Some platforms allow full depth and order-book interaction; others are quote-and-trade only, with no resting client orders.

Your backtests must align with what you can actually do in production. If you only have RFQ-based access, simulating continuous passive quoting in a limit order book is unrealistic. If your live access is through a single prime broker's aggregated book, simulating each underlying ECN separately may be unnecessary or even misleading.

Crypto: 24/7 Trading and Heterogeneous Venues

Crypto asset markets combine elements from several of the above worlds:

- **Centralized exchanges** with order-book matching and varying fee structures.
- **Derivatives venues** offering perpetual swaps, futures, and options, often with their own funding-rate and margin rules.
- **Decentralized exchanges** (DEXs) using automated market maker (AMM) models instead of traditional order books.

Distinctive features include:

- **24/7 trading**: there is no closing auction in the traditional sense; maintenance windows and outages are idiosyncratic.
- **Venue risk**: exchange solvency and custody risk are part of microstructure reality, not a separate concern.

- **On-chain settlement**: for DEXs, the matching and settlement occurs on a blockchain, where network congestion and gas fees affect execution.

Execution and routing implications:

- You may route across many exchanges to minimize spreads and access liquidity, while also managing transfer and funding frictions.
- For AMM-based DEXs, "liquidity" is not a set of resting orders but a pool whose price impact depends non-linearly on trade size; your backtests must model this function, not just a ladder.
- Latency includes not just network round-trip time but, for on-chain trades, block confirmation times.

If your backtests assume instant fills at midprice in crypto, you are ignoring not only order-book mechanics but also funding rates, slippage in AMMs, and potential exchange downtime.

Latency Geography: Where Your Orders Physically Go

So far we have focused on venue types within each asset class. Another crucial dimension is *where* those venues are located physically, and how your infrastructure is arranged relative to them.

Important concepts include:

- **Colocation**: placing your trading servers in the same data center as the exchange's matching engine, often within the same cage or room, to minimize latency.
- **Cross-connects**: dedicated, usually fiber, connections between cages or data centers, offering lower and more stable latency than public networks.
- **Regional data centers**: separate primary and secondary matching engines or access points in different cities or continents.

From a microstructure perspective, latency geography influences:

- Your queue position at a given price level: orders sent from a co-located engine will generally arrive ahead of those sent from distant locations.
- How stale your view of the order book is when you decide to trade.
- The risk that network disruptions isolate you from one or more venues.

For routing and system design:

- A single strategy might be deployed in multiple regions, each with its own gateways close to local venues, coordinated by a higher-level controller.
- Your backtests, if they aim to predict fills at sub-second scales, need at least a crude model of latency: the time between observing a quote and your order arriving at the book.
- Monitoring and failover procedures must be region-aware; a data center outage should not cause your entire system to behave unpredictably.

Latency geography is where market microstructure meets data-center engineering. Decisions about where to place servers are, in effect, decisions about the microstructure environment your orders will experience.

Contract Design and Its Impact on Execution

Across all of these venues and asset classes, *contract design*—the precise definition of what is being traded and on what terms—feeds directly into execution logic and risk control. Key aspects include:

- **Standardization vs. customization**: exchange-listed futures and options are standardized, while many OTC derivatives are bespoke.

- **Tick size and lot size**: the minimum price increment and minimum trade unit shape spread behavior and how easily you can adjust positions.
- **Clearing and settlement**: whether trades are centrally cleared, bilaterally settled, or settled on-chain; how margin, funding, and physical delivery work.

Practical implications:

- Your pre-trade checks must know, for each instrument, the correct tick sizes and lot sizes to avoid exchange rejections.
- Your risk engine must understand contract multipliers and margin rules to prevent over-leveraging.
- Your backtests must align with how positions will actually be rolled, settled, or delivered in production; ignoring these steps can hide significant costs and risks.

Contract design also shapes liquidity patterns. For example:

- In futures, liquidity often migrates from an expiring contract to the next one around a predictable "roll window."
- In options, near-the-money strikes and near expiries typically concentrate volume, while far-out-of-the-money strikes may be illiquid.
- In FX, certain tenors or pairings are standard and liquid, while others are only available OTC on a quote basis.

Your routing and execution algorithms should follow this structure rather than treating all listed instruments as equally tradable.

Bringing It Back to Backtests and Gateways

Linking this survey back to the central theme of the book, several guiding principles emerge:

1. **Model the venues you can actually use.** If your production setup routes only to a subset of exchanges or to a broker's aggregated book, your backtests should reflect that reality. Simulating idealized access to all global liquidity can overstate achievable performance.

2. **Treat routing as part of the strategy, not an afterthought.** In fragmented markets, *where* and *how* you route is as important as *when* you decide to trade. Backtests should embed a realistic routing logic, even if simplified, and gateways should implement the same logic with clear controls and monitoring.

3. **Respect latency geography.** A strategy tuned on data that implicitly assumes zero latency will behave differently when implemented in a specific data center, with real network paths to each venue. Even coarse latency modeling can significantly improve the realism of your simulations.

4. **Let contract design drive reference data and risk.** Tick sizes, expiries, multipliers, and settlement rules are not mere documentation; they are inputs to pre-trade checks, position management, and P&L calculation. Your system architecture should propagate this information from reference data into both the backtest engine and the live gateways.

5. **Use abstraction carefully.** It is often useful to build a *synthetic* view of the market in your research environment, but every abstraction hides something. Be explicit about what is being abstracted away (for example, venue fees, dark pool behavior, RFQ constraints) and ensure those simplifications are acceptable given your strategy's sensitivity.

In the next section, we will see how regulatory frameworks overlay this venue and asset-class landscape. Those rules—from market access requirements to audit trail obligations—further constrain how you design gateways, risk controls, and deployment procedures, and they often differ by region and asset class. Understanding venues and instruments is only half the story; understanding the rules under which they operate completes the foundation for safe, realistic live trading.

1.3 Regulatory Frameworks for Electronic Trading

In the first two sections of this chapter, we treated markets mainly as technical systems: collections of order books and venues connected by networks, with microstructure and latency shaping execution. In reality, those technical systems sit inside another structure: the regulatory framework.

For electronic trading, regulation is not just a legal backdrop. It directly determines:

- who may connect to a venue and under what conditions (*market access controls*),
- how algorithms must be tested and supervised (*testing and governance obligations*), and
- what safeguards and records your infrastructure must maintain (*safe system design*).

This section gives a practitioner-focused tour of the most relevant regulatory ideas, with emphasis on how they translate into concrete requirements for gateways, risk engines, monitoring, and backtesting practices. We will not attempt to be exhaustive or jurisdiction-specific; instead, we will highlight recurring patterns that show up in the U.S., Europe, and other major markets.

Why Regulation Matters to System Architecture

Before diving into specific regimes, it is worth being clear about the connection between regulation and design. As an algorithmic trader or system architect, you might be tempted to treat regulation as something your legal and compliance colleagues "handle." That is a mistake for at least three reasons.

First, many controls are explicitly mandated. Limits on order size, message rates, credit exposure, and access to kill-switches are not optional "nice-to-have" risk features. In most jurisdictions they are stated obligations for brokers and, increasingly, for firms that deploy automated trading systems.

Second, regulators expect reconstructibility. If something goes wrong, you must be able to show exactly what your systems did and why. That means:

- detailed logs of orders, modifications, and cancels,
- synchronized timestamps across components,
- records of configuration and code changes, and
- often, the ability to replay relevant data to reconstruct an incident.

Third, rules shape deployment processes. In many markets, you may not simply switch on a new algorithm in production:

- There may be formal requirements for testing environments and conformance certification.
- Significant changes to trading systems can trigger documentation, approval, or notification obligations.
- Supervisory responsibilities (who oversees what, and with what authority) must be clear and demonstrable.

The bottom line is simple: you cannot design serious electronic trading systems in a regulatory vacuum. The rest of this section makes that connection concrete.

The U.S. Landscape: SEC, CFTC, and FINRA

In the United States, three bodies are central for most electronic trading in listed instruments:

- The **Securities and Exchange Commission** (SEC), which oversees securities markets and exchanges (equities, many ETFs, listed options).

- The **Commodity Futures Trading Commission** (CFTC), which oversees futures, many swaps, and certain derivatives.
- The **Financial Industry Regulatory Authority** (FINRA), a self-regulatory organization that supervises broker-dealers.

Rather than list individual rules by name, we will organize the discussion around themes that show up repeatedly.

Market Access Rules and Pre-Trade Risk

If you are a broker-dealer providing clients with access to exchanges, or a firm with "direct" or "sponsored" access to a venue, you are expected to have effective *market access controls*. At a high level, these controls must:

- prevent orders that would exceed credit or capital limits,
- block "fat-finger" errors such as orders with clearly off-market prices or sizes,
- enforce reasonable limits on order and message rates, and
- avoid any activity that could destabilize the market or violate trading rules.

In system terms, this implies the existence of a **pre-trade risk layer** sitting between your strategy logic and the exchange gateways. That layer must be:

- **comprehensive**: covering all orders, including those generated by automated strategies;
- **reliable**: failures cannot cause "fail-open" behavior where checks are silently bypassed; and
- **fast**: implemented in a way that meets the latency demands of your trading style while still performing meaningful checks.

Examples of checks that typically fall into this layer include:

- *Max notional per order* and *max quantity per order*,
- *Price band checks* relative to current market reference prices,
- *Intraday position and P&L limits*,
- *Message throttles* to avoid saturating venues or violating their rate limits.

When designing gateways and backtests, it is not enough to think in terms of pure microstructure performance. You must design with these constraints in mind, because they will shape what orders you can send and when.

Kill-Switches and Emergency Controls

Regulators and venues expect that, if trading goes wrong, your firm (or your sponsoring broker) can rapidly halt activity. This typically means having:

- A **global kill-switch** that can stop all new orders and, often, cancel open orders across one or more venues.
- More granular switches to disable specific strategies, symbols, or gateways.
- Procedures and clear responsibilities for who can activate these controls and under what circumstances.

From a system-design perspective:

- The kill-switch function must be designed-upfront; you cannot bolt it on after an incident.
- Gateways must be capable of processing bulk cancels and rejects gracefully.
- Monitoring and alerting should be integrated so that unusual behavior (for example, runaway order rates or extreme P&L swings) can trigger or at least suggest activation of these controls.

When writing backtests and simulation tools, you should mirror this thinking: can you simulate the impact of triggering such controls? Do your strategy logs and dashboards make it clear when the system is in a "stopped" or "safe" state?

Supervision and Algorithmic Trading Controls

Electronic trading does not remove human responsibility. Regulation in the U.S. expects that:

- Automated strategies are **supervised** by qualified individuals.
- There is **documentation** describing what a given algorithm is intended to do, under what conditions, and with what risks.
- **Changes** to algorithms (including parameter changes that materially affect behavior) are controlled and reviewed.

This pushes your engineering organization toward:

- Formal **change-management processes**: code reviews, test evidence, deployment approvals, version control of configuration.
- Clear **strategy catalogs**: which algorithms are active, what symbols and venues they trade, what limits apply to them.
- Operational dashboards that give supervisors real-time insight into algorithm behavior.

Your backtest infrastructure is part of this picture: it should help produce evidence that an algorithm has been tested across a range of market conditions; that it behaves as intended; and that known failure modes and safeguards are documented.

European Frameworks: MiFID II and Beyond

In Europe, the Markets in Financial Instruments Directive II (MiFID II) and its associated regulations provide the main framework for electronic and algorithmic trading on EU venues. The details differ from

U.S. rules, but the themes will sound familiar, often with more explicit wording around algorithmic trading.

Broadly, MiFID II:

- defines **algorithmic trading** and **high-frequency trading** as specific regulated activities,
- requires firms engaging in such activities to have robust systems and risk controls, and
- places obligations on both trading firms and venues regarding testing, deployment, and monitoring of algorithms.

Let us highlight a few aspects that matter directly for system design.

Definition and Scope of Algorithmic Trading

Under MiFID II, algorithmic trading is broadly defined as using computer algorithms automatically to determine order parameters (such as timing, price, or quantity) with limited or no human intervention for each order. High-frequency trading is then defined as a subset involving high intraday message rates and low-latency infrastructure.

This has two practical consequences:

- Many strategies that you might casually call "automated" are formally considered algorithmic trading and subject to specific rules.
- High-frequency trading firms must meet additional requirements, such as providing liquidity in certain ways if they are market makers, and meeting stricter system-resilience standards.

As a result, your **architecture diagrams, system descriptions, and strategy catalogs** become regulatory documents. They will often be requested by venues or regulators when you seek access or during audits.

Testing and Conformance Obligations

MiFID II explicitly requires firms to:

- test algorithms in **controlled environments**, including stress and disorderly-market scenarios,
- ensure that changes to algorithms are **tested and approved** before deployment, and
- participate in **venue-level conformance testing** when required.

This implies that your backtesting and simulation stack must support more than just historical P&L studies. It should facilitate:

- replay of extreme events and halts,
- injection of abnormal market conditions (for example, gaps, spikes, data-feed dropouts),
- automated regression tests that can be run as part of a deployment pipeline.

Moreover, venues may provide specific **test environments** and scenarios you must pass before being certified for production connectivity. Your gateway implementations must therefore:

- support switching between production and test endpoints,
- implement protocol features fully enough to pass venue-specific test scripts, and
- log test results and any deviations for later reference.

Governance, Documentation, and Third-Party Dependencies

European rules place strong emphasis on governance around electronic trading:

- Firms must have **policies** covering algorithm development, testing, deployment, and monitoring.
- There must be clear **lines of responsibility** up to senior management for oversight of algorithmic trading.
- Use of **third-party technology** (for example, off-the-shelf algos or hosted platforms) does not remove a firm's responsibility; you must understand and control what those components do.

From a technical point of view, this encourages:

- good internal **documentation standards** for trading systems,
- configuration management that can show which version of which algorithm ran when,
- due diligence processes for external vendors, including understanding their controls and failure modes.

These requirements are not purely bureaucratic. They help align your internal practices with external expectations, reducing the risk that a technical failure becomes a regulatory failure as well.

Cross-Cutting Requirements: Audit Trails and Clock Synchronization

Across jurisdictions, a few technical themes recur because they are essential for understanding and supervising electronic trading.

Audit Trails and Order Lifecycle Reconstruction

Regulators and venues expect you to maintain **comprehensive audit trails**. At a minimum, these typically include:

- All order submissions, modifications, and cancels sent to venues.
- All acknowledgments, rejections, and execution reports received.

- Internal events that influence trading decisions (for example, parameter changes, strategy start/stop commands).

Each record should carry:

- precise timestamps,
- identifiers linking it to a strategy, trader, or client,
- enough context (such as symbol, venue, and quantities) to reconstruct what happened.

From an infrastructure-design perspective:

- Logging must be **reliable** and **tamper-evident**; you may need to store logs for several years.
- The system must be able to **reconstruct an order's lifecycle**: from initial decision to final fill or cancel, including all intermediate states.
- This sometimes leads firms to maintain separate **surveillance stores** or data warehouses optimized for investigation and regulatory reporting.

Backtest engines that model order lifecycles benefit from the same structure: if you design your simulation logs as if they had to serve as an audit trail, you will gain clarity about what the strategy did and why.

Clock Synchronization

Accurate timestamps are meaningless if each component in your system uses a different clock. To solve this, many regimes specify:

- synchronization of system clocks to a reference time (usually UTC),
- maximum allowable **drift** between system clocks and the reference,

- documentation of **time sources** and synchronization mechanisms.

In practical terms, your architecture must include:

- one or more reliable **time sources** (for example, GPS-based time servers, or high-quality NTP sources),
- synchronization services that distribute time to trading servers and gateways,
- monitoring and alerting for clock drift or sync failures.

This is not only a compliance issue. For any serious analysis of microsecond-to-millisecond behavior—such as queue positioning, race conditions between venues, or pathologies during fast markets—you must trust your timestamps. Clock discipline is part of market microstructure discipline.

Multi-Jurisdiction Trading and the Common Risk Layer

Most active trading firms operate across instruments and venues that fall under different regulators and rule sets. A single strategy might:

- trade U.S. equities and listed options (under SEC/FINRA rules),
- hedge with futures listed on an exchange under CFTC oversight,
- interact with European venues subject to MiFID II,
- and use FX instruments for cross-currency exposure management.

From a systems point of view, this raises several challenges.

Designing a Common Risk Layer

You do not want to build completely separate risk engines for each jurisdiction; that would be hard to maintain and reason about. Instead, most firms aim for a **common risk layer** that:

- implements core controls consistently across all venues (for example, global credit limits, firm-wide message limits),
- allows for **jurisdiction-specific** additions or stricter thresholds where required,
- provides a unified view of exposure and limits to traders and risk managers.

This encourages a modular design:

- Base modules implement generic checks (sizes, prices, exposure).
- Jurisdiction or venue modules add or adjust checks (for example, stricter price bands on a particular exchange, or specific obligations for a European high-frequency strategy).
- A routing layer ensures that every order passes through the relevant combination of modules.

Testing and Environments Across Regions

Trading across regions also implies multiple:

- **test environments**: U.S. exchange certification environments, European venue simulators, FX platform sandboxes, and so on,
- **deployment windows**: different session times and maintenance schedules,
- **regulatory calendars**: different holidays and reporting timelines.

Your deployment and cutover processes must respect these differences. For example:

- A code change affecting both U.S. and European equities might be rolled out first in test environments for each, then in one region's production, then the other.
- You may need region-specific runbooks documenting what to do if a venue rejects orders after a deployment.
- Monitoring dashboards should be region-aware, showing the relevant instruments, venues, and limits for each jurisdiction.

Seen in this light, regulation is one of the key drivers for having disciplined, automated deployment pipelines and robust testing frameworks: they are not only technical best practices; they are mechanisms for meeting your obligations to regulators and venues.

Regulation as a First-Class Design Input

We can now summarize the main message of this section: regulatory frameworks are not peripheral constraints to be checked at the end of a project. They are *first-class design inputs* for any serious electronic trading system.

Concretely, this means:

- When you design your **gateway layer**, you specify not only latency and throughput targets but also required pre-trade checks, kill-switch capabilities, and logging behavior.
- When you architect your **risk engine**, you align limits and controls with both your internal risk appetite and the minimum regulatory floor, often choosing to be stricter than the bare minimum.
- When you build your **backtesting and simulation tools**, you incorporate scenarios and features that directly address regulatory expectations around testing (stress, disorderly markets, incident reconstruction).

- When you set up your **operations and monitoring**, you explicitly map responsibilities, escalation paths, and documentation to regulatory concepts such as supervision and governance.

For quant developers and researchers, the practical takeaway is that a strategy's life cycle does not end when it looks good in a backtest. It also has to clear a parallel life cycle of controls, documentation, and tests defined by the markets in which you operate. Understanding the regulatory frameworks early, and building them into your design thinking, will make that path smoother, safer, and faster.

In the next section, we will return to the market's internal state machine: how venues move between pre-open, continuous trading, auctions, and halts, and how mechanisms such as price bands and limit-up/limit-down interact with the microstructure and regulatory ideas introduced so far.

1.4 Market States, Halts, and Price Bands

In the earlier sections we treated markets as if they were always in the same mode of operation: orders arrive, the book updates, trades occur, and your strategy interacts with this continuous flow. In reality, venues operate as *state machines*. They move through distinct trading states over the course of a day, and they sometimes change state abruptly in response to volatility or technical problems.

For a human trader watching a screen, these transitions are often obvious: the open, the close, a halt banner, an auction countdown. For an automated strategy or a gateway process, nothing is obvious unless you teach it to recognize and react to these changes. Being state-aware is as important as understanding the limit order book itself.

This section explains:

- the typical *market states* a venue passes through,
- how *halts* and *auctions* alter matching behavior,

- how *price-band mechanisms* (like limit up-limit down) constrain trading during volatile periods,
- and why your strategies, backtests, and gateways must track this state machine explicitly.

The Venue as a Trading State Machine

At a high level, you can think of each venue (and often each instrument on that venue) as being in one of a handful of core states:

- **Closed**: the venue is not accepting or processing regular-day orders.
- **Pre-open** or **pre-session**: orders may be accepted and queued, but continuous matching has not started.
- **Opening auction**: orders are collected and then crossed in a single batch to determine an opening price.
- **Continuous trading**: regular, real-time matching against the limit order book.
- **Intraday auction** (volatility or call auction): continuous trading paused; trading may resume via a batch cross.
- **Closing auction**: continuous trading ends, followed by a batch cross that sets the official close.
- **Halted** or **suspended**: trading is temporarily stopped, often due to volatility, news, or technical issues.

Different venues use different labels and subtle variations, but the pattern is broadly similar: time-driven transitions (open and close) punctuated by event-driven transitions (halts, volatility auctions).

From a system's point of view, these states are exposed via market data and control messages:

- special fields in reference or status feeds (for example, "trading status: halted"),

- event messages indicating the start or end of an auction,
- flags on quote or trade updates (for example, indicating auction-only prices).

If you do not read and interpret these signals, your strategy will treat all ticks as if they came from the same regime, which is a recipe for surprises.

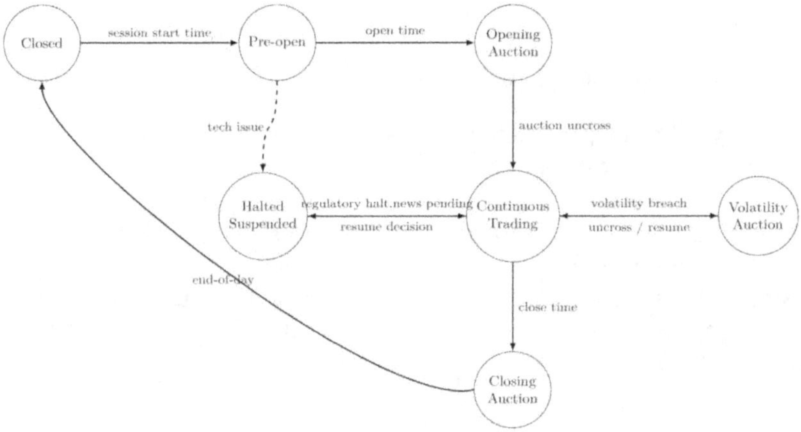

Thinking in terms of this state machine will guide the rest of our discussion: halts and auctions are not special cases; they are just particular states and transitions in a larger, structured process.

How States Are Represented in Market Data

Before we examine specific states, it is useful to understand how your systems will *see* them.

Venues typically broadcast state information through:

- **Instrument status feeds**: separate from the main quote and trade streams, often lower-frequency, summarizing whether each symbol is trading, halted, in auction, and so on.

- **Flags or condition codes** on messages: individual quote or trade messages may carry small codes indicating that they are part of an opening cross, a closing cross, or that trading is paused.
- **Administrative messages**: messages explicitly announcing halts, resumptions, or changes to price bands.

Your market data handler should parse and normalize these into a clear internal representation, such as:

- current trading state per symbol and per venue,
- timestamps of last state transitions,
- any relevant parameters (for example, indicative auction price, or current price bands).

A common mistake is to focus only on quotes and trades and ignore status and administrative messages. In backtests, this shows up as treating all days as continuous from first trade to last. In production, it shows up as strategies continuing to send orders during a halt or misinterpreting auction prints as continuous-trading prices.

Pre-Open and Opening Auctions

The **pre-open** and **opening auction** set the starting point for the trading day. Different venues implement these slightly differently, but the broad pattern is:

- Before the official open, the venue accepts orders. These orders may be tagged as "regular" or "auction-only" depending on the rules.
- No continuous matching occurs yet. Instead, the venue calculates an *indicative opening price* based on the order book it is building.
- At the opening time, an algorithm chooses a single price that maximizes executable volume (subject to tie-breaking rules). All eligible orders are crossed at that price.

- After the auction uncross, the venue transitions to continuous trading.

From a microstructure and systems perspective:

- During pre-open, the visible book may show only indicative prices and sizes, not firm bid/ask quotes in the usual sense.
- The order types you can submit may be constrained (for example, some venues treat market orders in pre-open as "market-on-open" instructions).
- There may be special rules for order cancellation and modification in the final seconds before the auction.

If your strategy trades near the open, your gateway must know whether a symbol is in pre-open or continuous trading, because:

- An order submitted in pre-open might not execute immediately even if it crosses the visible indicative price; it will wait for the auction.
- Market data during pre-open can be misleading if you interpret it as regular quotes.

Backtests should respect this:

- Simulated fills at or near the open should be based on auction mechanics, not just the first trade print.
- Strategies that use opening prices (for example, gap trades) should model the fact that they do not know the final opening price until the cross occurs.

Continuous Trading and Intraday Auctions

The main part of the trading day is **continuous trading**: orders arrive, the limit order book updates, and trades occur in real time whenever there is a match. This is the mode most strategies implicitly assume by default.

However, continuous trading can be interrupted by **intraday auctions**, also called volatility auctions or call auctions. These are typically triggered by:

- prices attempting to move too quickly or beyond predefined bands,
- order imbalances that would produce an extreme price,
- regulatory or venue-specific volatility controls.

When an intraday auction is triggered:

- Continuous matching is paused for that instrument (or, in rare cases, for the entire venue).
- The venue enters a call period, similar to pre-open, where orders are accepted and the indicative auction price is updated.
- At the end of the call period, a batch cross occurs at a single auction price, and the venue may return to continuous trading.

For your systems, this means that the trading state machine can leave continuous trading not only at the scheduled close, but also at unscheduled times. Your gateway should therefore:

- stop sending certain kinds of orders (for example, market orders intended for continuous matching) during the auction call period, unless you explicitly want auction participation;
- understand which order types are eligible for the auction and how they will behave;
- treat auction prints differently from continuous trades when updating models or risk.

In backtests, ignoring intraday auctions can lead to unrealistic assumptions about how quickly you could have entered or exited positions during volatile periods.

Closing Auctions and End-of-Day Behavior

The **closing auction** plays a special role because it sets the official close, which feeds into index calculations, fund NAVs, and many portfolio processes. Its mechanics resemble those of the opening auction:

- The venue announces a closing auction window.
- Orders can be submitted, modified, or cancelled according to specific rules (for example, market-on-close and limit-on-close orders).
- An indicative closing price is updated during the call period.
- At the end, a batch cross occurs, and regular trading for the day ends.

Execution desks and index funds often concentrate significant volume into the close. For algorithmic strategies:

- Liquidity before the close can dry up as participants move to auction-specific order types.
- Spreads and volatility may widen in the last minutes of continuous trading.
- Your pre-trade risk engine must respect cut-off times and size limits specific to closing auctions.

Backtests that treat the last trade of the day as just another continuous-trading print may misrepresent both the cost and the opportunity of trading into the close.

Halts and Suspensions

A **trading halt** or **suspension** is a stronger form of interruption than an intraday auction. Halts can be triggered by:

- regulatory requests (for example, pending news announcements),

- technical problems at the venue or with an instrument's issuer,
- extreme volatility at the instrument or market-wide level (for example, index-wide circuit breakers).

During a halt:

- The venue stops matching trades for the affected instruments.
- It may or may not accept new orders; often, existing orders remain but are not executable.
- Information about the reason and expected duration may or may not be fully transparent.

Some halts end with an auction (to re-establish a fair price), while others simply resume continuous trading.

Your systems must treat halts as first-class states:

- Gateways should suppress new orders that assume continuous matching and avoid sending cancellations that cannot be processed.
- Strategies should recognize that prices during a halt (often stale) are not meaningful for signal generation.
- Risk controls may tighten or force de-risking on related instruments (for example, hedges) if an underlying is halted.

In backtests, halts are often under-modeled or ignored entirely, yet they can dominate risk during stress events. At minimum, simulations should:

- block fills during halted periods,
- model the re-opening mechanism (auction vs. direct resume),
- reflect any price gaps that occur at re-open.

Price Bands and Limit Up-Limit Down Mechanisms

So far we have focused on *states* in which matching is entirely paused or batch-based. Many markets also use **price bands** that constrain how far and how fast prices can move during continuous trading.

Two common patterns are:

- **Static price limits**: fixed upper and lower bounds relative to a reference price (for example, previous close), beyond which trades are not allowed for a session.
- **Dynamic price bands**: bands around a moving reference price (such as a rolling average of recent trades), which adjust during the day.
- **Limit up-limit down** (LULD) mechanisms: for equities and related products, prices are not allowed to trade outside a band around a reference price; attempts to do so can trigger a pause or auction.

When an order would cause a trade outside the current band:

- It may be rejected outright.
- It may be accepted but automatically repriced to the band boundary.
- It may contribute to triggering a trading pause or volatility auction.

This has several direct consequences:

- Your pre-trade risk layer should be aware of current price bands to avoid sending obviously unfillable or auto-repriced orders.
- Your strategy's expectation of slippage and fill probability must change when the market is trading near a band edge.

- In backtests, you cannot assume that historical prints would have been reachable with arbitrary orders; some trades you imagine might have been impossible under the then-current bands.

Price bands are where regulatory concerns about disorderly markets directly affect microstructure. They interact closely with halts and auctions: trading near or beyond a band often leads into an intraday auction or formal halt.

Why Strategies and Gateways Must Be State-Aware

We can now tie these pieces back to system design and backtesting realism. Being explicit about market states is not optional; it is central to safe and accurate trading.

Strategy Logic

A robust strategy should:

- change its behavior depending on the current market state (for example, use different order types around auctions; reduce or pause trading into halts),
- know when its signals are invalid or unreliable (for example, ignoring prices during halts or auction-only phases),
- be configurable so that risk managers can enforce state-dependent limits (for example, disabling certain tactics during volatility auctions).

This does not mean every strategy must implement a complex state machine internally. Instead, your shared trading framework can expose a clear API: current state, time to next scheduled transition, and relevant parameters (such as indicative auction prices or price bands).

Gateway and Risk Layer Behavior

Gateways and risk engines must also be state-aware:

- Gateways should validate that an order is allowed in the current state, and with the current venue rules (for example, rejecting continuous-only order types during auction call periods).
- Risk layers should adapt limits based on state (for example, more conservative limits during reopening after a halt, or near market-wide circuit breakers).
- Monitoring and alerting should treat state transitions as first-class events, with clear logs and metrics.

A useful design pattern is to centralize state tracking in a dedicated *venue-state service* that consumes market data, maintains the state machine per symbol and venue, and publishes updates to strategies and gateways. This avoids each component having to re-implement partial, error-prone logic.

Backtesting and Simulation

Finally, backtests that ignore market states risk being misleading in precisely the environments where risk is highest. A more realistic simulation framework:

- derives state from historical status feeds or, when unavailable, from heuristics based on timestamps and known schedules;
- blocks or modifies order execution rules in ways that mimic actual halts, auctions, and price bands;
- allows you to stress-test strategies with synthetic state transitions beyond those seen historically (for example, longer halts or more frequent volatility auctions).

The goal is not to perfectly replicate every quirk of every venue, but to ensure that the major state-driven constraints and behaviors are present in your tests.

State Machines as a Unifying Concept

Limit order books, venue fragmentation, regulatory rules, and trading states may at first seem like separate topics. A useful way to unify them-

and to design systems around them-is to think in terms of nested state machines:

- **Order state machine**: for each order you send, tracking its lifecycle (new, resting, partially filled, filled, cancelled).
- **Instrument/venue trading state machine**: as described in this section (pre-open, auction, continuous, halted, etc.).
- **Strategy and risk state machine**: whether a strategy is active, paused, in fail-safe, or being rolled back after a deployment.

Your backtests and live gateways should respect all three layers. Only then will the edge you see in research have a fair chance of surviving contact with real markets that open, close, halt, and resume according to rules that are as much regulatory as they are technical.

In the next section, we will turn to the comparatively unglamorous, but absolutely essential, topic of instrument reference data and symbology. There we will see how static information-identifiers, calendars, tick sizes, corporate actions-forms the backbone that allows all of these state machines to operate consistently across data, risk, and execution systems.

1.5 Instrument Reference Data and Symbology

By now we have treated markets mainly in terms of dynamic behavior: order books, venue states, halts, auctions, price bands. Underneath all of that lies something quieter but just as important: the static and slowly changing data that tells your systems *what* they are trading, *how* it trades, and *when* it trades.

This information is often called *reference data*. It includes:

- identifiers and symbols,
- basic attributes such as currency, tick size, and lot size,

- trading calendars and session times,
- and the corporate actions that change an instrument over its life.

If microstructure and states tell you *how orders move*, reference data tells you *what those orders refer to*. Mistakes here do not usually show up as exotic slippage; they show up as rejected orders, wrong instruments, mis-valued positions, and incorrect regulatory reports. For a system you plan to move from backtest to live, getting reference data and symbology right is non-negotiable.

Why Reference Data Matters for Execution Systems

It is tempting to think of reference data as bookkeeping rather than part of trading. Consider a few concrete failures that stem from poor reference data:

- You send a limit order priced in dollars for an instrument actually quoted in *pence*.
- You size an order assuming a minimum lot of 1, but the venue enforces a minimum of 100.
- Your strategy trades a symbol that was reused after a corporate action, so backtests refer to a different company than the one trading live.
- A futures contract in your historical data quietly expires and rolls, but your backtest ignores expiries and treats the series as continuous, overstating liquidity and underestimating roll costs.

All of these are reference-data mistakes. They have nothing to do with the quality of your signal or the cleverness of your execution algorithm. They are also exactly the sort of errors that regulators, risk managers, and clients find hardest to forgive because they look avoidable.

A robust architecture treats reference data as a first-class component, with clear flows from external providers into internal symbol masters, into backtesting data sets, and into live gateways.

Identifiers and Symbology: Naming What You Trade

Every trading system must agree on names for instruments. The problem is that the outside world does *not* have a single naming scheme. Instead, you face a patchwork:

- **Local exchange symbols**: short tickers like AAPL or VOD, often unique only within one venue.
- **ISINs** (International Securities Identification Numbers): 12-character codes designed to be globally unique for a given security.
- **CUSIPs**, **SEDOLs**, and other local standards: U.S.-centric, U.K.-centric, or region-specific identifiers.
- **FIGIs** and vendor-specific IDs: identifiers created by data vendors or industry groups.

On top of that, derivatives such as options and futures embed extra structure:

- Expiry dates,
- Strikes,
- Contract type (call vs. put, physical vs. cash-settled),
- Underlying instrument and multiplier.

Venues and data vendors encode this in various ways: some use fixed field layouts; others compress everything into compact codes.

Symbology in Practice

Consider a simple U.S. equity:

- On exchange A, it trades under local symbol XYZ.

- On exchange B, it might also be XYZ, but with a different MIC (market identifier code).
- Its ISIN is unique globally and does not depend on venue.
- Your risk system might store it as an internal numeric ID.

For your *backtests*, this matters because:

- You may source historical data from multiple vendors, each using different identifiers.
- You must map these into a consistent internal ID to avoid treating the same instrument as two different ones or vice versa.

For your *live gateways*, it matters because:

- Order messages must carry the correct venue-specific symbol and other identifiers (for example, security IDs in native protocols).
- Market data subscriptions must be requested using whatever symbology the venue or vendor expects.
- Risk aggregation and reporting must combine positions across venues and data sources correctly.

A common pattern is to define an **internal instrument ID** and maintain a mapping table that, for each instrument, stores:

- all known external identifiers (ISIN, local symbol per venue, vendor IDs),
- asset class and instrument type,
- relationship to any underlying (for derivatives),
- and key trading attributes (currency, tick size, lot size, calendar).

Every strategy and gateway then operates on these internal IDs rather than raw exchange symbols. This provides a single source of truth and reduces the chance that different components "disagree" on what a symbol means.

Corporate Actions: How Instruments Change Over Time

Instruments are not static objects. Over their life, they may undergo events that change their price, quantity, or identity. These events are called *corporate actions*. Typical examples include:

- **Stock splits and reverse splits**: the number of shares outstanding changes, and the price adjusts inversely.
- **Cash dividends**: some value is paid out to shareholders; prices typically drop by the dividend amount on the ex-date.
- **Stock dividends and bonus issues**: shareholders receive additional shares instead of cash.
- **Mergers and acquisitions**: one company is absorbed into another, sometimes with a combination of cash and shares changing hands.
- **Spin-offs**: part of a company becomes a separate, newly listed entity.
- **Symbol and name changes**: the ticker or legal name changes while the underlying entity continues.

From a trading-system perspective, corporate actions have two major impacts: they affect *historical data and backtests*, and they affect *live positions and P&L.*

Corporate Actions and Historical Data

Most historical price series you obtain from vendors are either:

- **Unadjusted**: raw traded prices as they occurred.
- **Adjusted**: prices that have been mechanically adjusted backward in time to remove the jumps caused by splits and dividends.

For research, adjusted data are often more convenient because they create smoother series. But adjusted data can be dangerous if you do not understand how they relate to actual tradable prices:

- Backtests using adjusted prices may hide the true gaps and P&L effects of large corporate actions.
- If you mix adjusted prices for history with unadjusted prices in production, your models can mis-calibrate.

The safest approach is to:

- Store *both* raw prices and adjustment factors.
- Make your backtest engine capable of applying or removing adjustments on demand.
- Ensure that any performance metrics that cross the adjustment boundary are interpreted correctly.

For example, if a stock undergoes a 2-for-1 split, prices before the split should be halved if you want to plot a continuous adjusted series. But your simulation of orders and fills around the split day must respect the actual tick sizes and lot sizes that were tradable at the time.

Corporate Actions and Live Positions

Corporate actions also impact your live holdings:

- A split doubles the number of shares in your position and halves the price; your gross market value may remain roughly constant, but your order sizes and tick sensitivity change.
- A cash dividend results in a P&L event that needs to be recorded, often in a different cash account than your trading P&L.
- A merger may convert your position in one symbol into a combination of another symbol plus cash, which your systems must recognize and reflect.

Operationally, this means:

- Your reference data system must ingest corporate action notices (from exchanges, custodians, or data vendors) and propagate them ahead of effective dates.
- Your position-keeping and risk systems must apply these events to positions and P&L.
- Your backoffice and reporting tools must align with your front-office view to avoid unexplained breaks.

Strategies that hold positions across such events should be tested explicitly for behavior through corporate actions. For example, a strategy that automatically rebalances based on price and volatility should not interpret a split-induced price change as a true price move.

Tick Sizes, Lot Sizes, and Price Increments

Every instrument trades with discrete rules:

- **Tick size**: the minimum allowable price increment between distinct quotes.
- **Lot size** or **round lot**: the standard trading unit (for example, 100 shares for many equities).

Some instruments also have:

- **Odd-lot rules**: special treatment for trades smaller than the standard lot.
- **Block trading thresholds**: minimum sizes for certain types of off-book or negotiated trades.

Tick sizes are often more complicated than a single number per instrument. They can depend on:

- the instrument's price level (smaller ticks at lower prices, larger ticks at higher prices),
- the venue (tick sizes may differ between exchanges),
- the time (tick size regimes sometimes change after regulatory reforms).

Lot sizes can also vary by venue or market segment and can change over time.

Why Tick and Lot Sizes Matter

For backtests:

- You must ensure that simulated limit prices lie on valid tick levels, otherwise fills and quotes will not match any realistic book.
- If you are modeling spread capture, the tick size determines the minimum spread and thus the potential edge.
- When computing indicators or signals, using tick-inconsistent rounding can introduce subtle biases.

For live gateways:

- Pre-trade validation must reject or correct orders that violate tick or lot rules; sending invalid orders leads to rejections and wasted latency.
- Size and price calculations must be aware of instrument-specific conventions (for example, bond prices in fractions vs. decimals).

A robust reference data system therefore maintains a **tick-size table** and **lot-size table** per instrument, possibly per venue, and exposes this to both research and production components.

Trading Calendars and Session Definitions

Unlike crypto markets, most traditional venues do not trade 24/7. Each has:

- a **trading calendar**: business days when the venue is open,
- **holidays** and special non-trading days,
- regular **session hours** (for example, pre-open, regular session, after-hours),
- occasional **early closes** or special schedules.

Cross-asset and cross-region strategies often span multiple calendars at once: U.S. equity, European futures, Asian FX sessions, and so on. Misunderstanding calendars leads to:

- scheduling jobs (such as batch backtests, roll logic, or rebalancing) on days when no trading occurs,
- misinterpreting gaps in price series as information rather than non-trading days,
- sending orders during closed periods and receiving rejections.

In addition, for many venues, certain instruments trade in distinct sessions (for example, cash session vs. extended-hours), each with its own rules and allowed order types. These are closely linked to the market state machine discussed earlier but must be grounded in correct calendar and clock data.

Practically, you will want:

- canonical calendar definitions per venue and, where relevant, per instrument class,
- a library or service that answers questions like "is this timestamp inside the regular session for instrument X on venue Y?",
- support in your backtest engine for skipping non-trading periods intelligently.

Calendars are a bridge between the wall-clock time of your systems and the trading-time of your strategies. Get them wrong, and even the best-designed state machine will be out of sync with reality.

Reference Data Flows into Gateways, Risk, and Backtests

We have described pieces of reference data in isolation. To make them useful, you must consider how they flow through your architecture. Conceptually, you can think in terms of a pipeline:

1. **Ingestion from external sources**: exchanges, data vendors, custodians, and issuers publish reference data and corporate actions in their own formats.
2. **Normalization and validation**: your systems convert these into internal formats, resolving conflicts, filling gaps, and checking for consistency.
3. **Distribution to internal consumers**: trading gateways, risk engines, portfolio systems, and backtesting platforms all need access to a consistent view.

Some key design points:

- **Single source of truth**: maintain a central symbol master or reference data store that authoritative components read from, rather than letting each system maintain its own partial copy.
- **Versioning and history**: track how reference data change over time (for example, tick-size changes, symbol changes, corporate actions) so that backtests can reconstruct the environment as it was on a given date.
- **Validation rules**: detecting anomalies early (for example, duplicated ISINs, missing tick sizes, contradictory corporate action feeds) reduces downstream errors.

The connection to earlier sections should be clear:

- Microstructure modeling assumes correct tick sizes, lot sizes, and symbology.
- Venue and asset-class behavior is only meaningful if you know which instruments belong to which venues and under what trading calendars.
- Regulatory reporting relies heavily on correct identifiers, corporate action handling, and calendars.
- Market state machines are keyed by instrument and venue; if your IDs are wrong, your perceived state will not match reality.

Reference Data Hygiene and Operational Resilience

Finally, reference data quality is an operational resilience issue. Common failure modes include:

- **Order rejects**: sending invalid symbols, wrong tick sizes, or orders in closed sessions.
- **Wrong-instrument trades**: mis-mapped symbols leading to positions in unintended instruments.
- **Valuation errors**: mis-priced positions because of incorrect multipliers, currencies, or corporate action processing.
- **Reporting errors**: inaccurate regulatory or client reports due to mismatched identifiers or calendars.

To manage these risks, firms typically implement:

- **Change controls** for reference data, with approvals for significant changes (for example, symbol merges, tick-size table updates).
- **Monitoring and alerts** for suspicious patterns (for example, sudden jumps in tick size, missing prices on days that should be active).

- **Reconciliation processes** comparing front-office positions and prices to backoffice and custody records.

From a backtesting standpoint, reference data hygiene also matters:

- Clean, well-documented symbology mappings make it easier to extend strategies across asset classes and regions.
- Historical corporate action and calendar data enable realistic simulations of long-lived strategies and portfolios.
- Consistent tick-size and lot-size handling prevents accidental exploitation of impossible price points or sizes in simulations.

In short, reference data and symbology are the connective tissue that makes the dynamic machinery of electronic markets usable. Without them, you may have sophisticated models of order books, states, and regulations, but you will not be able to direct orders at the right instruments, at the right times, with the right sizes, or explain afterward exactly what happened.

As you move strategies from backtest to live execution, investing in a robust reference data foundation is one of the highest-leverage steps you can take. It reduces operational surprises, supports regulatory compliance, and allows your microstructure-aware models to operate in a world where names, calendars, and contracts are constantly—if slowly—changing.

Chapter 2

Data and Strategy Validation

Backtests don't fail in production because your Sharpe ratio couldn't add- they fail because your assumptions couldn't. This chapter walks from the very first tick you record to the last dollar you allocate, showing how to build data and strategy validation pipelines that are brutally honest about what the market will actually let you earn.

2.1 Market Data Acquisition and Normalization

In the previous chapter we treated backtesting at a fairly conceptual level: as a controlled experiment on history whose credibility depends entirely on the quality of the inputs. In this section we move one level down, into the plumbing that makes those inputs trustworthy. Our goal is to build market data pipelines that are *deterministic* (same inputs, same outputs every time) and *reproducible* (another researcher, or future you, can rerun a study and see the same data reality). That sounds abstract, but it has a very concrete meaning: no matter how messy the real-time venue feeds are—missing packets, clock drift, symbol changes, corporate actions—your research database should present a single, consistent, analysis-ready view of the market.

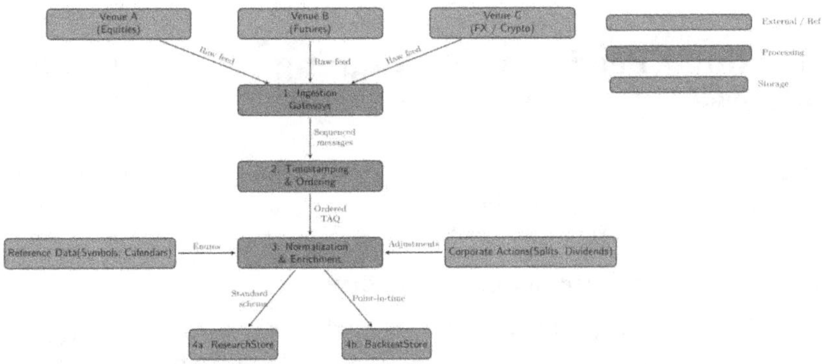

What "Research-Grade" Market Data Really Means

The term *research-grade* is used so often that it risks becoming a buzzword. In our context it has three very specific properties:

- **Causal**: At any historical decision time, the data reflects only what a trader could reasonably have known at that moment. There is no look-ahead leakage or restated information silently injected into the past.
- **Deterministic**: Given the same raw inputs, the pipeline will generate the same cleaned and normalized outputs. Randomness is not part of the cleaning logic.
- **Complete enough**: While no dataset is perfect, gaps, errors, and anomalies are known, measured, and either corrected or explicitly flagged so that strategies can account for them.

A backtest that ignores these properties will nearly always look better than it should. Mid-price fills with no fees, perfectly continuous time series, and a universe that only contains today's survivors all create an unrealistically smooth reality. The purpose of the acquisition and normalization pipeline is to push your data *away* from that fantasy and toward the noisy, inconvenient world your live strategies will face.

Choosing Feeds and Aligning the Tradable Universe

Before any code is written, you must decide what "market reality" you want to reconstruct. That choice has three main dimensions: which venues, which feed types, and which instruments.

Venues: where your orders will actually trade.

If your strategy trades U.S. equities through a smart order router, your fills may land on any of a dozen exchanges and alternative trading systems. For a futures strategy, you may have a single dominant venue but separate feeds for the central limit order book and the block market. In FX and crypto, liquidity is fragmented across many electronic communication networks and exchanges.

A good rule of thumb: *your research data should mirror your execution scope*. If you will route to Venues A, B, and C, you should at minimum have reliable trades and quotes from those venues or a consolidated feed that truthfully combines them.

Feed types: direct versus consolidated.

Direct feeds come from each venue independently. They usually offer the richest information (full depth of book, detailed flags), lowest latency, and highest complexity. Consolidated feeds (for example, securities information processors in some equity markets or third-party consolidated vendors) provide a merged view—often best bid and offer across venues—with less detail but simpler handling.

For *high-frequency* or microstructure-sensitive strategies, direct feeds are often necessary; your fills depend on which queue you were in on which venue. For *lower-frequency* strategies (intraday or daily bars), a well-constructed consolidated feed can be sufficient and far easier to maintain.

Instrument universe: tradable, realistic, and stable.

The universe you use in research should:

- Include instruments that were actually tradable for your intended size.
- Reflect the listings and delistings that occurred over time.
- Respect any regulatory or internal restrictions (for example, no shorting certain names).

At this stage you are defining not just a list of symbols, but a long-term contract: "these are the instruments for which the firm promises to maintain research-grade history." That contract has cost implications; each additional venue, feed, or asset class multiplies your data engineering burden.

Ingestion: Capturing the Raw Streams

Once you know which feeds you need, the first technical challenge is ingestion: converting raw network packets into an ordered stream of structured messages.

We typically distinguish three classes of messages:

- **Trades**: Actual transactions with price, size, and flags (for example, whether they occurred at the bid or ask).
- **Quotes**: Updates to the order book—changes in available size at each price level.
- **Reference**: Symbol definitions, trading status changes, halts, and resumptions.

The ingestion gateway (Stage 1 in the figure) has two main responsibilities.

1. Loss-aware decoding.

Real-time feeds may drop packets, arrive out of order, or be temporarily unavailable. The gateway must:

- Track sequence numbers for each channel to detect gaps.

- Mark intervals as "incomplete" when gaps occur.
- Persist the raw binary payloads (where licensing permits) so that you can re-decode with improved parsers in the future.

The key here is honesty. If you lost messages, the downstream pipeline must *know* that; fabricating plausible data to "fill in" gaps defeats the purpose of research-grade history.

2. Immutable raw storage.

Immediately after decoding, you should store the messages in an immutable, append-only format. This might be compressed columnar files, a write-optimized database, or even structured log files. The point is to have a permanent, unchanging record of "what the feed told us at the time," separate from any later normalization or corrections.

This raw layer is your ground truth; when bugs are discovered, you can regenerate higher layers from it. Without such a layer, you will be tempted to patch data in place, and reproducibility will erode.

Time, Ordering, and Causality

Time is the axis along which your backtests run, so mis-handling timestamps is one of the most subtle ways to corrupt results.

There are three common notions of time in a trading system:

- **Exchange time**: The time the venue assigns when the event occurs in its engine.
- **Gateway time**: The time your edge gateway notes on receiving the message.
- **Strategy time**: The time when your strategy logic becomes aware of the event and can act.

In historical data, we usually have at least exchange time; sometimes we also have receipt time. Strategy time is a function of your internal processing and is usually modeled in the backtester rather than stored in the data.

The timestamping and ordering stage (Stage 2 in the figure) aims to reconstruct a consistent sequence:

Use exchange time for market reality.

For most backtesting purposes, exchange time should be the primary timestamp on trades and quotes. It reflects the order in which the matching engine processed events. Exchange clocks can drift, but venues typically manage their own time coherently enough to trust the ordering within a venue.

Use receipt time to model latency.

If you have accurate gateway timestamps, you can later model the delay between when an event happened and when your systems learned about it. That matters enormously for high-frequency strategies; at millisecond scales, even the path from the matching engine to your colocation rack is nontrivial.

Preserve causality across venues.

Consolidating multiple venues complicates ordering. A trade on Venue A might have exchange time 10:00:00.001, while a quote update from Venue B has 10:00:00.000 but arrived later. Your pipeline must define deterministic rules for cross-venue ordering, for example:

- First, sort by exchange time.
- If two messages share the same timestamp, break ties using feed sequence numbers or a consistent venue priority.
- If exchange timestamps are missing or known to be unreliable for a feed, fall back to receipt time with clear documentation.

The goal is not to achieve perfect physical causality—that is impossible with limited information—but to have a *well-defined, repeatable* ordering that all downstream consumers can rely on.

Normalization: From Venue-Specific to Firm-Standard

Each venue speaks its own dialect: symbol formats, message types, flags for trade conditions, and so on. The normalization and enrichment stage (Stage 3) translates these dialects into a single, firm-wide schema.

Common message schema.

A clean starting point is to define two core tables or streams:

- A **trades** schema with fields such as instrument identifier, timestamp, price, size, side (from aggressor perspective, if available), and condition flags.
- A **quotes** schema with fields for bid/ask prices and sizes at the top of book, and optionally a compact representation of deeper levels.

On top of that, you may define aggregated views—for example, one-minute bars—but these should be derived from the core trades and quotes in a deterministic way.

Symbol mapping and stable identifiers.

Relying on raw venue symbols (like short tickers) is dangerous. Symbols can be reused, change spelling, or clash across venues. Instead, assign each instrument a *stable internal identifier* and maintain mapping tables that link venue symbols and dates to that identifier.

For example, if a stock changes its ticker from ABC to XYZ on a given date, both symbols map to the same internal ID, with validity intervals. If a futures contract rolls from the March to the June expiry, those are distinct internal IDs, but linked via a family or root identifier.

This mapping is a central component of the reference data feeding into normalization (the purple node above Stage 3). Any backtest should rely on the stable IDs, not on raw symbols, so that symbol changes over time do not segment a time series unintentionally.

Venue codes and side conventions.

Similarly, venues and order sides should be expressed using consistent internal enums. If one venue reports "B" and another "BUY" and a third uses numeric codes, you should translate them all into the same internal representation. This sounds trivial, but inconsistent flags are a recurring source of subtle bugs in execution and slippage analysis.

Currencies, units, and calendars.

For multi-asset and multi-region trading, normalization also covers:

- **Currencies**: Record the currency of price and notional explicitly; do not assume everything is in your base currency.
- **Units**: Distinguish between price per share, per contract, per lot, or per basis point of notional. Document contract multipliers for futures and options.
- **Trading calendars**: Attach each instrument to one or more calendars that define regular sessions, holidays, and partial days. This will later guide bar construction and session-based analysis.

A normalized dataset should make it impossible to confuse a price of 10 dollars per share with 10 basis points of yield; the units and context must be explicit.

Dealing with Imperfections: Gaps, Outliers, and Oddities

No matter how good your feeds and parsers are, you will encounter defects. A robust pipeline does not pretend these do not exist; it detects, labels, and often corrects them in systematic ways.

Common issues include:

- **Gaps**: Periods when trades or quotes are missing due to feed or network problems.
- **Stale quotes**: Bid and ask that remain unchanged for an unusually long time in an otherwise active market.
- **Outlier prices**: Trades far away from the prevailing market, often due to error trades or late prints.
- **Status changes**: Halts, suspensions, or auctions during which normal trading rules do not apply.

Your normalization layer should attach quality flags to each record: "in gap interval," "trade excluded from official statistics," "quote during halt," and so on. These flags allow researchers to filter appropriately for their strategies. For example, a daily bar strategy may tolerate some short gaps, while a market-making model may exclude any period with known quote issues.

It is tempting to patch data by simply deleting "bad" records or forward-filling missing ones. Resist doing this silently. Any transformation that changes raw economic content must be:

- Documented (what rule, applied where).
- Reversible or at least traceable (you can audit what changed and why).
- Parameterized so you can test how sensitive your strategies are to those choices.

The Contract Between Data Layer and Backtester

Everything we have described so far is in service of a clear contract between the data layer and the backtest engine. That contract says:

- **What the backtester can rely on.**
- **What the backtester must never assume.**

A reasonable set of guarantees from a well-designed data layer might include:

- Within each venue and instrument, trades and quotes are in a deterministic order consistent with venue timestamps and sequence numbers.
- All records contain stable instrument identifiers, venue codes, currencies, and units.
- Known gaps and anomalies are flagged; no attempt is made to fabricate missing trades.
- Corporate actions and symbol changes are represented in reference tables that can be joined by instrument and date.

- The process that built the dataset is versioned (code version, configuration, source raw data) so that the same history can be regenerated.

In return, the data layer should make explicit what it *does not* promise:

- It does not guarantee that you will see every trade that ever occurred, especially for markets with opaque or off-exchange activity.
- It does not promise perfect cross-venue causality; the ordering across different venues is based on reasonable rules, not omniscient knowledge.
- It does not convert all feeds to a common latency profile; modeling your own signal and order delays remains the backtest engine's job.

By stating these boundaries, you avoid a common failure mode where a researcher silently assumes properties that the data simply does not have (for example, assuming best bid and offer represent the full trading interest).

Designing for Determinism and Reproducibility

Two qualities separate an ad hoc data setup from an institutional-grade pipeline: determinism and reproducibility.

Deterministic transformations.

Every step in the pipeline—decoding, timestamping, normalization, aggregation—should be a pure function of its inputs and a declared configuration. There should be no hidden randomness, manual edits, or dependence on external mutable state.

Practically, this means:

- All corrections and adjustments are expressed as transformation rules, not one-off database updates.

- Configuration files (for example, symbol mapping rules, calendars) are version-controlled alongside code.
- Aggregations (like bar construction) are fully specified: which trades to include, how to handle sessions and gaps, and how to treat auctions or opening prints.

If a transformation needs a tie-breaking rule (for instance, selecting among multiple trades with the same timestamp), the rule must be fixed and documented. "Whatever the database returns first" is not acceptable.

Reproducible builds of the data universe.

A mature setup treats the data universe much like compiled software. You define:

- The raw inputs (feeds and versions, date range).
- The code version of the pipeline.
- The configuration version (mapping tables, calendars, corrections).

From these, you produce a named, timestamped "data release" that serves as the reference for research and risk reports. When you improve the pipeline—for example, by adding better outlier detection—you can build a new release, compare it with the old one, and gradually migrate strategies.

This practice has two major benefits:

- It allows you to reproduce old results, even years later, because the data and pipeline versions are preserved.
- It gives you a structured way to upgrade data quality without accidentally shifting the ground under live strategies mid-flight.

From Pipeline to Practice

The acquisition and normalization pipeline may feel far removed from the excitement of alpha discovery and live trading, but it is where most of the hidden edge or hidden landmines lie. A careful design gives you:

- Confidence that your backtests are not quietly exploiting data artifacts.

- A common language across teams (research, execution, risk) for what "the market" looked like at any time.

- The ability to debug live issues by replaying history with the same deterministic transformations.

In the next sections we will build on this foundation. With a stable, normalized view of prices and quotes, we can confront data quality more systematically: enforcing point-in-time integrity, eliminating look-ahead and survivorship biases, and designing validation tests and dashboards that continuously monitor your market reality. Only once that reality is solid does it make sense to ask whether a strategy truly adds value on top of it.

2.2 Data Quality, Look-Ahead and Survivorship Bias

In the previous section we built a deterministic market data pipeline: raw venue feeds are ingested, timestamped, normalized, and stored in a stable schema. That gave us a coherent picture of "what happened" in the market. We now add a second, equally important layer: discipline about *when* information became available and to *whom*. A backtest must not merely replay prices; it must respect the information set a trader actually had at each decision time.

This section develops that discipline. We will clarify what we mean by *data quality* in a trading context, introduce *point-in-time integrity*, and then examine two of the most damaging distortions: look-ahead bias and survivorship bias. Throughout, the key idea is simple but strict: your strategies must not benefit from information that did not exist yet, and they must not pretend that only the winners ever existed.

Four Dimensions of Data Quality

Classical data management frameworks describe data quality along many dimensions, but in trading four are especially relevant:

1. **Completeness**: Are important records missing?
2. **Accuracy**: Are the records that exist correct?
3. **Timeliness**: When did each piece of information become available?
4. **Consistency**: Do different datasets tell the same story?

The first two are intuitive. If half a day's trades are missing, you know you have a problem. If the price of a stock is recorded as one thousand instead of ten, the error jumps off the chart. Timeliness and consistency, however, are more subtle and are exactly where most backtests fail in practice.

Timeliness: the invisible axis.

Timeliness is not just about having "fresh" data in real time. In backtesting, it is about reconstructing the lag between an economic event and its appearance in your dataset. For example:

- A company's earnings announcement happens at 16:05, but your vendor's fundamental database records it at end-of-day.
- A stock is added to an index effective next Monday, but the announcement about the inclusion was released two weeks earlier.
- A corporate action (stock split) is announced today, becomes effective in two weeks, and is applied to your historical prices only after the fact.

If your backtest uses the final, cleaned, restated dataset without modeling these lags, it is almost certainly using information "too early."

Consistency: aligning overlapping worlds.

Trading strategies often draw on multiple data sources: prices and quotes, corporate actions, fundamental data, analyst estimates, index memberships, news, and sometimes alternative data. Each of these has its own conventions and timing. Consistency means that when you join them, you preserve a coherent narrative.

For example, suppose your price database already reflects a stock split effective on June 1, but your fundamentals database still shows pre-split earnings per share for a few days. A naive join may mix post-split prices with pre-split fundamentals, yielding ratios that look attractive but are meaningless. Without explicit care, such inconsistencies can systematically favor certain names in a backtest.

Point-in-Time Integrity: Replaying the Information Set

To manage timeliness and consistency, we introduce the idea of *point-in-time integrity*. At each decision time in your backtest—say 10:00 on a particular trading day—you want to be able to reconstruct exactly what a reasonably well-informed trader could have known.

This has two implications:

1. Every data item in your research database must carry not just a "valid-from" date (what period of history it refers to) but also an "as-of" or "effective in our systems" timestamp (when it became available).
2. Your backtest engine must query data *as of* the decision time, not as of today. It should ignore any information whose as-of time is in the future relative to the simulation clock.

Valid time vs. as-of time.

It helps to think in terms of two timelines:

- **Valid time**: the period in history that the data describes. For a balance sheet as of December 31, the valid time is that date.
- **As-of time**: when you, the trader or system, first see or could use that data.

These differ because information is reported with delay, may be corrected later, and sometimes is restated years after the fact. A point-in-time database preserves both notions, allowing you to answer questions like:

> "On March 15, when we rebalanced the portfolio, what did we believe the company's earnings were at that moment, given all the filings and corrections we had seen so far?"

This is the lens you must use for backtesting. If a restatement in 2024 corrects earnings from 2020, your 2020 backtest should *not* see the corrected numbers. It should see the original numbers and, if you are modeling it, the restatement only starting from the date when it was published.

Why this matters for strategy evaluation.

Many appealing signals live in these lags and revisions. For instance:

- Strategies based on "earnings surprises" can look extremely profitable if they know, at the moment of the announcement, not just the headline number but also the final, cleaned time series of revisions.
- Value strategies built on price-to-earnings or price-to-book ratios may appear to avoid value traps if they implicitly use restated fundamentals that were not available at the time.
- Event-driven strategies that trade around index inclusions and deletions may look better if they trade on the effective date using knowledge of the event that was only widely known later.

Point-in-time integrity forces you to measure performance against a realistic, delayed, sometimes messy information flow, not against hindsight-perfect data.

Look-Ahead Bias: Seeing the Future by Accident

Look-ahead bias arises whenever a strategy's decisions in the backtest are influenced by information that was not actually available at the time in history when those decisions are simulated. It is easy to introduce and often surprisingly hard to detect.

We can distinguish several common forms.

Using future prices directly.

The most blatant form is when a rule accidentally references future prices. Examples include:

- Computing a signal at the close using the same day's closing price, then assuming you trade at that close. In reality, you would know the closing price only after the close.
- Constructing features based on future returns (for example, labeling data by whether the stock went up over the next week) and then, by mistake, letting those future return labels leak into today's decision rule.

The remedy is to define a clear "decision cut-off" time for each strategy and ensure that all inputs used for decisions are lagged appropriately. If you decide at 15:59 based on intraday data, you must not use the 16:00 close price to make that decision.

Post-hoc fundamentals and restatements.

More insidious is look-ahead in fundamental or reference data. Common pitfalls:

- Using annual financial statements as if they were available at the fiscal year-end, rather than on the date they are actually filed and disseminated.
- Using a fundamentals database that silently overwrites old numbers with restated values, without preserving the original reports.
- Aggregating analyst estimates or ratings in a way that includes updates that arrived after your decision time.

Here, point-in-time integrity is the cure. Your dataset must preserve the history of changes. When your backtest looks up a value on a given date, it should only consider reports with as-of times prior to that date.

Index and membership look-ahead.

When you use index constituents (for example, "trade only S&P 500 names") you must be careful not to define membership based on today's constituents and project that back in time. Doing so implicitly assumes you knew in advance which names would remain in the index and which would be deleted.

The correct procedure is:

- Use a point-in-time record of index additions and deletions, with effective dates and announcement dates.
- For each simulation date, include only those constituents that were actually in the index at that time, based on information available as of that date.

If you instead filter your universe by "stocks that are in the index today" and then backtest over the last ten years, you are looking at a world where only survivors exist and where you never encounter names that dropped out due to poor performance or corporate events. That is survivorship bias layered on top of index look-ahead.

Survivorship Bias: A Universe with No Graveyard

Survivorship bias occurs when your dataset includes only instruments that survived to the present and omits those that delisted, merged, went bankrupt, or otherwise disappeared. Backtests run on such a "cleaned" universe almost always overstate returns and understate risk.

How survivorship bias creeps in.

The most common channel is the choice of universe:

- Many free or inexpensive datasets contain only currently listed stocks, ignoring those that delisted in previous years.
- Index constituents may be available only for recent periods, leading to a past universe composed of today's members only.
- Fundamental and price histories might silently drop symbols once they are delisted, because they are no longer "active."

Another, more subtle channel involves corporate actions. If delisted stocks are present but their final months of trading are incomplete, distorted, or misaligned with corporate action data, they may be filtered out by quality screens, effectively removing poor performers from your sample.

Why survivorship bias is dangerous.

The bias is not symmetric. Companies that delist due to bankruptcy or poor performance tend to have been bad investments prior to delisting. Removing them makes almost any long-only strategy look better. It reduces drawdowns, volatility, and tail losses. It may also overstate the benefit of certain signals that, in real time, would have led you into names that later failed.

The risk team cares deeply about this. If your backtests ignore the graveyard of failed names, your capital allocation will be based on a rose-tinted view of history. When the real world starts to resemble the forgotten tail of the distribution, your portfolio may suffer losses you never saw coming in the lab.

Building a survivorship-free universe.

To remove survivorship bias, your universe construction must:

- Include all instruments that were tradable at any point during the backtest window, regardless of their current status.
- Maintain full history up to the last trading day, including corporate actions, halts, and the final delisting event.
- Tag instruments with their lifecycle status (active, merged, delisted, suspended) as a function of time.

This is where the normalized identifiers from the previous section matter. If a company changes ticker symbols, undergoes a merger, or spins off a subsidiary, these events should be captured in reference data, not erased from history. Your backtest may then choose how to handle such events (for example, liquidate positions at the last available price), but it must not act as if the company never existed.

Practical Techniques for Enforcing Data Discipline

Having described the problems, we now turn to practical controls you can build into your pipeline and backtesting environment.

Stale-tick and sanity filters.

Stale or abnormal prices can create artificial opportunities if not flagged. For example, if quotes are frozen during a halt but trades continue elsewhere, naive mid-price calculations could show a huge spread, suggesting profitable arbitrage that did not really exist.

You can implement:

- **Stale-quote flags**: mark quotes as stale if they have not updated for a configurable period while other activity is present.
- **Price sanity checks**: flag trades that deviate too far from recent mid-prices or that are tagged by the venue as special (for example, late prints or off-market crosses).
- **Halt awareness**: incorporate trading status messages so that bars built during halts are clearly identified.

Backtests can then exclude or treat differently periods or events with low data quality, rather than unknowingly basing signals on them.

Corporate action alignment.

Corporate actions—splits, dividends, rights issues—must be applied consistently to prices, volumes, and fundamental data. Two key principles help:

- **Explicit adjustment factors**: maintain tables of split and dividend factors with effective dates and, if available, announcement dates. Use these to adjust historical prices and volumes in a reproducible way.
- **Coordinated adjustment**: ensure that ratios like earnings per share, shares outstanding, and price-to-earnings are computed on data that has been adjusted in a consistent manner. Avoid mixing pre- and post-split figures.

Again, store not just the final, fully adjusted time series, but also the underlying corporate action history so you can reconstruct the point-in-time view of what a trader would have seen.

Versioned joins and delayed availability.

When joining disparate datasets—for example, price and fundamentals—adopt a "delayed join" discipline:

- For each record in a slow-moving dataset, such as quarterly earnings, associate an availability date (filing date, or later if vendor lag is known).
- In backtests, when you query fundamentals as of a given day, only include records whose availability date is on or before that day.

This simple rule eliminates a large class of look-ahead errors. It also forces you to think carefully about the realistic delay between an event and your ability to react to it.

Data validation dashboards.

It is not enough to design rules; you must monitor whether they are working. Many firms maintain dashboards that track, for example:

- Fraction of missing or flagged data per day, per instrument, per venue.
- Distributions of returns and volumes, highlighting days with unusual spikes that may signal data issues.
- Counts of corporate actions processed and any mismatches with vendor summaries.

These dashboards serve two purposes: operational (catching feed or vendor problems quickly) and research-oriented (helping analysts judge whether an apparent anomaly is economic or merely a data artifact).

What the Backtester Must Assume and Refuse

As in the previous section, it is useful to spell out the contract, now extended with point-in-time guarantees.

A backtester that respects data quality should:

- Query all auxiliary data (fundamentals, index membership, corporate actions, reference data) using as-of times anchored to the simulation clock.
- Resist the temptation to "patch in" today's knowledge to fix past anomalies, unless the patch is modeled as a real-time correction occurring at a specific date.
- Treat missing or low-quality data as a first-class input: strategies may choose to reduce exposure or skip trades when the information set is too thin or unreliable.

Conversely, the backtester should *refuse* to:

- Use datasets that lack basic timing fields (for example, fundamentals without filing dates) as if they were point-in-time.
- Build universes based on today's active instruments without explicit historical membership rules.
- Evaluate strategies only on periods and instruments with perfect data, then casually extrapolate to the full universe.

When such shortcuts are unavoidable—for instance, when only limited history is available for a new market—they should be labeled as provisional and treated with skepticism in capital allocation decisions.

From Clean Data to Honest Experiments

Data quality, look-ahead, and survivorship are not cosmetic issues. They go to the heart of whether your backtests are honest experiments or rehearsed plays in which the actors already know the ending. A pipeline that carefully timestamps and normalizes feeds, yet ignores when information became available and who survived, will still produce misleadingly smooth results.

By imposing point-in-time discipline and eradicating survivorship bias, you accept a more uncomfortable history: one in which information arrives late, is sometimes wrong, and can be revised; one in which some instruments fail spectacularly and vanish. But this is the history your live strategies must navigate.

In the next section we will add another layer of realism: the costs of turning signals into trades. With data timing and universe issues under control, we will examine transaction costs, slippage, and market impact—the frictions that separate idealized backtest P&L from what your broker will actually fill.

2.3 Transaction Costs, Slippage, and Market Impact

In the previous sections we treated data as if it were an accurate, point-in-time record of what the market offered, and we built backtests that respected that record. In this section we take the next step: we stop pretending that every simulated order trades at the last price or the mid-price, and we start asking what the market actually *gives* you when you show up with size and urgency.

A strategy that looks excellent when it "fills at mid" can easily be untradable once you incorporate realistic costs. The purpose of this section is to give you a disciplined way to translate an idealized backtest into something that resembles a real blotter: with fees, spreads, slippage, partial fills, and impact all explicitly accounted for in the PnL path.

We will proceed in four layers:

1. Understand the taxonomy of transaction costs and how they show up in executions.

2. See why mid-price or last-price fills systematically overstate PnL.

3. Build simple but useful models of slippage and market impact, and link them to trading conditions.

4. Integrate these models into the backtest loop so that signal, execution, and cost all co-evolve.

Throughout, the guiding principle is conservative realism: you want assumptions that are tight enough to reflect your likely experience in the market, but not so pessimistic that they rule out everything except buy-and-hold.

A Taxonomy of Transaction Costs

Transaction costs are everything you pay to turn a trading decision into a position change. They fall into three broad categories.

Explicit fees and commissions

These are the easiest to understand:

- Brokerage commissions (per share, per contract, or per order).
- Exchange and venue fees, often different for adding vs. removing liquidity.
- Regulatory and clearing fees, taxes, and stamp duties in some markets.

They are usually published in fee schedules and are relatively stable over time or change in discrete steps. Because they are so visible, they often get *too* much attention relative to other costs that are less obvious but larger in magnitude.

The bid-ask spread

Every tradable instrument has two quoted prices at a point in time:

- The best bid: the highest price at which someone is currently willing to buy.
- The best ask (offer): the lowest price at which someone is currently willing to sell.

The difference between them is the spread. If you want immediate execution:

- A buy order pays the ask.
- A sell order hits the bid.

If your backtest assumes that every trade happens at the mid-price (halfway between bid and ask), then every aggressive order is implicitly given "half a spread" of free PnL relative to reality. In liquid equities, that half-spread might be a fraction of a cent; in less liquid names, futures near the close, or small-cap crypto, it can be a meaningful fraction of a percent.

Spread costs are not fixed. They vary with:

- Liquidity (tight in large caps, wide in small caps).
- Volatility (spreads often widen in fast markets).
- Time of day (wider near the open/close, tighter mid-session).
- Market regime (crisis vs. calm).

Hidden costs: slippage, queue position, and opportunity

Even if you know the spread and the fees, there are additional "hidden" costs:

- **Slippage** The difference between the price you intended to trade at (for example, the price at the time of your signal) and the actual execution price you receive. Slippage includes spreads, but it also reflects short-term price moves and your own impact.
- **Queue position** On an order book, many orders may be standing at the same price. Whether you get filled when the market trades at your price depends on where you are in the queue. Backtests that assume a fill as soon as the market touches your limit price ignore this.

- **Opportunity cost** Sometimes you do not get filled at all. You wanted to buy, the price moved away, and your order never executed. You paid no explicit cost, but your strategy may have lost the chance to earn its expected return.

From a PnL perspective, all of these belong under the umbrella of "execution shortfall": the deviation between the PnL your signals would have earned under ideal fills and the PnL you actually realize.

Why Mid-Price Fills Inflate Backtest PnL

In the data layer you now have normalized trade and quote data that faithfully record what the market looked like. In a naive backtest, you might do the following:

- Generate a signal at time t on bar or event close.
- Assume you can instantly execute at the last trade price or at the mid-price at time t.

This is unrealistic in two key ways.

Ignoring the direction of aggression

If your strategy is buying on positive signals and selling on negative signals, it is usually *taking* liquidity, not providing it. That means:

- Buys tend to trade at or above the ask.
- Sells tend to trade at or below the bid.

By filling both at the mid-price, you are:

- Giving your buys a better price than they deserve (bid + half-spread instead of full ask).
- Giving your sells a better price than they deserve (ask - half-spread instead of full bid).

Over many trades, this systematically adds a spread-related uplift to your results.

Ignoring time between signal and fill

In a realistic engine, the path from signal to execution includes:

1. Signal computation (even if just microseconds or milliseconds).
2. Order construction and risk checks.
3. Transmission to the gateway and then to the exchange.
4. Matching engine processing and queuing.

While all this is happening, prices are moving, and the order book is changing. If your strategy reacts to fast short-term patterns, even small latencies can turn a predicted edge into a disadvantage. A backtest that fills at the exact same timestamp as the signal cannot see this erosion.

These two effects-aggression and latency-are enough to make mid-price simplifying assumptions dangerous. They must be replaced with explicit cost models.

Building Intuitive Slippage and Impact Models

We now build from simple to more realistic models of slippage and market impact. Think of each model as a lens you can plug into your backtest. You can start with a coarse lens and gradually refine it as your strategy, data, and venue knowledge improve.

A basic spread-plus-fee model

The simplest step up from mid-price is:

- Aggressive marketable orders:
- Buy fills at best ask plus a small markup.

- Sell fills at best bid minus a small markdown.
- Limit orders: assume fills only when the market trades through your price, and treat them as slightly better than or equal to the passive side of the spread.

Layer on:

- Per-share or per-contract commissions.
- Per-order minimum fees.
- Exchange add/remove liquidity fees or rebates.

This model already enforces that:

- You pay at least half a spread on average when you take liquidity.
- Trading in wider-spread names is more expensive.
- Trading more frequently raises absolute costs even if trade size is small.

For many slower, higher-holding-period strategies, such a spread-plus-fee model captures the bulk of the cost story.

Introducing market impact

Market impact is the price change *caused by your own trading*. Intuitively:

- A small, patient order in a deep, liquid book barely moves the price.
- A large, urgent order relative to available liquidity pushes the price away from you.

To make this tractable, practitioners often scale order size by a liquidity proxy such as average daily volume (ADV) or the depth at the inside levels of the order book.

A common conceptual pattern is:

- For orders smaller than a few tenths of a percent of ADV, assume only spread and small slippage.
- As size grows toward several percent or more of ADV, assume slippage grows more than proportionally.

Rather than formalizing this with equations, it is helpful to picture it:

- On the horizontal axis: order size as a percentage of ADV.
- On the vertical axis: realized execution price relative to the mid or decision price.
- For small sizes, the curve is flat and close to the spread.
- For larger sizes, the curve bends upward for buys (downward for sells), reflecting growing impact.

In a backtest, you can encode this qualitatively:

- If order size is tiny relative to ADV, use a base slippage assumption tied to half the spread.
- If order size enters a "medium" band, add extra slippage proportional to size.
- If order size is large, add a more-than-proportional penalty to reflect difficulty sourcing liquidity.

This shape-gently sloping for small size, sharply increasing for large size-is precisely what the visual in this section will emphasize later.

Regime dependence: volatility, liquidity, and time of day

Impact is not the same on a calm morning and during a volatile news event. Three dimensions matter:

Volatility. When prices are moving rapidly, spreads tend to widen and depth may thin. Your order interacts with a more fragile book, so the same size tends to move the price more, and your fills are more uncertain.

Liquidity. Even at the same volatility level, some instruments are naturally thinner than others. A small-cap stock or illiquid future can be pushed around with much smaller notional size than a large-cap or a major index future.

Time of day. Many markets have U-shaped intraday liquidity: thin and jumpy at the open, deeper in the middle of the session, thinner again near the close or during lunch hours in some regions. An impact model that ignores this will underestimate costs when your strategy trades at difficult times.

A more sophisticated backtest cost model adjusts slippage parameters based on these regimes:

- Higher volatility → widen your assumed spread and slippage.
- Lower depth → treat even moderate orders as large relative to the book.
- Unfavorable times of day → move your assumed size-versus-cost curve upward.

Even if you do not have full depth-of-book data, you can often approximate these effects from top-of-book quotes and trade sizes, calibrated on historical fills where available.

Integrating Costs into the Backtest Loop

Cost modeling is not a final "haircut" you apply to a strategy's PnL after the fact. To be meaningful, costs must be integrated into the backtest itself so that they influence:

- Which trades are taken.
- When they are taken.
- How large they are.

From signals to orders

In earlier sections, we focused on signals: when to be long, short, or flat. In a cost-aware backtest, each signal must be translated into specific orders:

- Market vs. limit vs. pegged or conditional orders.
- Single-shot orders vs. sliced execution over multiple bars or events.
- Aggressiveness choices: cross the spread immediately or wait and try to provide liquidity.

Your cost model then acts on these orders:

- For a market order, it computes the expected execution price given current spread, estimated impact, and regime.
- For a limit order, it determines if and when a fill is likely, and at what price, given order book evolution and queue position assumptions.
- For a sliced execution, it accumulates the slippage and partial fills across the slices.

This order-centric view makes the backtest resemble the real trading system more closely and ensures that cost estimates are tied to concrete execution choices.

Adjusting realized PnL path

Once each simulated order has an execution price and realized size, you can compute:

- Trade-by-trade PnL: the difference between sale and purchase prices, net of all costs.
- Path-wise equity curve: how these trade PnLs accumulate over time.

The key is to apply costs at the time of trade, not retroactively. By doing so:

- You correctly penalize high-turnover periods where frequent trading amplifies spread and impact losses.
- You see the drag of transaction costs on volatility and drawdowns, not just on final return.
- You can attribute performance between "raw signal edge" and "execution drag."

This attribution is crucial. Many promising signals are viable only if you can execute them cheaply. A cost-aware backtest reveals whether your proposed speed and size of trading are compatible with your cost assumptions.

Feedback into strategy design

A robust workflow does not stop at "apply cost model and accept or reject strategy." Instead, it uses cost results to refine the strategy itself. Common feedback loops include:

- **Turnover discipline.** If costs consume a large fraction of the gross edge, consider:

- Increasing holding periods.
- Imposing a minimum signal threshold before trading.
- Using position inertia (only trade when the desired position changes meaningfully).

- **Size scaling.** If impact explodes beyond a certain size:

- Cap per-instrument or per-order size relative to ADV.
- Spread risk across more instruments to stay under impact thresholds.

- **Timing and venue selection.** If costs are high at certain times or venues:
- Avoid trading at those times unless the signal is exceptionally strong.
- Prefer venues with better historical fill quality or lower fees.

By iterating between strategy design and cost-aware backtesting, you converge toward strategies whose edges survive realistic execution frictions.

Calibration and Stress-Testing of Cost Assumptions

All cost models are approximations. To keep them from becoming sources of hidden optimism, you must both calibrate and stress-test them.

Calibration to historical executions

If you have access to historical executions from your own or similar trading activity, you can:

- Compute realized slippage as the difference between your execution price and a reference price at decision time.
- Group these observations by:
- Order size relative to ADV.
- Volatility and spread regime.
- Time of day and venue.
- Estimate average and worst-case costs in each bucket and adjust your model parameters to match.

Even a rough calibration-such as verifying that your assumed slippage per unit of size is not lower than what you have historically experienced-helps avoid underestimation.

Conservative stress scenarios

Because past conditions do not cover all futures, you should deliberately stress cost assumptions:

- Increase spreads and slippage by a factor (for example, 1.5x or 2x) across the board.
- Assume thinner liquidity and higher volatility simultaneously.
- Enforce stricter limits on maximum tradable size in stressed regimes.

You then recompute the backtest under these stressed costs:

- If a strategy only works under the lowest-cost scenario, it is fragile.
- If it remains attractive under harsher but plausible assumptions, it is more robust.

Stress-testing costs is particularly important for strategies whose edge is only a few basis points per trade. For them, minor model errors can flip expected value from positive to negative.

Putting It All Together

By the end of this section, you should see transaction costs not as an afterthought, but as a central part of strategy evaluation:

- The data and backtest frameworks you built earlier define what the market *offered*.
- Transaction cost, slippage, and impact models define what the market will *give* you when you act on those offers with real orders.

In practice, you will likely adopt a layered approach:

1. Start with a basic spread-plus-fee model to rule out obviously overactive or low-edge ideas.
2. Introduce size-dependent slippage and impact as you move toward higher capacity and shorter-horizon strategies.
3. Refine parameters using historical executions and venue statistics.
4. Stress-test cost assumptions to ensure your strategy's viability is not an artifact of optimistic modeling.

Once you have a strategy that survives this process, you can meaningfully compare it to others and decide how much capital, if any, it deserves. In the next section, we will broaden our focus from individual trades and costs to the design of the overall backtest experiment itself-how to evaluate strategies in a way that is statistically rigorous and resistant to overfitting, so the remaining edges you see have a chance of surviving contact with live markets.

2.4 Robust Backtest Design

In the previous sections we focused on getting the inputs right. We built a disciplined data pipeline, enforced point-in-time integrity, and translated trading signals into realistic executions with spreads, fees, and impact. Now we turn to the engine that ties all of this together: the backtest itself.

A backtest is not a movie of the past; it is a controlled experiment conducted on historical data. A robust design makes sure that the experiment respects how the market actually works (latency, microstructure, order lifecycles) and how statistics work (sample size, multiple testing, out-of-sample evaluation). The goal is simple but demanding: an in-sample success should have a fighting chance of surviving contact with live trading.

We will build this idea in four steps:

- Clarify the role of a backtest and its common failure modes.

- Introduce walk-forward and time-aware cross-validation.
- Embed realistic order and market microstructure behavior into the simulation.
- Control overfitting and ensure reproducibility.

Throughout, keep this mental test in mind: if you showed your backtest setup to a skeptical execution trader, would they recognize their world in it, or would they see a fantasy?

What a Backtest Is (and Is Not)

At its core, a backtest answers the question: "If I had traded this strategy, with these rules and this execution style, in this market history, how would I have done?" This may sound straightforward, but several subtle issues lurk behind each part of the question.

The strategy must be fully specified

A strategy is more than a signal formula. It includes:

- How you turn raw data into signals (including transformations and delays).
- How you map signals into positions and orders (position sizing, leverage, position limits).
- How you execute orders (market vs. limit, slicing, venue choice, urgency).
- How you manage risk (stop-losses, take-profits, position caps, portfolio-level limits).

A robust backtest requires that these elements be explicit, not implicit assumptions in your head or in hidden parts of the code.

The environment must be credible

The environment is the simulated market you trade in. It is built from the research-grade, point-in-time data you prepared earlier, plus models of:

- Latency between decision and execution.
- Order book behavior (quotes, trades, spreads).
- Transaction costs, slippage, and impact (as discussed in the previous section).

A naive environment might let you "teleport" orders into the past and trade on information that was not yet available. A robust environment forces your strategy to live in the same time and space constraints as a real trader.

The evaluation must be honest

Finally, a backtest needs honest evaluation:

- You must separate the historical period used to design and tune the strategy from the period used to test it.
- You must account for how many different ideas or parameter sets you tried before finding a "winner."
- You must summarize performance with more than just one headline statistic; you need to understand drawdowns, turnover, cost sensitivity, and more.

If any of these three pillars—strategy specification, environment credibility, or evaluation honesty—is weak, impressive PnL curves can be illusions.

Time-Aware Validation: Walk-Forward as the Backbone

In many fields, model evaluation uses random splits: you shuffle your data and reserve a random subset for testing. In trading this is inappropriate because time ordering matters. You cannot use tomorrow's data to help you tune a model that you claim would have traded today.

Instead, robust backtest design uses time-aware validation. The most practical version for trading is called *walk-forward analysis*.

The idea of walk-forward analysis

Walk-forward analysis tries to mimic how you would operate in production:

- Use an initial historical window as a "training" period to design and calibrate your strategy.
- Freeze the strategy configuration and trade it forward in the next block of time, recording performance. This is a "test" period.
- Slide the window forward: extend the training period by including the just-tested data, re-tune if needed, then test again on the subsequent block.
- Repeat until you reach the end of your available history.

Train windows are always strictly before their corresponding test windows. At no point does a test window leak back into its own training.

This procedure yields a sequence of out-of-sample performance segments. Concatenated, they provide a more realistic estimate of how your strategy would have evolved over time, including adjustments you might make as you learn from new data.

Design choices in walk-forward setups

Several design choices matter:

Window lengths.

- A very short training window may not give enough data to calibrate the strategy, especially for low-frequency signals.
- A very long training window may include outdated regimes and slow your reaction to structural shifts.

You typically choose training and test lengths based on:

- The holding period of the strategy (shorter for high-frequency, longer for monthly rebalance).
- The typical length of stable market regimes in your universe.

Overlapping vs. non-overlapping windows.

- Non-overlapping test windows are simpler and provide clean segments of performance.
- Overlapping windows (where each new test period overlaps the previous one in calendar time) can provide more "samples" of out-of-sample behavior but require more care in interpretation.

Recalibration frequency.

Recalibrating too often can lead to chasing recent noise; too rarely and the model can become stale. Your walk-forward design should reflect how frequently you realistically plan to adjust parameters in production.

Visualizing walk-forward over time

Because this concept is central, it helps to visualize how training and test windows march forward over historical data. The diagram below shows a time axis with alternating training and test segments, each labeled, making it clear that tomorrow's test data never appears in today's training set.

Respecting Latency and Microstructure in the Engine

With the temporal structure of evaluation in place, we turn to the mechanics inside each walk-forward experiment. A robust backtest engine must simulate how orders interact with the market over time, not simply "snap" trades to prices.

Event-driven vs. bar-based engines

There are two broad styles of backtest engines:

Bar-based engines.

These operate on aggregated bars (for example, 1-minute or daily OHLCV). At each bar:

- You compute signals from past bars.
- You decide on trades.

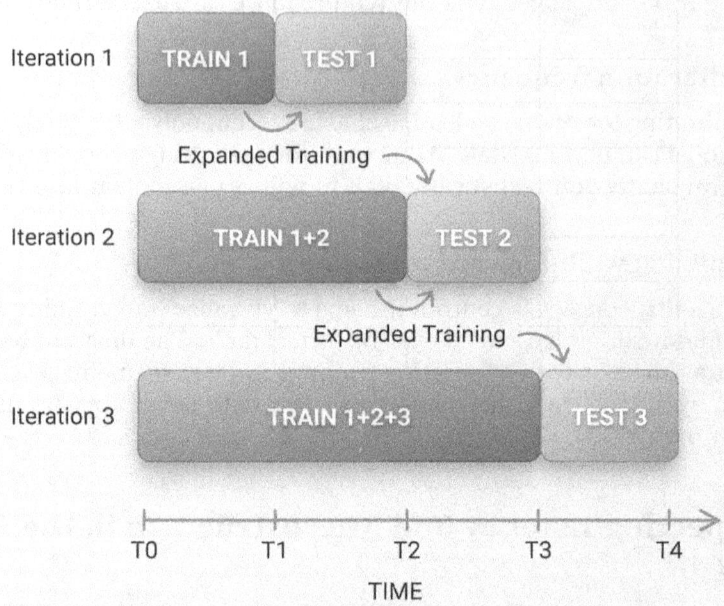

- You execute those trades at some assumed price derived from the bar (open, close, volume-weighted average, etc.).

Bar-based engines are simpler and computationally cheap, but they hide intra-bar dynamics: the sequence of quotes and trades within the bar that real orders would interact with.

Event-driven engines.

These operate on the actual stream of events:

- Quote updates (bid/ask changes).
- Trades.

- Your own orders and fills.

At each event, you update signals (if appropriate), decisions, and the state of the order book and your orders. Event-driven engines can represent microstructure and latency much more faithfully, but they are more complex and resource-intensive.

Which style you choose depends on your strategy's time scale:

- For intraday or high-frequency strategies, event-driven simulation is usually essential.
- For slower, daily or weekly strategies, a carefully designed bar-based engine may suffice, as long as you avoid inconsistent assumptions about when signals are known and when trades occur.

Modeling the order lifecycle

Regardless of engine style, you must represent the lifecycle of an order:

- **Signal time.** A signal is computed at a specific time using only data available up to that time.
- **Decision and routing delay.** There is a delay between signal and order arrival at the exchange: computation, risk checks, and network transmission.
- **Queueing.** Once at the venue, your order joins the order book. Limit orders wait in a price-time queue; market orders consume available liquidity.
- **Fills and partial fills.** Fills may occur all at once or in multiple pieces over time, as other participants trade against your order.
- **Amendments and cancellations.** You may cancel or modify outstanding orders in response to new information or risk constraints.

A naive backtest often skips most of these steps, jumping directly from signal to full fill at a favorable price. A robust design implements at least a coarse representation of each phase, especially for strategies sensitive to microseconds, milliseconds, or seconds.

Latency and stale information

Latency is more than just a delay; it changes what information your decisions are based on. For example:

- You compute a signal from a quote at time t.
- Due to processing and network delays, your order reaches the exchange at time t plus a few milliseconds.
- By then, the quote may have changed; perhaps the price has moved, the spread has widened, or the depth has thinned.

If your backtest assumes that the market at time of order arrival is identical to what you saw at signal time, you are granting yourself an informational and timing advantage that does not exist in reality. A better approach is to:

- Explicitly model the time between signal and order arrival.
- Use the market state at order-arrival time, not signal time, to determine fills and costs.

Even in bar-based engines, you can approximate this by:

- Using only data up to the bar close to compute the next bar's orders.
- Executing trades at the next bar's open or volume-weighted average, instead of the same bar's close.

This simple shift enforces a minimum one-bar latency and avoids lookahead.

Queue position and fill uncertainty

For limit orders, whether you get filled when the market touches your price depends on your position in the queue and on how much volume trades at that price. A realistic backtest will not assume a fill just because the price prints at your level. Instead, it will:

- Track how much volume is ahead of you in the order book at your price.
- Reduce that queue as trades occur.
- Only grant you a fill once enough volume has traded to reach your position.

If your data does not provide full depth, you can approximate queue position by:

- Assuming you join the back of the visible top-of-book size.
- Using historical fill ratios at touch for similar orders to estimate your fill probability.

Even a rough queue model is better than the optimistic assumption that every touch is a fill.

Statistical Rigor and Multiple Testing

Once your backtest mechanics are realistic, you still face a powerful adversary: randomness. Noise in financial data can easily produce patterns that look like edges in-sample but vanish out of sample. Robust backtest design must therefore include basic statistical discipline.

Overfitting by parameter tuning

Most strategies have parameters: lookback windows, thresholds, decay rates, and so on. It is tempting to sweep over many combinations and pick the one with the best historical PnL.

The more parameter combinations you try, the higher the chance that one of them will look good purely by luck. To reduce this risk:

- Use relatively simple models with as few free parameters as needed.
- Restrict parameter ranges based on economic or microstructure reasoning, not just performance.

- Evaluate candidate parameter sets in out-of-sample walk-forward tests, not just in the in-sample period where they were chosen.

Multiple strategy and feature searches

Overfitting does not only occur in numeric grids. It also occurs when you:

- Try many alternative features or signals.
- Test many asset universes or subsets.
- Experiment with numerous variations of position sizing or risk rules.

If only the "best-looking" results survive to a final report, you are implicitly selecting on performance. A robust research process counters this by:

- Keeping a research log of all ideas tried, not just the successful ones.
- Being skeptical of strategies that only emerged after extensive trial-and-error on the same dataset.
- Validating final candidates on genuinely untouched data or in paper-trading environments before committing capital.

Using multiple metrics, not just returns

A statistically honest evaluation uses multiple lenses:

- Return per unit of risk (for example, Sharpe-like measures).
- Drawdown depth and duration.
- Turnover and cost load as a share of gross alpha.
- Stability over time: does performance depend on one exceptional period?

- Behavior across market regimes: bull, bear, high volatility, calm.

A strategy that earns high returns but only in one or two short windows, or only by trading with extreme leverage, is less trustworthy than one with modest returns but consistent behavior across time and regimes.

Walk-forward analysis is especially helpful here: by examining metrics in each out-of-sample segment, you can see whether performance is consistent or whether it degrades sharply after the initial design period.

Reproducibility and Determinism

Finally, robustness is not only about realism and statistics; it is also about engineering discipline. A backtest whose results you cannot reliably reproduce is of limited use, no matter how carefully designed in theory.

Versioning of data and code

Your backtest depends on:

- The exact versions of your market data (including corrections and adjustments).
- The exact version of your backtest engine and strategy code.
- The configuration that ties them together (parameters, universes, cost models).

To make runs reproducible:

- Store data snapshots or use point-in-time data services that can reconstruct past states.
- Use version control for code, with tags corresponding to significant backtest runs.
- Save configuration files alongside results, not just in memory or temporary scripts.

Determinism in distributed environments

Many backtest platforms use parallel processing to speed up simulations across instruments, time slices, or parameter sets. Parallelism can introduce subtle non-determinism if you are not careful. For example:

- Floating-point accumulation order differences can cause small numerical discrepancies.
- Random sampling (for example, in stochastic models or resampling procedures) can change from run to run unless seeds are fixed.

A robust design aims for deterministic behavior:

- Fix random seeds and record them with each run.
- Structure the engine so that operations that affect PnL do not depend on non-deterministic iteration orders.
- Where exact bit-level repeatability is not practical, ensure that differences between runs are immaterial for decision-making.

Audit trail and diagnostics

A good backtest is accompanied by a clear audit trail:

- Logs of key events (strategy configuration, major parameter choices, data range used).
- Summaries of data quality checks performed.
- Diagnostics about execution modeling (for example, fill rates for limit orders, average slippage, distribution of latencies).

These artifacts allow you to revisit past results years later and understand exactly what was done, spot mistakes, and build incrementally rather than repeatedly reinventing.

Taken together, these ingredients—time-aware validation, realistic latency and microstructure modeling, statistical discipline, and reproducibility—turn your backtest from a fragile storytelling tool into a robust experimental platform. With such a platform in place, you can approach the final steps of strategy validation with more confidence: understanding where PnL really comes from, how sensitive it is to your assumptions, and how to monitor strategies in live trading so that they are shut down or scaled back before small problems become trading disasters.

2.5 Strategy Risk, Sensitivity, and PnL Attribution

By this point in the chapter, you have built a credible pipeline from data to strategy: the market data is research-grade, the backtests respect point-in-time information, executions include realistic costs, and the simulation engine honors latency and microstructure. The next question is not "Does the backtest make money?" but something more demanding:

> *Why does this strategy make money, how fragile is that edge, and how much capital can we responsibly allocate to it?*

Answering this requires you to move from raw performance curves to structured diagnosis. You must decompose PnL into understandable pieces, probe how those pieces change when assumptions shift, and define clear conditions under which the strategy should be scaled up, scaled down, or turned off.

This section develops three ideas in turn:

- PnL attribution: breaking returns into components that can be interpreted and monitored.
- Sensitivity and robustness: understanding how performance changes when key inputs or market conditions change.
- Risk and capital decisions: translating attribution and sensitivity into position limits, risk thresholds, and reallocation rules.

The goal is to turn a promising backtest into a strategy that fits coherently into a portfolio and can be supervised with discipline once live.

What PnL Attribution Is Trying to Answer

PnL attribution is the process of explaining where your performance comes from in a way that is both numerically accurate and conceptually meaningful. It should help you answer questions like:

- Is the strategy mainly riding broad market trends, or is it extracting a more idiosyncratic edge?
- Are profits dominated by a few instruments, venues, or times of day?
- How much of the gross edge is being eaten up by transaction costs and slippage?
- Is performance driven by good signals or by aggressive risk-taking (for example, high leverage, concentrated bets)?

A useful way to think of attribution is as a layered breakdown. At the top you have total PnL; at lower layers you split it into components that correspond to distinct economic or microstructural forces. Each layer should be:

- **Additive:** components sum to the total.
- **Interpretable:** each component answers a clear question.
- **Actionable:** large or changing components suggest concrete responses.

Without such structure, it is easy to misdiagnose a strategy that is temporarily lucky, structurally flawed, or quietly becoming more risky than intended.

Decomposing Strategy Returns

There is no single "correct" way to decompose PnL, because strategies differ widely. However, several recurring layers appear across many electronic trading approaches. We will introduce them from coarse to fine.

Directional versus non-directional components

At the coarsest level, you can separate:

- **Directional PnL:** profits or losses that come from being long or short in instruments that move up or down. Trend-following, carry trades, and most long-only or long-short equity strategies have a strong directional component.
- **Market-neutral or microstructure PnL:** profits that do not rely heavily on broad market moves, such as earning the bid-ask spread as a market maker, cross-sectional mean reversion, or relative-value arbitrage between closely related instruments.

Practically, you can estimate the directional component by measuring how much of your PnL moves with well-known risk factors, such as:

- Overall equity indices or bond indices.
- Style factors like value, momentum, size, or quality.
- FX carry or term-structure curves in rates.

Whatever is left after accounting for these broad drivers can be viewed as more idiosyncratic. A strategy that appears market-neutral but in fact earns most of its returns from hidden directional bets is riskier than it seems: a regime change in those hidden factors can quickly erase the apparent edge.

Carry, roll-down, and spread components

Many strategies, especially in fixed income, FX, and derivatives, earn or pay "carry":

- Positive or negative interest rate differentials between currencies.
- Yield differences between bonds of different maturities or credit quality.
- Option theta and volatility risk premia.

Here, PnL can often be decomposed into:

- *Carry*: the income you earn from simply holding the position through time, assuming no changes in prices or yields.
- *Roll-down or convergence*: gains or losses from instruments moving along a curve or converging toward a reference value as time passes.
- *Price shocks*: unexpected changes in yields, spreads, or implied volatility.

This breakdown clarifies whether your strategy is truly forecasting changes (for example, predicting tightening of a credit spread) or mainly collecting a risk premium that is exposed to occasional large shocks (for example, spread widening in a crisis).

Microstructure and execution components

For electronic strategies, microstructure and execution matter enormously. You can separate:

- **Pre-cost alpha:** PnL that the *signal* would earn if trades executed at a reference price, such as mid-price at decision time.
- **Execution drag:** the loss due to transaction costs, slippage, and market impact relative to that reference.

Execution drag can be further split:

- Explicit fees and commissions.

- Spread costs (average half-spread or more paid).
- Adverse selection and impact (prices moving against you around your trades).
- Missed opportunities (signals that would have made money but did not trade because orders were not filled).

This layer ties directly back to the cost modeling in the previous section. If you discover that a large share of gross alpha is being consumed by execution drag, you have at least three levers:

- Slow down the strategy (reduce turnover).
- Improve execution (change order types, venues, or urgency).
- Tighten the signal (trade only when expected edge is clearly above cost).

Cross-sectional breakdowns

In addition to these economic layers, attribution should also answer "where" questions:

- **By instrument:** which names, contracts, or pairs contribute most to PnL and risk?
- **By sector, country, or asset class:** are returns concentrated in specific segments of the universe?
- **By venue:** do certain exchanges or liquidity pools systematically generate better or worse execution results?
- **By time of day or session:** does performance cluster in particular intraday windows?

These breakdowns help detect hidden concentrations and fragilities. For example:

- A "diversified" equity strategy might actually derive most of its PnL from a narrow sector.

- A cross-asset strategy could be heavily reliant on one venue's particular microstructure quirks.

- Intraday PnL may come mainly from opening or closing auctions, which can behave differently in stress.

Once you have these attributions, you can start asking whether the concentrations are intentional (and priced accordingly) or accidental (and thus a source of unsuspected risk).

Understanding Strategy Fragility Through Sensitivity Analysis

Attribution tells you where PnL is coming from under your *current* assumptions and historical sample. Sensitivity analysis asks a harder question: *How does that picture change when key knobs are turned or when the environment differs from the backtest?*

Think of sensitivity as gently but systematically poking the strategy to see where it bends or breaks. There are several useful axes to poke along.

Sensitivity to transaction costs and impact

Because electronic strategies often operate with thin net edges (tens of basis points or less), small changes in transaction costs can flip sign. You should therefore:

- Re-run backtests with transaction costs uniformly scaled up, by say 50% or 100%.

- Stress the cost model more selectively in challenging regimes: higher volatility, wider spreads, thinner liquidity.

- Examine not only final return but also turnover, trade count, and the fraction of signals that remain attractive under higher-cost assumptions.

A robust strategy typically retains acceptable performance under moderately more conservative cost assumptions. If instead the strategy collapses as soon as you move away from the most optimistic cost model, then its edge is fragile, and deployment should be reconsidered or limited.

Sensitivity to latency and execution speed

Latencies change with infrastructure, routing decisions, and market load. To gauge sensitivity:

- Introduce additional delays between signal formation and order arrival (for example, double your best estimate of live latency).
- Change execution style from fully aggressive to more patient, or vice versa, and observe PnL changes.
- For high-frequency or intraday strategies, test the effect of slight randomization of order timing to capture the impact of jitter.

If performance is highly sensitive to small increases in latency or minor changes in execution policy, the strategy is effectively a race: it only works if you consistently beat other participants to the same trades. That may or may not be an acceptable business proposition, but it is a very different risk profile from a strategy that is robust to moderate timing degradation.

Parameter robustness

Any non-trivial strategy has parameters: lookback horizons, volatility targets, thresholds for entering or exiting positions, and so on. A common pattern of overfitting is that performance spikes at a particular parameter value but deteriorates quickly as you move away from it.

Parameter sensitivity analysis involves:

- Varying one parameter at a time around the chosen value and observing how performance metrics change.

- For key pairs of parameters, scanning a grid of values to see whether there is a broad plateau of good performance or a narrow ridge.

- Repeating this analysis in multiple walk-forward windows or on different market segments.

Strategies that perform well over a wide region of parameter space are generally more trustworthy than those that require fine tuning. In other words, you prefer a "flat hill" of good performance to a sharp, isolated peak.

Regime and stress sensitivity

Markets go through regimes: bull and bear phases, volatility spikes and lulls, liquidity expansions and contractions, structural changes in regulations or trading technology. A strategy that thrives only in one regime is inherently fragile.

You can study regime sensitivity by:

- Tagging historical periods by regime (for example, high vs. low volatility, crisis vs. calm) and computing PnL attribution separately in each.

- Identifying periods of known stress (for example, major market shocks, flash crashes, sudden illiquidity) and examining how the strategy behaved.

- Creating synthetic stress tests by, for example, widening spreads, increasing gaps between prices, or introducing more frequent trading halts in the simulation.

The objective is not to demand that every strategy perform well in every regime. Rather, it is to understand *which* regimes your strategy depends on, how it behaves in adverse conditions, and whether those behaviors are acceptable within your portfolio and risk appetite.

From Diagnostics to Risk Limits and Capital Allocation

PnL attribution and sensitivity analysis are only fully valuable if they feed into clear risk and capital decisions. In practice, this means defining risk measures, limits, and rules that link strategy behavior to concrete actions.

Core risk measures at the strategy level

For each strategy, you should track at least:

- **Volatility and drawdowns:** not just average returns, but the typical and worst historical path of losses.
- **Leverage and concentration:** exposure relative to capital, broken down by asset, sector, and factor.
- **Cost and slippage drift:** how realized execution drag compares to the assumptions used in the backtest.
- **Turnover and liquidity footprint:** how frequently the strategy trades and what fraction of daily volume it represents in its instruments.

These measures connect directly to risk limits. For example, you might impose:

- A maximum allowable drawdown over a given horizon before the strategy is reviewed or halted.
- A cap on gross or net exposure, or on leverage.
- A cap on participation rate (for example, never trade more than a given percentage of average daily volume).

Kill switches and de-risking rules

A "kill switch" is a pre-defined condition under which the strategy should be shut down or significantly de-risked. Good kill-switch rules are:

- **Simple:** based on a small number of clear indicators.
- **Observable:** can be monitored in near real time.
- **Aligned with your diagnostics:** tied to the ways you know the strategy can fail.

Examples of such triggers include:

- *Performance-based:* a drawdown exceeding a specified threshold, especially if concentrated in a short time or accompanied by a deterioration in hit rate.
- *Execution-based:* realized slippage or fill rates deviating materially from expectations, suggesting that microstructure conditions have changed.
- *Regime-based:* volatility or spreads exceeding levels where sensitivity analysis indicated the strategy becomes unstable.

Importantly, kill switches should be decided *before* going live, using insights from backtest attribution and sensitivity. Changing them ad hoc in response to stress undermines their value.

Capital allocation and reallocation across strategies

In a multi-strategy environment, each strategy competes for capital. PnL attribution and risk diagnostics guide how much capital each should receive:

- Strategies with stable, well-understood sources of PnL, robust sensitivity profiles, and acceptable risk-adjusted returns can be scaled up.
- Strategies whose edge appears narrowly concentrated, highly regime-dependent, or very sensitive to costs and latency may warrant reduced capital or experimental status.
- Highly correlated strategies should not each receive full capital as if independent; attribution to common factors helps avoid double-counting the same risk.

Reallocation should be systematic rather than reactive. For example:

- Periodically (for instance, monthly or quarterly), review each strategy's recent performance in the context of its historical pattern and sensitivity expectations.
- Increase or decrease capital based on whether realized behavior matches the profile established in backtests and early live runs.
- Consider portfolio-level limits on exposure to specific factors or microstructure risks that can be hit by multiple strategies simultaneously.

Striking the right balance between persistence and adaptability is key. You do not want to yank capital away at the first drawdown if the drawdown is consistent with historical behavior. Equally, you do not want to keep funding a strategy whose live behavior has clearly diverged from its validated profile.

Closing the Loop: Monitoring and Continuous Validation

The journey from backtest to live strategy does not end at deployment. Instead, deployment starts a continuous validation loop:

- **Monitor live PnL attribution.** Replicate, as far as possible, the same breakdowns you used in research: by factor, asset, venue, time of day, and cost component.
- **Track sensitivity indicators.** Compare current conditions (costs, spreads, volatility, participation rates) to the ranges explored in sensitivity analysis.
- **Detect drift.** Identify when the mix of PnL components or the relationship between pre-cost and post-cost PnL changes meaningfully.
- **Respond via risk rules.** Apply kill switches, de-risking, or reallocation rules when triggers are hit, and record the rationale.

Over time, this loop also feeds back into improved research:

- Live PnL attribution highlights which components are more or less stable than originally thought.
- Observed sensitivities during real market stress refine your assumptions for the next generation of strategies.
- Cases where kill switches were triggered become valuable "case studies" for improving both backtest design and risk frameworks.

In this way, strategy risk, sensitivity analysis, and PnL attribution are not just end-of-pipeline reports; they are integral parts of a living process that keeps your trading systems aligned with evolving markets and with your firm's risk appetite. Combined with the data, execution, and backtest design disciplines developed earlier in the chapter, they form the final layer of defense between seductive historical PnL and robust, sustainable live performance.

Chapter 3

Connectivity and Market Data Infrastructure

Markets are not just matching engines and algos; they are timing machines. This chapter steps beneath the trading logic into the wiring, clocks, and controls that determine what you actually see and when you see it. You'll design a market data fabric that is precise enough for compliance, fast enough for alpha, and predictable enough that a backtest can be replayed as if the market were happening again-on demand.

3.1 Networks, Time Sync, and Clock Compliance

In the previous chapter we treated connectivity mostly as a question of reachability: can you open and maintain robust sessions to venues, brokers, and data vendors, and can you move orders and market data between components without loss? In this section we add a more demanding requirement: *deterministic time*.

Electronic markets are not just about which messages arrive, but *when* they arrive and how confidently you can prove that timing later to yourself, to risk managers, and to regulators. Time is the first-class dependency under every other metric in this book: latency measurement, fair sequencing of orders, backtest alignment with live data, and post-trade surveillance all assume that your clocks are correct and consistently interpreted.

We will work from the physical edge of your network inwards, designing a timing substrate that spans the exchange cross-connect, your colocation racks and core data centers, and finally your wide-area links. Along the way, we will contrast retail-grade time synchronization with the precision and governance that a serious trading operation requires.

Why "Good Enough" Time Is Not Enough

Most general IT systems are content with what we might call "wall-clock correctness": if servers agree on the current time within a second or so, applications are fine. Traditional NTP (Network Time Protocol) against a few public internet time servers usually suffices.

Trading systems live in a different universe:

- Market data messages and orders are often only microseconds apart.
- Venue rules and regulations may require timestamping to the microsecond or better, with documented accuracy relative to a reference time.
- Strategy logic and risk checks rely on time deltas: how long since the last quote, how long an order has been resting, how long a gateway took to respond.
- Post-trade analytics and surveillance reconstruct event timelines across many systems and venues; if clocks disagree, causality becomes ambiguous.

If two gateways disagree by even a few hundred microseconds, a post-mortem might show an order apparently arriving *before* the quote that triggered it. A compliance team, regulator, or counterparty may contest your narrative, and you will have no defensible way to prove the actual sequence.

This is why we talk not just about time synchronization, but about a *deterministic timing substrate*: an engineered, monitored, and governed system of clocks, networks, and processes that make your timestamps *trustworthy*.

From Retail NTP to Layered Timing Architectures

Before we discuss designs, it helps to outline the basic actors:

- **Reference clocks**: Devices that derive time from an external standard such as GPS, GNSS, or PTP delivered over a trusted network.
- **Distribution clocks**: Network devices (often switches or dedicated timing appliances) that relay time into your network while compensating for known delays.
- **Client clocks**: Hosts and appliances—feed handlers, gateways, databases, risk engines—that ultimately attach timestamps to events.

A simple corporate NTP setup might use a few internet-based NTP servers as references, a couple of internal servers as distributors, and all hosts as clients. For trading, this is fragile and often not precise enough:

- The internet path to public NTP servers adds variable latency and jitter.
- The internal hierarchy is often poorly documented, with hidden single points of failure.
- NTP itself, while robust, is not optimized for sub-microsecond synchronization across a data center.

By contrast, a *layered timing architecture* for trading typically uses:

- GPS-disciplined grandmaster clocks in each major site.
- PTP (Precision Time Protocol) for high-accuracy distribution within the data center.
- NTP as a complementary, lower-precision layer for less critical systems and as a fallback.
- Boundary and transparent clocks in switches to minimize and account for network-induced delay.
- Careful segregation of timing traffic from ordinary production flows.

We will build such a hierarchy step by step, then add the observability and governance that make it dependable in practice.

An End-to-End Time Synchronization View

Before diving into each component, it is useful to visualize the entire timing path: how reference time enters your environment, how it is distributed, and how it attaches to actual packets and events.

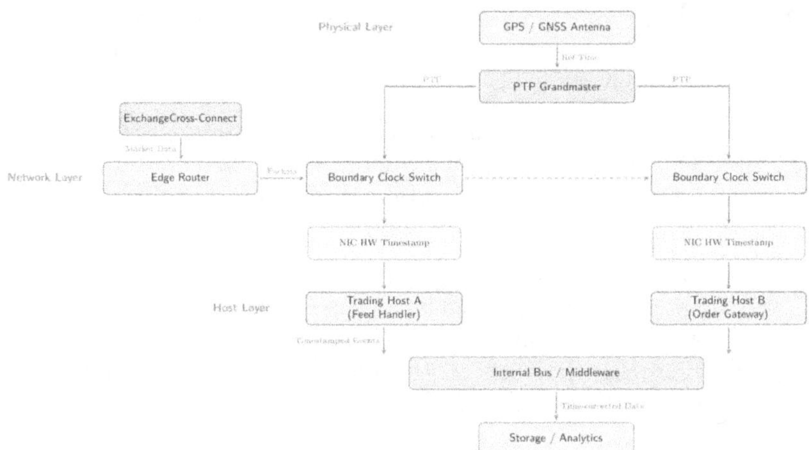

This picture emphasizes three ideas that will recur throughout the chapter:

- Time enters your environment through a small number of reference devices.
- Time is distributed through a dedicated hierarchy of network elements.
- Timestamps are applied as close to the wire as possible, then carried faithfully through internal systems.

Designing the Clock Hierarchy

Reference and Grandmaster Clocks

At the top of the hierarchy sit your reference clocks. In a colocated environment, these are typically GPS-disciplined PTP grandmasters located either in the same site as your trading racks or in a nearby timing room.

Key design choices include:

- **Redundancy:** Use at least two independent grandmasters per site, ideally with separate GPS antennas and diverse power and network paths. The loss of a single grandmaster should not degrade the entire facility.
- **Holdover performance:** When GPS is temporarily unavailable (for example, indoor antenna issues or external interference), the grandmaster should maintain a stable clock for a reasonable period. High-quality oscillators (such as OCXO or, at the top end, rubidium) help.
- **Role segregation:** Avoid letting an ordinary application server act as a PTP grandmaster. Treat grandmasters as specialized infrastructure with tightly controlled configuration and change processes.

Even firms that are not colocated can benefit from a similar pattern in their primary data center, using GPS or leased time services as the reference.

Boundary and Transparent Clocks

Below the grandmasters, your network switches become active participants in time synchronization.

- A *boundary clock* switch receives time from a grandmaster and then acts as a PTP master for devices connected downstream. It separates timing domains and reduces the load on the grandmaster.
- A *transparent clock* switch does not act as a master itself but measures and corrects for the time spent inside the switch, improving accuracy for clients further downstream.

In a trading data center, top-of-rack switches for trading hosts often run boundary clock mode, fed by distribution switches that themselves synchronize directly against the grandmasters. This creates a tree: grandmaster at the root, distribution switches as intermediate nodes, and access switches at the leaves.

Design goals for this layer:

- **Short and simple paths:** Minimize the number of hops between grandmaster and host. Each additional hop adds complexity and potential error.
- **Dedicated timing VLANs:** Carry PTP traffic in a separate VLAN or QoS class from normal data. This reduces interference from market data bursts and management traffic.
- **Diverse paths:** Where practical, provide alternate timing paths so that a single switch failure does not isolate a group of hosts from accurate time.

Host-Level Synchronization

At the leaves of the tree are your trading hosts: the machines that actually send orders, process market data, run risk, and store logs. These hosts must synchronize their internal clocks to the timing hierarchy *and* must correctly expose that time to software and hardware components.

Key points:

- **PTP client daemons:** On hosts that demand sub-microsecond precision, run a PTP client (for example, a specialized daemon) configured to use local boundary clocks as masters.
- **NTP as backup:** Keep NTP configured as a secondary source, ideally pointing at the same site's time servers. If PTP fails, hosts can fall back to NTP with a graceful degradation rather than an abrupt jump.
- **Kernel and NIC support:** Modern NICs and kernels can timestamp packets at the hardware level; the PTP client should program the NIC's clock, not just the host's software clock, so that in-flight packet timestamps are meaningful.

It is useful to think of each host as having multiple clocks: a hardware NIC clock, a kernel clock, a user-space notion of time, and perhaps separate clocks in accelerators or FPGAs. The job of your timing architecture is to ensure that these are all tightly aligned with the reference.

Isolating Time Traffic from Production Flows

Timing traffic competes for the same physical mediums as normal application packets, but you should not let application bursts dictate the quality of your clocks. There are three main isolation techniques:

Logical Separation: VLANs and QoS

Place PTP packets on dedicated VLANs or logically separate interfaces where practical. Configure Quality of Service (QoS) so that timing packets have high priority and low latency, even when market data or order traffic spikes. Timing packets are typically small and infrequent, so giving them priority has negligible cost but big stability benefits.

Physical Separation for Critical Links

For extremely demanding environments, run separate physical links for PTP between grandmasters and key boundary switches, or even separate timing networks. This ensures that no amount of production traffic can interfere with timing, though it increases cost and operational complexity.

Rate Limiting and Policing

Protect timing interfaces against accidental floods. Misconfigurations or software bugs can cause storms of PTP traffic that distort clocks. Use rate limiting and control-plane protection features on switches to keep timing traffic within expected bounds.

Measuring Offset, Jitter, and Skew

Design alone does not guarantee correct time. You must measure and monitor key indicators:

- **Offset**: The difference between a client's clock and its reference.
- **Jitter**: The short-term variability of that offset.
- **Skew or drift**: The systematic tendency of a clock to gain or lose time when left free-running.

Per-Host Metrics

On each host, your PTP and NTP daemons can expose:

- Current offset from the master.
- Estimated jitter or dispersion.
- Frequency adjustments being applied to the local clock.

Export these metrics into your central observability system. Set service-level objectives such as "99.9% of the time, offset must be within 100 microseconds of the grandmaster" for critical trading hosts, and less strict bounds for non-latency-sensitive systems.

Cross-Host Cross-Checks

Relying only on the client-reported offset can be misleading if an entire timing domain drifts together. Cross-checks help:

- Compare timestamps from independent sources (for example, logs from two different systems that both record the same external event).

- Maintain a small number of hosts that also synchronize to an external time source via a different path (for example, a separate grandmaster, or a high-quality WAN-delivered time feed) and monitor divergences.

The goal is to detect not just local noise, but systemic shifts that could affect your entire environment.

Timestamping at the Right Places

Once clocks are well synchronized, you must decide *where* to assign timestamps to events. There are several natural points:

- At the **network interface**: NIC hardware can append timestamps to packets as they arrive or depart.
- At the **gateway or feed handler**: software can record when it finished reading a message from a socket or buffer.
- At the **middleware or storage layer**: systems can timestamp as they enqueue, forward, or persist messages.

In low-latency trading, you want the earliest feasible timestamp—usually at or near the NIC—for two reasons:

1. It captures wire time with minimal influence from variable software processing.
2. It allows you to break down end-to-end latency into network, kernel, and application components.

However, later layers should still include their own timestamps so that you can reconstruct the path of each event. For example, a market data packet might carry:

- A NIC-level ingress timestamp.
- A feed-handler decode timestamp.

- A bus-publish timestamp.
- A strategy-consumption timestamp.

All of these depend on the same timing substrate; if clocks drift, your entire latency picture becomes untrustworthy.

Regulatory and Compliance Expectations

Regulation has increasingly codified what was once just a technical best practice. While specifics vary by jurisdiction and asset class, a few themes are common:

- **Accuracy requirements:** Timestamps on reportable events (orders, trades, quotes) must be accurate to within a specified bound relative to an external standard (for example, within 1 microsecond or 100 microseconds of UTC).
- **Consistency across systems:** Order management, execution venues, and reporting systems must be able to reconstruct coherent timelines; large unexplained offsets can be grounds for concern.
- **Auditability:** Firms must retain records of how their clocks were synchronized, which devices served as time sources, and when configurations changed.

This drives two additional requirements beyond basic engineering:

Documented Clock Configurations

Treat your timing infrastructure like any other regulated control:

- Maintain an inventory of grandmasters, boundary clocks, and critical PTP/NTP servers, including hardware models, locations, and firmware versions.
- Keep version-controlled configuration files for PTP and NTP daemons, with change history and approvals.

- Map which systems rely on which timing servers; this dependency graph is invaluable in incident response.

Retention of Time-Sync Logs

Log files from PTP and NTP processes are often not considered "business-critical" and can be accidentally rotated away. For trading, they are part of your evidentiary trail.

Define policies such as:

- Retain summarized time-sync metrics for several years, aligned with trade record retention.
- Archive detailed logs around significant incidents, such as major outages or cutovers.
- Ensure logs are tamper-evident; signing or secure storage can help.

In a regulatory review or dispute, being able to show exactly how your clocks behaved during a questionable period can make the difference between a manageable explanation and a serious finding.

Governance: Operating Clocks as a Critical Service

Even excellent technical design can be undermined by ad hoc operations. Clocks need explicit governance.

Change Management

Clock-related changes—firmware upgrades on grandmasters, switch replacements in timing paths, configuration changes in PTP daemons—should:

- Go through the same change control process as major trading system releases.
- Be scheduled during low-risk windows where possible.
- Include pre-change and post-change offset measurements and alerts.

It is particularly important to test for step changes in offsets after modifications. A misconfigured delay value in a boundary clock, for example, can systematically skew downstream hosts.

Handling Daylight Saving and Leap Seconds

Two kinds of calendar events can cause trouble:

- **Daylight saving time changes**: Local wall-clock jumps forward or backward, but UTC remains continuous.
- **Leap seconds**: An extra second is inserted (or, in theory, removed) from UTC.

Best practices include:

- Run trading systems on UTC internally; treat local time only as a display concern for humans.
- Rely on your timing infrastructure (grandmasters, PTP/NTP) to handle leap seconds according to a single, documented policy (for example, smearing versus step insertion).
- Test your systems in a simulation environment that replays previous DST or leap-second transitions.

Strategies and risk checks that naively compute time differences based on local wall time can misbehave around these events; using UTC everywhere greatly reduces such surprises.

Disaster Recovery and WAN Links

Your timing story must also hold under disaster-recovery (DR) scenarios. Typical patterns:

- Each major site (primary, backup, regional) should have its own reference clocks. WAN links should not be the only source of time.
- During failover, hosts in the DR site must seamlessly switch to local grandmasters without large time steps.

- WAN-delivered time (for example, PTP over a carrier network) can serve as a supplemental source but should be carefully monitored for asymmetries and variable delays.

Remember that the goal is not merely to keep *some* time available, but to keep a time base that allows you to reconstruct cross-site event ordering with confidence.

Explaining Your Timing Story

Finally, a practical test of your design is whether you can explain it clearly to non-engineers:

- To a risk committee: how timing errors could cause trading risk, and what controls you have in place to prevent and detect them.
- To auditors and regulators: how your architecture meets stated accuracy requirements and how you document compliance.
- To developers and quants: what assumptions they can safely make about timestamp quality and how to interpret multiple timestamps on a single event.

A concise "timing runbook"—one or two pages with diagrams, key metrics, and operational procedures—is often more powerful than a thick but unread configuration manual. It turns a complex technical system into an understandable, governable control.

In this section we treated time as the invisible backbone of your connectivity and market data infrastructure. We moved from the limitations of casual NTP setups to a layered architecture built on GPS-disciplined grandmasters, boundary and transparent clocks, and host-level synchronization via PTP and NTP.

We emphasized physical and logical isolation of timing traffic, the importance of measuring offset, jitter, and skew as first-class operational metrics, and the need to timestamp events as close to the wire as practical while propagating time-correct information through middleware and storage.

Finally, we connected these engineering choices to regulatory expectations and governance: clock configurations and logs as audit artifacts, structured change management, and careful handling of calendar anomalies and disaster-recovery scenarios. With this deterministic timing substrate in place, the next sections can safely build higher-level market data and order-routing pipelines, confident that the timestamps they depend on are both accurate and defensible.

3.2 Feed Handlers and Order Book Construction

In the previous section we treated time as a first-class dependency: every packet entering your environment is tagged against a carefully engineered clock hierarchy. We now turn to the layer that consumes those packets first—the feed handler—and to the structure it produces—the order book.

From a trading strategy's perspective, a feed is "just" a sequence of quotes and trades. From an infrastructure perspective, a feed is a fragile, high-speed data stream that must be turned into a *reliable, gap-free, and auditable* representation of the market. That job belongs to your feed handlers and order book builders.

This section will proceed in four steps:

1. Define what a feed handler is and its core responsibilities.
2. Explain the main types of exchange feeds and their implications.
3. Walk through the end-to-end pipeline from raw packets to validated books.
4. Discuss design choices and trade-offs in book construction for trading and research.

Throughout, we assume you have the deterministic timing substrate described earlier, so that every stage can timestamp events meaningfully.

What a Feed Handler Really Does

A feed handler is the trading system's "ears." It is not a single function, but a pipeline whose job is to convert raw exchange transport into a clean internal view of the market. Concretely, a production-grade feed handler must:

- **Manage sessions** to the exchange or vendor: logon, heartbeats, sequence resets, and recovery.
- **Receive and demultiplex packets** from the network (often multicast, sometimes unicast), across one or more network interfaces.
- **Decode messages** from the venue's native format into an internal representation.
- **Check and enforce sequence continuity**, detecting gaps and out-of-order messages.
- **Recover state** by combining snapshots (full or partial) with incremental updates.
- **Maintain order books** that reflect the current state of bids and offers, at either price level or individual order level.
- **Publish normalized data** to downstream consumers (strategies, risk engines, recorders) with strict latency and jitter budgets.

Missing any of these responsibilities introduces risk. For example, if you do not detect sequence gaps quickly and accurately, your view of the market may silently diverge from the real state, and strategies will trade on fiction.

Varieties of Market Data Feeds

Exchanges and vendors offer several categories of feeds. Understanding their differences is essential when designing handlers and books.

Top-of-Book Versus Depth Feeds

- **Top-of-book (TOB) feeds** provide the best bid and offer (BBO), sometimes with associated sizes and last trade information. They are compact and relatively simple to process, but they discard information about depth beyond the first level.
- **Depth feeds** provide multiple levels of the order book on each side, for example, the best five or ten price levels. They allow more detailed liquidity modeling and slippage estimation, at the cost of higher message rates and more complex book maintenance.

Order-by-Order Feeds

Some venues go further and provide *order-by-order* feeds:

- Each add, modify, or cancel of an individual order is broadcast.
- The exchange assigns unique identifiers to orders and uses them in subsequent messages.

These feeds are the richest and most demanding: they allow you to construct an order-level view (who arrived when, which orders executed against which), but they require careful handling of identifiers and more memory.

Multicast Versus Unicast Delivery

On the transport side:

- **Multicast feeds** send each market data packet once, and multiple consumers subscribe. This is common for high-bandwidth depth or order-by-order feeds.
- **Unicast feeds** deliver a private stream to each consumer. They are often used for lower-bandwidth or more customized feeds, or for control paths such as snapshot requests.

Multicast is efficient but offers no guaranteed delivery: packets may be dropped. Unicast can be more reliable but may not scale to very high update rates. Feed handlers must be designed with these characteristics in mind, especially for loss detection and recovery.

The Feed Handler Pipeline: From Packets to Books

With this context, we can describe the pipeline a feed handler implements. Conceptually, it is a sequence of stages that transform data and add guarantees at each step.

Stages and Responsibilities

A typical pipeline includes:

1. **Ingress and timestamping** at the NIC and kernel.
2. **Packet capture and framing** into individual market data messages.
3. **Message decoding** from binary wire format into internal structures.
4. **Sequence validation and gap detection**.
5. **Snapshot handling and reconciliation** with incrementals.
6. **Order book update** (price-level or order-level).
7. **Publication** of a normalized view to internal buses.

Each stage has both functional requirements (decode correctly, maintain invariants) and non-functional ones (stay within latency and jitter budgets, avoid memory bloat, expose metrics).

A Visual View of the Pipeline

To anchor these ideas, it is helpful to see the flow from raw packets to books.

We now look more closely at the key stages.

Ingress, Framing, and Low-Jitter Behavior

At ingress, packets arrive on one or more NICs, ideally with hardware timestamps anchored to your PTP-based timing fabric. The primary tasks at this stage are:

- Efficiently moving packets from the NIC into user space.
- Grouping packet payloads into discrete exchange messages (framing).
- Preserving the arrival order as seen on the wire.

Controlling Jitter

Jitter is the variability of delay between packet arrival and processing. Strategies sensitive to microstructure depend not just on low average latency, but on predictable processing times.

To keep jitter low:

- Avoid unnecessary context switches; pin key threads to CPUs.
- Isolate feed-handling CPU cores from other workloads.
- Pre-allocate buffers so that memory allocation does not introduce sporadic pauses.

The exact techniques are implementation-specific, but the design goal is simple to state: for a given update rate, the time from wire arrival to decoded message should be tightly clustered, not occasionally spiking due to unrelated system activity.

Message Decoding and Normalization

Exchange protocols are diverse: some use binary formats with fixed layouts, others mix fixed and variable fields, and a few still rely on text-based messages. Your feed handler must decode these into a uniform, internal representation.

Venue-Specific Decoding

Decoding includes:

- Interpreting headers (length, message type, sequence number).
- Parsing body fields (price, quantity, side, order ID, trade flags).
- Handling optional or extension fields gracefully.

Here correctness is crucial: a single misinterpreted field can invert the meaning of a message, for example, treating a cancel as a new order. Robust handlers validate basic invariants (such as non-negative sizes, plausible price ranges) and flag or discard obviously corrupt data.

Normalization

Once decoded, events are mapped into an internal schema that is consistent across venues. For example:

- Unified field names for price, quantity, instrument, side.
- Common enumeration values for event types (add, modify, delete, trade).
- Standard units (for example, prices in decimal rather than integer ticks, sizes in standardized quantity units).

Normalization is an investment: it allows you to write strategy and risk code once instead of separately for each venue schema. It also provides a stable contract so that venue upgrades do not ripple uncontrollably through your systems.

Sequence Validation and Gap Handling

Market data feeds are usually *sequenced*: each message carries a sequence number that increments monotonically. This is your primary tool for detecting packet loss and out-of-order delivery.

Enforcing Monotonic Sequences

For each feed or channel, the handler tracks the last applied sequence number. When a new message arrives:

- If its sequence is exactly one greater, processing continues normally.
- If it is higher than expected, a gap has occurred.
- If it is lower than expected, it is either a duplicate or out-of-order and must be handled according to the venue's rules.

By treating sequence gaps as first-class events, you avoid silently corrupting your book. A pristine-seeming order book built on a broken sequence is more dangerous than an explicit error.

Gap Detection and Recovery Strategies

Upon detecting a gap, the handler should:

- Mark the affected instrument or channel as *stale* or *uncertain*.
- Trigger recovery actions, such as requesting a snapshot from the exchange or vendor, or waiting for retransmission if the protocol supports it.
- Optionally, propagate a "data quality" signal downstream so that strategies can adjust behavior (for example, widen spreads, reduce size, or pause trading) on stale instruments.

Recovery may not be instantaneous. During that window, you must decide whether to allow trading decisions based on potentially incomplete data. This is a risk decision as much as an engineering one and should be explicitly agreed with risk management.

Snapshots and Incremental Updates

Most depth and order-by-order feeds are delivered as a combination of:

- **Snapshots:** a full (or large partial) view of the current book state at some point in time.
- **Incremental updates:** a stream of changes to that state.

The challenge is to reconcile the two so that your internal book always represents a coherent state of the exchange.

Cold Start: Building from Snapshot + Incrementals

When a feed handler starts up, it usually must:

1. Request or subscribe to a snapshot.
2. Note the snapshot's reference sequence number or timestamp.
3. Buffer incrementals that arrive while the snapshot is being received.
4. Once the snapshot is complete, apply buffered incrementals with sequence numbers greater than the snapshot point, in order.

Only after this process can the handler claim to have a correct live book.

Recovery After Gaps

After a sequence gap, the process is similar:

- Stop applying incrementals beyond the gap point.
- Obtain a fresh snapshot.
- Resume from the snapshot's reference point, applying subsequent incrementals.

Depending on venue design, recovery may involve multiple channels (for example, one for snapshot, one for incrementals). Coordinating them correctly is a core responsibility of the handler.

Order Book Construction Strategies

Once decoded, validated, and reconciled, updates are applied to an in-memory representation of the order book. There are two main families of book:

Price-Level Books

A price-level book aggregates all orders at the same price. For each side (bid and ask) and each visible price level, it maintains:

- The total visible quantity.
- Possibly counts or statistics about contributing orders.

Advantages:

- Compact: memory scales with number of price levels, not number of orders.
- Fast to update when the feed is already price-level (many venues send "set size at price" or "add/remove size at price" messages).
- Sufficient for many strategy types, especially those concerned with top-of-book and immediate depth.

Order-Level Books

An order-level book maintains each individual order. For each order you may track:

- Price, quantity, and side.
- Exchange order ID.

- Time of arrival and possibly time in force or other attributes.

Advantages:

- Enables detailed microstructure analysis (queue position, order lifetime, cancellation patterns).
- Useful for compliance and surveillance (who traded with whom, in what sequence).

Costs:

- Memory usage grows with number of individual orders, which can be very large in active instruments.
- Update logic is more complex, especially for partial fills and order modifications.

Many firms maintain both: a lighter price-level book for low-latency strategy decisions and a richer order-level book (possibly with slight additional latency) for research and post-trade analysis.

Maintaining Invariants and Detecting Corruption

Regardless of book type, your construction logic should enforce basic invariants:

- No negative quantities at any price level.
- Side ordering is preserved: highest bid strictly below lowest ask in non-crossed markets, unless the venue explicitly allows crossed or locked books.
- Sequence numbers applied in strict order, with no skips unless intentionally recovered.
- Book state reflects a sum of all processed events since the last known-good snapshot.

When an invariant is violated, the handler should:

- Log enough context for later investigation (instrument, sequence number, recent messages).
- Mark the instrument as suspect and, if necessary, trigger a resynchronization from snapshot.
- Decide, according to policy, whether to continue publishing data for that instrument.

Silent corruption is the worst outcome. It is better to declare a book "down" temporarily than to feed incorrect prices to your strategies.

Publishing to Internal Buses: Latency and Jitter Budgets

After the book is updated, its state (or incremental changes) must be distributed to internal consumers. This may happen over an internal message bus, shared memory, or other mechanisms. Two concerns dominate:

Latency Budgets

You should define clear targets such as:

- Median time from packet ingress to book update.
- 99th or 99.9th percentile times for the same.

These budgets guide engineering decisions throughout the pipeline. For example, if your strategies target sub-millisecond response times, you might allocate:

- A few tens of microseconds for ingress and decoding.
- A similar amount for sequence validation and book updates.
- The remainder for gateway and strategy processing.

Without explicit budgets, it is easy for "small" changes (for example, extra logging or debug features) to erode performance until tails become unacceptable.

Backpressure and Loss Avoidance

If downstream consumers cannot keep up, the feed handler faces a choice:

- **Drop messages** to preserve current data (for example, keeping just the latest snapshot and skipping intermediate updates).
- **Apply backpressure** by slowing or queuing updates, which risks increasing latency.

Well-designed systems favor explicit backpressure policies over silent loss. For instance, you might allow some components (like archival recorders) to fall behind, but protect latency-sensitive consumers by giving them priority or a separate data path.

Supporting Both Trading and Research

A common mistake is to design feed handlers only for live trading and treat research needs as an afterthought. This leads to painful mismatches between what strategies do in production and what researchers can see in historical data.

To avoid this, design from the start so that:

- The same normalized data model is used for both live and replayed data.
- Historical recorders capture enough detail (including sequence numbers, timestamps, and flags for data quality) to reconstruct the book to the same standard as in real time.
- Versioning of schemas is explicit: when the internal model changes, you can still interpret older data.

This alignment allows backtests and simulations (covered in the next section) to exercise strategies against realistic, book-consistent data that reflects actual feed behavior, including gaps and recoveries.

Feed handlers and order book builders transform high-speed, sometimes unreliable exchange feeds into a clean, gap-free, and auditable view of the market. They stand on the timing substrate built earlier, using precise timestamps to measure latency and maintain consistent event ordering.

We have broken their responsibilities into stages: ingress and low-jitter packet handling, robust decoding and normalization, strict sequence validation with gap recovery, careful reconciliation of snapshots and incrementals, and disciplined order book construction at either price or order level. Finally, we emphasized that these components must serve both live trading and research, using normalized models and rich historical capture.

In the next section, we will leverage this accurate, well-timestamped book data to build replay and simulation environments, turning recorded markets into a controllable laboratory for testing strategies before they face live conditions.

3.3 Market Data Replay and Simulation

In the previous sections we built two foundations: a deterministic timing substrate and a set of feed handlers that turn noisy, exchange-native messages into clean, validated order books. We now put those ingredients to work in a different setting: a laboratory where you can replay and manipulate markets without risking capital.

The goal of this section is to show how recorded and synthetic market data can be turned into a *controllable* environment for testing and validating strategies, gateways, and risk controls. We will pay particular attention to determinism (being able to reproduce a run exactly), realism (making replay feel like the live market), and safety (ensuring replay traffic never leaks into the real world by mistake).

Why Naïve Log-Replay Is Not Enough

Many teams start with a simple idea: "We have log files of market data and orders. Let us read them back and feed them to our strategy." This approach usually fails to capture the subtleties that matter in electronic markets, for two main reasons.

First, naïve replay often ignores **time**. Instead of respecting the gaps between messages, it sends them as fast as the replay process can read from disk and push to the network. For latency-insensitive backtests this might be acceptable, but for anything that depends on microstructure—such as queue dynamics, race conditions, or interaction across venues—the timing distortions can dramatically change outcomes.

Second, naïve replay tends to ignore the **full pipeline**. It might feed data straight into a strategy library, bypassing the very gateways, feed handlers, risk checks, and buses that will run in production. This leaves you blind to integration risks: configuration errors, performance bottlenecks, or subtle differences between simulated and live paths.

A proper replay and simulation environment aims to:

- Preserve, or intentionally and transparently modify, inter-arrival times.
- Exercise the *same* components and code paths that you use in live trading.
- Offer controls to speed up or slow down time, to change market intensity, and to inject special scenarios.
- Provide enough metadata and logging so that you can exactly reproduce an earlier test run.

In other words, we want a wind tunnel for trading systems, not just a tape recorder.

Defining Clock-Accurate Replay

The key concept in a serious replay framework is *clock-accurate replay*. To understand it, recall that each recorded market event has at least two important timestamps:

- The **exchange time**, often embedded in the message itself, representing when the event occurred at the venue.
- The **arrival time** in your system, typically captured by your NIC hardware and feed handlers relative to your internal clock.

For most strategy development and infrastructure testing, arrival time is the more relevant measure: it reflects the exact stream and pacing of data as your systems saw it.

A replay is clock-accurate if:

- The sequence of events is the same as in the original recording.
- The gaps between events, measured in your chosen time scale, are preserved (or modified in a controlled way, such as consistently scaled by a factor).

For example, if two updates in the original day were 200 microseconds apart, a 10-times-faster replay would deliver them 20 microseconds apart. The relationship is preserved, only scaled.

Clock accuracy is important because many strategies are not purely "state-based" (reacting only to the current book), but also "time-based" (reacting to the speed and pattern of changes). A burst of orders arriving in a millisecond is not the same as the same orders spread over a second.

Sources of Data: Recorded Versus Synthetic

Replay environments typically draw from two families of data.

Recorded Live Data

Recorded data is captured during actual trading sessions:

- Full tick-level market data, ideally including order book updates, trades, and relevant control messages.

- Optional internal signals, such as your own orders, fills, and gateway events.
- Precise timestamps from your timing substrate.

Recorded data gives you authenticity: it includes real-world oddities such as exchange glitches, network microbursts, and rare market conditions that synthetic models may not anticipate.

Synthetic or Simulated Data

Synthetic data is generated according to models or rules. This might include:

- Simple patterned flows (for example, a steady Poisson order arrival process).
- More sophisticated microstructure models calibrated to historical data.
- Explicitly extreme scenarios: sudden liquidity vanishing, exaggerated spread widening, or correlated shocks across instruments.

Synthetic data gives you control: you can dial up or down specific phenomena, repeat them with variations, and explore "what if" cases that have not (yet) occurred in the wild.

A mature lab uses both: recorded data to verify that strategies behave as expected in real markets, and synthetic data to explore robustness beyond what history offers.

Storage and Indexing for Replay

Before you can replay anything, you must store it in a way that supports fast, flexible access. The raw format that exchanges use on the wire is not usually suitable as-is for large-scale, long-term analysis.

Designing a Storage Format

A practical storage schema should:

- Preserve all fields necessary to reconstruct books and measure timing (prices, sizes, sides, sequence numbers, timestamps, and event types).
- Capture provenance: which venue, which feed, which data center path.
- Support optional annotations, such as data quality flags (for example, "gap detected and recovered").

Common choices include compact binary formats with accompanying metadata, or columnar storage for analytics. The exact format matters less than the discipline of always recording complete, consistent information.

Indexing by Time, Instrument, and Venue

To support replay scenarios, you want to query data flexibly. For example:

- "Give me all events for instrument X on venue Y between 09:30 and 09:35."
- "Give me a synchronized view of instruments X and Z across venues A and B around a specific news event."

Indexes on time, instrument, and venue make such queries efficient. They also enable multi-stream replay, where you must coordinate events from multiple feeds in a coherent timeline.

Replay Engines: Respecting and Manipulating Time

With recorded data stored and indexed, the replay engine orchestrates the flow back into your systems. Conceptually, it sits where the exchange would normally be and plays the role of a synthetic venue.

Time Bases and Scaling

The replay engine must define a *replay time* that is related to the original recording time. Common patterns include:

- **Real-time replay:** One second of recorded time equals one second of replay time.
- **Accelerated replay:** One second of recorded time equals a fraction of a second (for example, 10 times faster).
- **Slowed replay:** Useful for step-by-step debugging of complex interactions.

Whichever scheme you choose, it must be:

- **Stable:** The mapping between recorded and replay time should not change unpredictably mid-run.
- **Transparent:** The scaling factor and reference points should be logged and part of the test configuration, so runs can be reproduced.

Synchronizing Multiple Streams

Real strategies often consume data from multiple venues and asset classes. A proper replay must preserve cross-stream relationships:

- If a futures quote and a cash equity trade happened 2 milliseconds apart in real life, they should have the same 2-millisecond relationship (after any time scaling) in replay.
- If your original system stamped arrivals from different venues with a shared clock, the replay engine can use those arrival times to merge streams.

Concretely, the engine merges sorted event streams across all requested instruments and venues, then schedules them according to replay time. This ensures that strategies see the same relative ordering and timing they would see in production.

Feeding Replay Through Production Gateways

One of the most important design principles is that replayed data should traverse the *same* pipelines as live data, wherever practical.

Reuse, Do Not Recreate

Instead of writing a special "test path" that feeds strategies directly from files, you should aim to have the replay engine emit packets or messages that look like they came from the real exchange:

- In a network-based setup, the replay engine sends packets over a lab network to the same feed handlers used in production. You may reuse the same binary protocol, multicast groups, and message framing.
- In an internal bus-based setup, the engine publishes events onto the same internal topics used by live normalized feeds, with a clear tag indicating that they are simulated.

This reuse ensures that any integration bugs, configuration errors, or performance regressions in your feed handlers, gateways, and risk engines are exposed during testing rather than in production.

Marking Replay Versus Live

While reusing pipelines, you must guarantee that replay events cannot be mistaken for live ones. Tactics include:

- Running replay in completely segmented environments with no route to real venues or brokers.
- Tagging events with a "simulation" or "replay" flag in metadata fields that strategies and risk components can inspect.
- Using different network subnets, multicast groups, or logical topics for replay feeds, with explicit configuration in consumers.

The goal is a strict separation of concerns: the functional path is as similar as possible, but the operational risk of accidental live trading on replay data is eliminated.

Stress and What-If Scenarios

Beyond simple replays of past days, you will want to ask richer questions: What happens if liquidity halves? What if order flow doubles? How do gateways behave in a volatility spike?

Amplifying Order Flow

Given recorded data, a replay engine can modify intensity:

- **Time compression:** In addition to global scaling (for example, 10 times faster), you can compress specific intervals (such as around market open) to simulate more extreme bursts.
- **Duplication and perturbation:** You can duplicate certain periods with small variations in price or size to create multiple similar, but not identical, bursts.

The key is transparency: the engine must record how it altered the original data so that test results can be interpreted correctly.

Injecting Rare Events

Some situations are too rare to rely on history alone:

- Crossed or locked markets (best bid above best offer, or equal).
- Sudden disappearance of top-of-book liquidity.
- Exchange-level halts or outages.
- Severe, but transient, time synchronization issues or feed gaps.

To test these, you can overlay synthetic events onto recorded streams, creating hybrid scenarios. For example:

- During a calm recorded day, inject a sudden widening of spreads and surge of cancellations over a short interval.
- Simulate an exchange pausing a subset of instruments by freezing their data while others trade normally.

By observing strategy and infrastructure responses to these injections, you can refine risk controls, throttling mechanisms, and human escalation playbooks.

Deterministic Versus Stochastic Simulation

Not all tests aim at the same outcome. It is useful to distinguish two modes.

Deterministic Replays for Regression

Deterministic replay means that, given the same input data and configuration, the system under test produces the same outputs—down to the order and timing of orders and risk decisions. This is ideal for:

- Regression testing after code changes.
- Confirming that strategy behavior has not changed unintentionally.
- Comparing alternative implementations of a gateway or risk module.

Determinism requires careful control of any randomness in the system (for example, fixed random seeds) and of external influences (for example, stable environment configuration). Replay engines should support this mode explicitly, including the ability to pause, step, or rewind.

Stochastic Simulations for Robustness

At other times, you want variety rather than exact repeatability. Stochastic simulation deliberately introduces randomness:

- Order arrivals drawn from probabilistic models.
- Price paths following stochastic processes or empirical distributions.
- Randomized timing and venue-specific noise.

The goal here is not to reproduce any particular day, but to explore many plausible futures and see how strategies behave across them. You might, for example, run hundreds of simulated days under slightly different conditions to estimate the distribution of slippage or drawdowns.

In this mode, *statistical* reproducibility matters more than exact event-by-event replication. The lab should still be able to regenerate a particular random sequence if needed (for debugging), but the emphasis is on ensembles of runs.

Observability and Metrics in the Lab

A good replay environment is not just a data source; it is also an observability platform. During replay and simulation, you should collect:

- Latency distributions at key hops (ingress, decoding, book updates, strategy decisions).
- Order and trade statistics (fill rates, rejection reasons, message rates).
- Resource usage (CPU, memory, network bandwidth) under various stress levels.

Because the lab uses the same timing substrate and instrumentation as production, you can directly compare metrics. For instance, you might verify that a new gateway build under replayed market-open conditions stays within 80% of CPU budgets and maintains tail latency below a pre-defined threshold.

Operational Safety and Governance

As with time synchronization and live feeds, a replay and simulation environment benefits from clear governance.

Environment Boundaries

Document which networks, hosts, and services belong to:

- Pure simulation (no real money or customer orders).
- Paper trading or shadow environments (orders generated but not sent to venues).
- Live trading.

Ensure that routing, authentication, and user permissions make it difficult or impossible to cross boundaries accidentally. For example, a user in the lab should not be able to connect to a production gateway without explicit, audited steps.

Reproducible Test Scenarios

Treat test scenarios as assets:

- Store configurations (data ranges, instruments, scaling factors, injected events) in version-controlled form.
- Give important scenarios stable names (for example, "Equities Open Stress v3") that can be referenced in change management and risk committees.
- Require that material strategy changes or major infrastructure upgrades pass a standard suite of such scenarios before approval.

In doing so, you move from ad hoc experimentation to a disciplined, repeatable validation process.

In this section we extended the story of connectivity and market data from live systems into the laboratory. Starting from precisely timestamped feeds and well-constructed order books, we built a framework for clock-accurate replay and flexible simulation.

We saw that naïve log-replay is insufficient for serious electronic trading work: without respect for time and without exercising real pipelines, tests provide false comfort. Instead, a robust lab records data with rich metadata, indexes it for flexible access, replays it through the same gateways and buses used in production, and supports both deterministic and stochastic modes.

Finally, we framed replay and simulation as governed activities, subject to the same discipline as live trading: clear environment boundaries, reproducible scenarios, and strong observability. With such a laboratory in place, teams can explore strategies and infrastructure changes with confidence before any order touches a real market.

3.4 Security, Authentication, and Key Management

So far in this chapter we have treated connectivity and market data as an engineering problem: how to move messages with accurate time and minimal loss. We now add an equally important lens: security.

Your timing substrate, feed handlers, and replay systems together form a high-value target. If an attacker can tamper with them, they can mislead strategies, disrupt risk controls, or leak sensitive data. Even without a malicious actor, weak authentication and ad-hoc key management can leave you exposed under regulatory scrutiny.

In this section we will focus on three pillars:

- **Mutual TLS (mTLS)** to authenticate and encrypt connections.
- **Network segmentation** to contain damage and reduce attack surfaces.
- **Key and credential management** to protect the secrets that anchor your identity.

We will keep the discussion grounded in the concrete components you have already built: exchanges and vendors at the edge, internal buses carrying normalized books, gateways and risk engines, and replay or research environments.

What Is at Stake? A Brief Threat Model

Before choosing tools, clarify what you are protecting and from whom. For a trading firm, high-value assets in the connectivity fabric include:

- **Market data streams** that reveal detailed microstructure and your interpretation of it.
- **Order flow and strategy behavior**, often carried over the same networks and buses as market data.
- **Configuration and timing signals**, such as PTP control traffic and feed handler settings.
- **Audit and replay logs** that reconstruct past decisions.

Potential adversaries span:

- **External attackers** on the public internet or connected networks, scanning for exposed ports and weak TLS configurations.
- **Insiders** with legitimate access who might overreach intentionally or accidentally.
- **Compromised dependencies**, such as vendor appliances or third-party services that sit in your data path.

The main security properties you need are:

- **Confidentiality** so that eavesdroppers cannot see your market data or order flow.
- **Integrity** so that messages cannot be altered undetectably on the wire or inside your network.

- **Authenticity** so that both ends of each connection know who they are talking to.
- **Availability** so that essential feeds, gateways, and timing services keep working even under attack.

mTLS, segmentation, and strong key management are tools to achieve these; they are not goals in themselves.

Mutual TLS as the Default Transport Security

TLS (Transport Layer Security) is ubiquitous on the internet for encrypting connections from clients to servers. *Mutual* TLS extends this idea: both client and server present certificates and verify each other's identity, not just the client's verification of the server. For regulated trading systems, mTLS is often the right default for non-multicast flows.

Where to Use mTLS

You should aim to use mTLS for:

- **Order gateways** connecting to venues, brokers, and clearing interfaces over TCP.
- **API-based market data feeds** provided over unicast TCP or web sockets.
- **Internal services**, such as normalized market data buses, risk services, and admin APIs.
- **Control planes** for your replay engines, configuration services, and orchestration.

Multicast feeds are harder to protect with TLS because of their many-to-many nature and high throughput; here, you rely more on network segmentation, access control lists, and sometimes IPsec at the network layer. But wherever you have a point-to-point channel, mTLS should be the norm.

How mTLS Secures Your Fabric

mTLS helps you in three ways:

- **Encryption** prevents passive eavesdropping. A party who can see packets on an untrusted link learns nothing about prices, orders, or internal identifiers.
- **Endpoint authentication** prevents impersonation. A gateway can verify that the server really is the venue or internal bus it expects, and vice versa.
- **Fine-grained authorization** becomes possible because you can bind roles or permissions to specific certificates or certificate attributes.

For example, an internal market data bus might only accept connections from clients that present certificates belonging to the "FeedConsumer" role for a particular business unit. If a compromised host tries to connect using a generic certificate, the handshake will fail.

Certificate Lifecycle and Rotation

mTLS is only as strong as your certificate hygiene. In practice, that means:

- **Short-lived certificates** where feasible, so that compromised credentials age out quickly.
- **Automated issuance and renewal**, using a well-governed internal certificate authority (CA) or a secure integration with an external PKI.
- **Controlled subject naming**, so that certificate subjects and subject-alternative-names clearly identify hosts, services, or users.
- **Planned rotation procedures** that avoid downtime. For example, roll out new certificates and trust anchors in parallel, then deprecate the old ones once all parties support the new chain.

You should also audit where certificates are stored. Private keys on local disk, especially on multi-tenant hosts or shared containers, are easy targets. That leads us to key management.

Key and Credential Management as a First-Class Discipline

Encryption and authentication rely on secrets: private keys, API tokens, passwords, and occasionally symmetric keys for other protocols. Mismanaging these is one of the most common and damaging security failures.

Principles of Good Key Management

Several simple but powerful principles guide a robust design:

- **Minimize the number of secrets**: Do not create new keys casually. Reuse well-managed CAs and key hierarchies where appropriate.
- **Centralize storage, decentralize use**: Store secrets in a limited number of hardened systems, but make it easy for authorized services to obtain short-lived credentials as needed.
- **Limit blast radius**: Structure your keys so that compromise of one certificate or API key limits the damage to a small set of systems or privileges.
- **Instrument everything**: Log key issuance, rotation, and use; monitor for anomalies.

Hardware Security Modules and Secure Enclaves

For the highest-value keys—root CAs, venue gateway client certificates, keys used for regulatory reporting, or signing of critical logs—you should use a *Hardware Security Module* (HSM) or equivalent secure enclave. These devices:

- Generate keys inside tamper-resistant hardware.
- Perform cryptographic operations (such as signing or decrypting) without letting the private key leave the device.
- Enforce access controls and rate limits on key use.

HSMs can be physical appliances in your data center or cloud-based services with hardware-backed isolation. Integrating them means that even if an application host is compromised, the attacker cannot simply copy private keys and use them elsewhere.

For less critical secrets or where HSM integration is not practical, you can use software-based secure stores (for example, a secrets manager) protected by strong authentication and network controls. But you should still avoid embedding secrets in configuration files, code repositories, or container images.

Role-Based Access Control for Secrets

You should treat access to keys and credentials with the same rigor as access to trading systems themselves. For example:

- A developer building a new feed handler might have permission to request test environment certificates, but not production ones.
- Only a small, audited group should be able to trigger issuance of venue-facing gateway certificates.
- Automated deployment pipelines might have narrowly scoped permissions to fetch specific secrets for specific services.

Make these policies explicit using role-based access control (RBAC) and tie them into your organizational identity system. Regularly review who has which roles, and remove access when people change jobs or projects.

Segmented Networks: Building Safe Zones

While mTLS and strong keys secure individual connections, you also need to shape the overall network so that an attacker who breaches one area cannot roam freely. This is the purpose of *network segmentation*.

High-Level Zones

A typical segmentation scheme divides your network into zones with different trust levels and functions. For example:

- **DMZ (Demilitarized Zone)** Externally facing systems that talk to venues, brokers, vendors, and sometimes the public internet. These hosts are most exposed and should have the minimal necessary internal reach.
- **Trading zone** Internal systems that handle live market data, order generation, and pre-trade risk checks. This zone is tightly controlled and monitored.
- **Back-office zone** Systems for settlement, reconciliations, and reporting. Often less latency-sensitive, but still sensitive in terms of data.
- **Research and replay zones** Environments where analysts and quants experiment, sometimes with large datasets and simulation tools.

Clear network boundaries between these zones are enforced by firewalls, layer-3 routers, and sometimes micro-segmentation at higher layers.

Principles of Segmentation

Design your segments with a few guiding rules:

- **Least privilege connectivity**: Only allow the minimum traffic necessary in and out of each zone. For instance, a feed handler in the DMZ might be allowed to connect to internal normalized data buses, but not to back-office databases.

- **One-way data flows where possible**: Use one-directional links or strict ACLs for flows that should not reverse, such as copying market data from trading into research, but not the other way around.
- **Separate control and data planes**: Keep management and monitoring traffic on distinct networks or VLANs from trading data, so that a compromise of one plane does not easily grant control of the other.

Segmentation is not just about blocking hackers. It also limits the scope of configuration errors and software bugs. For example, if someone misconfigures a replay engine, segmentation can prevent it from sending test orders or data into production gateways.

Isolating Replay and Research Environments

Replay and simulation environments, discussed in the previous section, deserve special attention. They often have:

- Wide access to historical market data and internal logs.
- Powerful tools that can generate synthetic flows.
- Users (quants, researchers) who are more experimental in nature.

To avoid accidental or malicious crossover:

- Place replay engines and research tools in their own network segments with no direct path to live trading gateways.
- Use separate authentication realms or roles for lab versus production, so credentials cannot be reused across boundaries.
- Label and monitor these environments clearly, so that any attempt to route from them into live systems raises immediate alerts.

This way, you preserve the realism of using production-like pipelines in the lab without exposing live systems to undue risk.

Security as Observability: Logging and Audit Trails

Security is not just about keeping attackers out. It is also about being able to answer questions like "What happened?" and "Who did what?" after the fact. In trading, regulators and internal risk committees will ask these questions whenever there is a serious incident.

What to Log

Key security-relevant events in the connectivity and market data stack include:

- **Authentication events**: Successful and failed mTLS handshakes, API logons, and credential uses.
- **Authorization decisions**: Connection attempts that were denied because of missing roles, expired certificates, or invalid permissions.
- **Key lifecycle events**: Creation, rotation, revocation, and deletion of certificates and secrets.
- **Configuration changes**: Updates to firewall rules, routing, feed subscriptions, and timing infrastructure.

Each log entry should include a reliable timestamp (from your timing substrate), an identity (which system or user), and enough context to reconstruct intent.

Protecting the Logs Themselves

Logs are part of your evidence. They must be tamper-resistant:

- Store logs in append-only systems or sign log chunks so that modifications are detectable.
- Replicate logs to separate storage domains (for example, different zones or even different regions) so that an attacker who compromises one environment cannot erase all traces.

- Control access: only a limited, audited group should be able to read sensitive logs, and an even smaller group should manage retention and archival policies.

In some designs, you might use HSM-backed keys to sign particularly important logs (such as those related to risk overrides or manual trading interventions), so that they can be shown to regulators as strong evidence.

Weaving Security into Operational Playbooks

Security measures are only effective if operations teams understand and apply them consistently, especially under stress. You should embed the concepts we have discussed into concrete playbooks.

Incident Response for Connectivity Surfaces

For incidents involving gateways, feeds, or timing systems, playbooks should cover:

- **Initial containment**: How to quickly restrict or shut down external connections without crashing internal systems.
- **Verification**: How to use logs and monitoring to distinguish between misconfiguration, infrastructure fault, and active attack.
- **Escalation**: Whom to call (security, networking, trading desks, compliance) and in what order.
- **Recovery**: How to safely restore services, including revalidating keys and certificates if compromise is suspected.

These runbooks should be tested in drills, ideally using your replay environment to simulate realistic load and behavior during a "security event."

Key Compromise and Certificate Revocation

You should also have a specific plan for suspected key compromise:

- Rapidly **revoke** affected certificates in your CA or PKI.
- Push updated trust bundles to all relevant systems so they stop accepting compromised identities.
- Generate and deploy new keys and certificates following a controlled process.
- Review logs to assess the window of exposure and identify any suspicious connections during that time.

This is one of the clearest interfaces between security and compliance: regulators will often ask to see evidence that you can respond quickly and systematically to credential issues.

Security as an Ongoing Process

Finally, it is important to recognize that security of the connectivity fabric is not a one-time project. Protocols evolve, cryptographic algorithms age, vendors change APIs, and your own systems grow more complex.

To keep pace:

- **Regularly review** TLS configurations, deprecating weak cipher suites and protocols.
- **Schedule penetration tests** or red-team exercises that specifically target gateways, feed handlers, and timing infrastructure.
- **Integrate security checks** into deployment pipelines, so that services cannot be rolled out without valid certificates, correct mTLS settings, and approved network policies.
- **Educate developers and quants** about how their components authenticate and pass data, so they do not inadvertently bypass controls for convenience.

By treating security, authentication, and key management as integral parts of your connectivity and market data architecture, rather than bolt-on features, you strengthen both your technical resilience and your regulatory posture.

3.5 Performance, Latency, and Capacity Testing for Data Paths

Up to this point, we have focused on building the *correct* connectivity and market data stack: accurate clocks, robust feed handlers, realistic replay environments, and secure channels. In production, however, correctness alone is not enough. The system must also perform reliably under the full weight of real markets.

This section is about turning your architecture into measurable guarantees. You need evidence that the entire data path—from the exchange port, through your cross-connect, network, feed handlers, buses, gateways, and finally into consumer applications—can:

- Sustain expected and stressed loads without loss.
- Deliver predictable latency, especially in the tails.
- Provide enough *headroom* to survive cutovers, failovers, and extreme market events.

We will begin by defining the key performance metrics and why they matter for trading, then design end-to-end tests that exercise real paths rather than isolated components. We will cover capacity planning and regression testing, and end with guidance on how to communicate these results to both engineers and non-technical stakeholders.

What to Measure: Metrics That Matter in Markets

Traditional IT performance monitoring often focuses on averages: average CPU load, average request latency. In electronic markets, averages are misleading. During quiet periods you may look excellent, but most of your risk is concentrated in short bursts—market open, auctions, news shocks—when data rates and latency demands spike.

You need metrics that capture both central behavior and tails.

Throughput and Burst Capacity

Throughput is the volume of data your system can handle per unit of time, often measured in:

- Messages per second (for example, market data updates).
- Packets per second (at the network edge).
- Bytes or bits per second (bandwidth).

For markets, it is critical to consider:

- **Sustained rate**: the rough baseline during continuous trading.
- **Burst rate**: short periods where message rates are many times higher, such as at the opening cross or a major news release.

Your design must handle both without dropping messages or allowing unbounded queue growth.

Latency and Its Distribution

Latency is the time between an event at the edge (for example, a packet arriving from an exchange) and some downstream reaction (for example, a strategy receiving an updated book). In this section we especially care about:

- End-to-end latency: from exchange port to consumer application.
- Per-hop latency: network, feed handler, bus publish/subscribe, gateway.

Instead of reporting only the average (mean) latency, you should look at:

- **Median (p50)**: typical behavior.
- **High percentiles** (p99, p99.9): tail behavior, where rare but dangerous delays live.

A system with low median but very high p99 can produce unpredictable trading behavior at exactly the worst moments.

Jitter and Tail Spikes

Jitter is the variability of latency over time. Even if the average is acceptable, large fluctuations can confuse strategies that expect stable behavior. For example, a strategy that computes short-term volatility or quote fade rates might misinterpret system-induced jitter as market behavior.

You want not just low median latency, but low variance and tightly controlled tails.

Packet Loss and Message Drops

Loss can occur at several layers:

- Network packet loss due to congestion or interface saturation.
- Message drops in feed handlers or buses when internal queues overflow.
- Deliberate sampling or coalescing, if used, that discards information.

For most trading use cases, especially around top-of-book and immediate depth, loss should be extremely rare and always intentional (for example, a known sampling stage). Silent, unmonitored drops are unacceptable.

Designing End-to-End Benchmarks

With metrics defined, we can now design tests. The key principle is simple but often violated: *test full paths, not just components*.

Synthetic Edge Generators

At the network edge, near your exchange cross-connect or in a realistic lab environment, you deploy synthetic packet generators. They should:

- Produce packets that match real exchange formats and symbol mixes.
- Respect plausible inter-arrival distributions (not simply constant gaps).
- Support configurable bursts to mimic market open, auctions, and news events.

Where possible, calibrate these generators to real historical data (measured via your replay environment) so that the distribution of message sizes and update patterns is realistic.

Exercising the Real Pipeline

The generator then feeds:

- Your actual network devices (switches, routers, firewalls).
- The same feed handlers you run in production.
- Your normalized market data buses.
- Downstream strategy containers, risk engines, and recorders.

By using the identical code paths and configurations, your tests expose:

- Hidden bottlenecks, such as slow serialization libraries in bus publishers.

- Configuration mismatches between environments (for example, different buffer sizes in lab versus production).
- Interactions between components, such as backpressure cascades when a downstream consumer stalls.

Isolated microbenchmarks (for example, "this function can decode 1 million messages per second") are still useful, but only as supporting evidence. End-to-end behavior is what the market sees.

Representative Workloads

You should test at least three workload profiles:

- **Baseline**: Typical daily activity in your primary instruments and venues, including average open and close volumes.
- **Stressed but plausible**: Conditions around major economic releases or volatility spikes that have occurred historically.
- **Extreme cutover scenarios**: Combined with failovers, replays, or system restarts, simulating worst-case operational stress.

The aim is not to survive every imaginable catastrophe, but to know where your limits lie and to keep them comfortably beyond expected peaks.

Separating Network, Feed Handler, and Application Bottlenecks

If a test fails—for example, tail latency doubles under stress—you need to know *where* the problem is. This is where the timing substrate and instrumentation from earlier sections pay off.

Multi-Point Timestamping

By tagging events at multiple points, you can decompose latency:

- At NIC ingress: timestamp when packets first hit your host.
- After decoding: timestamp when a market data message is parsed and normalized.
- At book update: timestamp when the internal order book reflects the change.
- At publication: timestamp when the message leaves the bus towards consumers.
- At consumer: timestamp when a strategy or risk engine receives and processes the update.

By subtracting consecutive timestamps you can estimate per-hop latency distributions. If NIC-to-decode is stable but decode-to-publish has a fat tail under load, you know that the bottleneck lies in decoding or bus publishing, not the network.

Correlation IDs Across Paths

Use correlation IDs or sequence numbers to tie together events across components:

- For market data: carry a feed sequence number or internal ID through logs at each stage.
- For orders and acknowledgments: include an ID that is logged by gateway, venue simulator (in tests), and strategy.

With these identifiers, you can reconstruct complete journeys of individual messages and reason about where time was spent, rather than relying on coarse aggregate metrics alone.

Headroom and Capacity Planning

Performance metrics are not just for today; they inform your capacity plans for tomorrow. You want to answer questions like: "If we double the number of traded instruments or add three new venues, will we still meet our latency and loss targets?"

From Business Expectations to Resource Needs

Translate business plans into load assumptions:

- Number of instruments and venues you intend to trade.
- Expected growth in message rates due to market adoption or new products.
- Increased internal consumers (more strategies, more analytics).

Then, using your benchmark results, estimate:

- CPU and memory requirements for feed handlers and buses.
- Network bandwidth and packet-per-second capacity, including overhead for control traffic.
- Storage and I/O needs for logging and historical recording.

It is better to treat these as ranges with uncertainty rather than precise numbers. Plan for the high end, especially in parts of the system that are expensive or slow to scale, such as colocation space or specialized hardware.

Defining Headroom

"Headroom" is the margin between your tested safe operating point and your expected production peak. For example:

- If you expect a peak of 500,000 messages per second on a key multicast channel, you might want verified capacity for at least 1 million messages per second with tail latency still within agreed thresholds.
- If your gateway can handle 20,000 orders per second in tests with p99 latency under 500 microseconds, you may choose to operate under a hard cap of 10,000 orders per second in live trading.

Headroom absorbs:

- Unexpected market extremes.
- Degradations from configuration drift or minor code changes.
- The additional load that occurs during cutovers and failovers (for example, when multiple components restart and resubscribe).

Understanding Tail Latency with Visuals

To make tail behavior and headroom concrete, it is useful to visualize latency distributions under baseline and stressed conditions, alongside system throughput.

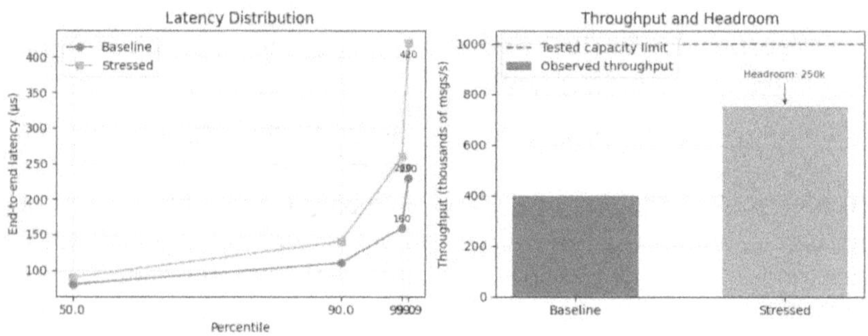

Such a figure tells a richer story than a single "average latency" number. You can see, for example, that under stress:

- Median and p90 latencies remain acceptable.
- p99 and p99.9 tails stretch noticeably, but still within defined risk thresholds
- Throughput is high but still leaves a clear margin below the tested capacity limit, indicating headroom.

Visuals like this are effective in discussions with risk committees and senior management.

Regression Testing: Guarding Against Performance Drift

Once you have established acceptable performance, you must keep it. Small code changes, library upgrades, or configuration tweaks can easily nibble away at latency and capacity margins without anyone noticing.

Performance Baselines

Record baseline metrics under well-defined scenarios:

- Specific data sets or synthetic patterns.
- Controlled hardware and configuration.
- Clear versions of all relevant software components.

Store these results with the same care as functional test suites. When you make changes, run the same scenarios and compare:

- Have median or tail latencies shifted significantly?
- Has throughput decreased under identical load?
- Are resource utilization patterns (CPU, memory, network) meaningfully different?

Set quantitative thresholds for acceptable drift. For example, "p99 latency may not increase by more than 10% under the standard 'Equities Open' scenario without explicit review and sign-off."

Automating Performance Checks

Integrate performance tests into your deployment pipeline where feasible:

- For small changes, run lighter, faster tests that still exercise critical paths.

- For major releases, run full end-to-end benchmarks, possibly overnight.

If automated tests detect regressions beyond thresholds, block promotion to production until the issue is understood. This may slow individual releases but greatly reduces the risk of surprises in live trading.

Testing for Cutovers and Failovers

A central theme of this book is how to move from backtest or old systems to new ones safely. Performance testing must explicitly address cutovers and failovers: moments when you might temporarily run multiple paths in parallel or rapidly shift load from one system to another.

Parallel Run Scenarios

In a parallel run, both old and new stacks process the same market data. You may:

- Feed both through identical market data paths, doubling the internal consumer count.
- Route a fraction of orders through the new gateway while the old gateway remains active.

Your performance tests should simulate:

- The increased load on internal buses and feed handlers from dual consumers.
- Any additional logging or comparison logic used to validate equality of outputs between paths.

Confirm that tails remain acceptable and that there is still headroom for market stress events during the parallel period.

Failover and Recovery Tests

Similarly, test failover scenarios:

- A primary data center feed handler or bus goes down, and clients reconnect to a secondary.
- A gateway cluster node fails and orders reroute to others.

Measure:

- Time to detect failure and complete failover.
- Latency and loss characteristics during the transition.
- Whether queues build up dangerously on surviving components.

These are not just operational questions. They directly affect trading risk: a prolonged or unstable failover can leave strategies blind or slow during crucial windows.

Communicating Results to Stakeholders

Finally, rigor in measurement is only useful if it can be understood and acted upon. Different audiences need different views.

For Engineers and Architects

Provide:

- Detailed latency breakdowns by hop and component.
- Resource utilization profiles under test scenarios.
- Clear evidence of bottlenecks and their root causes.

This information guides optimization and architectural evolution. It should be precise, technical, and reproducible.

For Risk Committees and Management

Translate the same results into higher-level assurances:

- Statements like "Under conditions equal to or exceeding the worst five days of the past year, the market data path maintained p99 latency under X microseconds with zero unintentional loss."
- Visuals showing headroom: observed peaks versus tested limits.
- Evidence that cutover and failover scenarios have been exercised and passed predefined criteria.

These summaries turn raw telemetry into confidence that new strategies, venues, or infrastructure can be safely deployed.

In this section we closed the loop on the connectivity and market data infrastructure chapter by focusing on performance and capacity. We defined the metrics that matter in trading—throughput, latency distributions, jitter, loss, and headroom—and designed end-to-end tests that exercise the real data path from exchange port to consumer applications.

We saw how multi-point timestamping and correlation IDs let you attribute latency to specific components, how capacity planning and headroom provide buffers for growth and stress, and how performance regressions can be caught before they reach production. Finally, we emphasized that cutover and failover scenarios deserve explicit performance validation and that results must be communicated in forms suitable for both technical and non-technical stakeholders.

With accurate time, reliable feeds, secure channels, realistic replay environments, and now quantified performance guarantees, you are equipped to move strategies from backtest to live execution with a systematic understanding of the infrastructure that supports them.

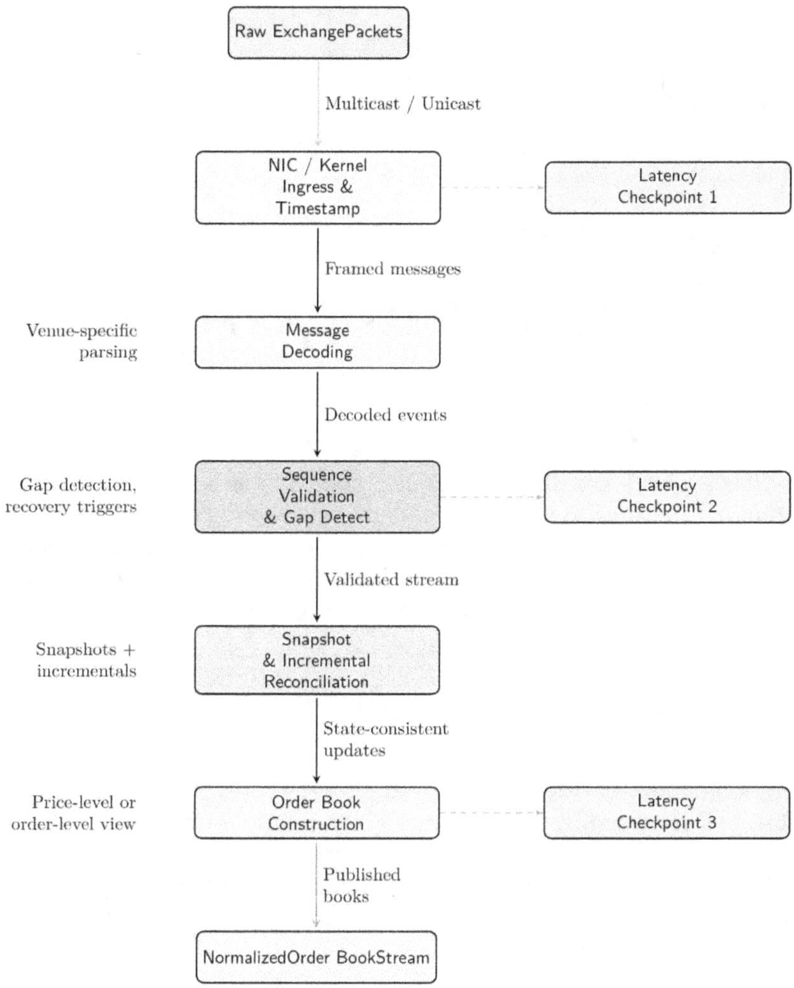
Raw ExchangePackets
Multicast / Unicast
NIC / Kernel Ingress & Timestamp
Latency Checkpoint 1
Framed messages
Venue-specific parsing
Message Decoding
Decoded events
Gap detection, recovery triggers
Sequence Validation & Gap Detect
Latency Checkpoint 2
Validated stream
Snapshots + incrementals
Snapshot & Incremental Reconciliation
State-consistent updates
Price-level or order-level view
Order Book Construction
Latency Checkpoint 3
Published books
NormalizedOrder BookStream

Chapter 4

Order Gateways and Session Management

Backtests never see sequence gaps, canceled sessions, or throttled gateways-live markets do. This chapter walks from the clean, abstract idea of "an order" to the messy reality of protocols, sessions, and safeguards that keep orders flowing, observable, and recoverable when the tape gets hectic or infrastructure fails.

4.1 Order Lifecycle and State Machine

When a strategy decides to trade, it does not simply "send an order and get a fill." Between that initial intent and the final outcome, the order passes through a series of well-defined states at the strategy, gateway, broker, and venue. If those states are not modeled carefully and consistently, you lose the ability to answer basic questions such as:

- How many shares are currently working in the market for this strategy?
- Which orders are still cancelable, and which are already terminal?

- Where did a missing fill or duplicate fill come from?

This section builds a precise, venue-agnostic order state model that you can implement in your own gateways. The goal is that every share is traceable from the moment your strategy decides to trade, through every partial fill and cancel attempt, to a final reconciled position. We focus on concepts that remain stable even though exchanges, brokers, and protocols vary widely.

Why a Canonical Order State Model Matters

Electronic markets expose many different views of "the same" order:

- The *strategy* keeps an internal object representing its intent (e.g., buy 10,000 shares at $25.10).
- The *gateway* enriches, risk-checks, and forwards that intent to one or more venues.
- The *broker or exchange* maintains its own order book and execution logs.
- A *drop copy* or post-trade feed streams independent confirmations.

Each domain uses its own identifiers and state labels, and each can lag the others for short periods. Without a unifying model, it is easy to misinterpret what is actually working in the market, and to either carry more risk than you think (stray live orders) or less (believing something is still working when it has already been canceled or fully filled).

A canonical order lifecycle gives you:

- A common vocabulary across teams, systems, and venues.
- Clear rules for valid state transitions.
- Well-defined "reconciliation boundaries" where you check that internal and external views agree.

We will first define the core states, then place them in a state machine that is robust to real-world messaging issues.

Canonical Order States

Although each venue has its own nuances, most order flows can be expressed in a compact set of states. We group them into three families: *working*, *terminated*, and *error/intermediate*.

1. New (or Pending New).

The strategy has requested an order, and the gateway has submitted it to a venue or broker, but no acceptance has yet been confirmed. You know what you *asked* for, but not yet what the venue has *accepted*.

Conceptually:

- Intent formed, risk checked.
- Message sent outward.
- No external acknowledgment (ack) or rejection received yet.

2. Acknowledged (Accepted).

The venue or broker confirms that it has accepted the order. The order now exists in an external book. From this point on, you must assume the order can trade until you see a cancel or terminal event.

Key idea: "Accepted" is the point where external risk begins. Before that, the order is only an internal intention.

3. Rested (Working).

After acceptance, the unfilled portion of the order is *rested* in the venue's order book. It may be immediately marketable (and thus fill quickly) or non-marketable (waiting in the queue). In practice, you often treat "Acknowledged" and "Rested" as a combined "working" state, but separating them helps when reasoning about timing, especially in very fast markets.

4. Partially Filled.

Some, but not all, of the order quantity has been executed. The order remains live for the residual quantity. Two quantities must be tracked carefully:

- *Original quantity*: what you initially asked for.

- *Cumulative filled quantity*: how much has actually traded so far.

The *leaves quantity* (still working) is simply the difference between those two in your internal model.

5. Filled.

The entire order quantity has been executed. There is no residual working. The order transitions to a terminal state; it cannot generate further fills, cancels, or replaces.

6. Pending Cancel / Pending Replace.

You have requested to:

- Cancel the remaining quantity, or
- Modify parameters such as price or quantity (a "replace").

The venue has not yet confirmed the outcome. While pending, the previous working order is still *in effect* from a risk perspective unless the venue's semantics say otherwise. This is one of the most subtle and venue-specific parts of the model, so the canonical state machine must be conservative: if in doubt, treat the order as still live until you receive explicit confirmation.

7. Canceled.

The order (or its remaining quantity) has been canceled successfully. No further trading can occur against it. Note that some fills may still arrive after the cancel request time but before the exchange's effective cancel time; your model must handle those without contradiction.

8. Rejected.

The order, cancel, or replace request is refused by some external system (pre-trade risk system, broker, or exchange). A new order that is rejected never becomes live; a cancel or replace rejection means the original live order remains in effect.

9. Expired.

The order terminates due to a time condition, such as:

- Time-in-force (e.g., day order at market close).

- Good-till-date or good-till-session boundaries.

Expired is also terminal; it behaves like a cancel that the venue initiated according to its rules.

A Canonical State Machine

We now connect these states in an order state machine. The diagram below captures the major transitions seen in most equity and futures venues.

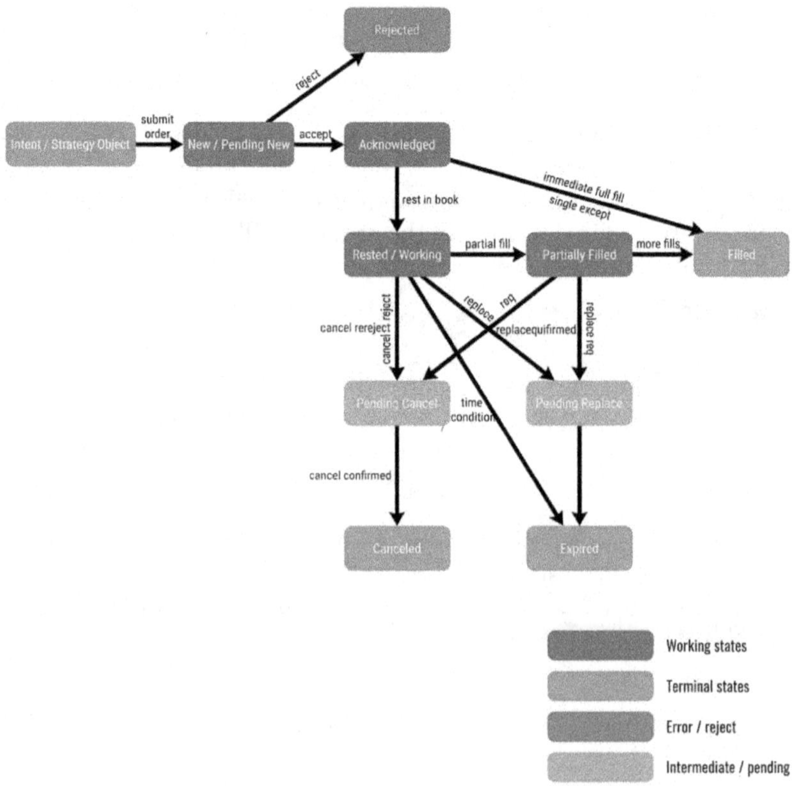

This diagram compresses a lot of detail, so we unpack the main design choices next.

Strategy View vs. Venue View

An important theme is that your internal state machine is not the same as the venue's. Instead, it is your *best consistent interpretation* of what the venue is doing, based on messages received so far.

Two principles guide the mapping:

1. **Conservatism about risk.** When internal and external views disagree temporarily, you should assume more exposure rather than less until reconciliation proves otherwise. For example, when a cancel is pending, you still treat residual quantity as live.

2. **Monotonicity of information.** Information about an order should become only more precise over time. You do not "forget" fills or revert to an earlier, less informative state.

Consider a cancel request:

- The *strategy* moves the order from Rested/Partially Filled to Pending Cancel as soon as it sends the cancel.

- The *venue* may still treat the order as fully working until it processes that cancel.

- For risk, your system must assume fills may still occur until a cancel confirmation or terminal state is received.

Designing your state machine with this asymmetry in mind prevents dangerous assumptions about when risk actually ends.

Key Invariants in the Lifecycle

Once we have the basic states in place, we impose invariants that must hold at all times across the lifecycle. These invariants turn a loose model into a reliable risk control.

Quantity and Fills

- **Cumulative filled quantity never decreases.** Once a fill is recorded, it is permanent. If the venue later sends a "bust" or "cancel trade," you handle it as a separate corrective event rather than decrementing historical fills.
- **Leaves quantity is derived, not authoritative.** The working quantity is derived from original quantity minus cumulative filled minus any explicitly canceled portion. You do not maintain an independent "leaves quantity" field that could drift out of sync.
- **Each individual execution is counted exactly once.** Duplicate execution reports (due to resends or replay) must not cause overstatement of fills.

These rules ensure that summing all fills across orders produces a coherent position history.

Immutability of Core Attributes

After an order is accepted (Acknowledged), certain attributes should be treated as immutable within that order instance:

- Side (buy/sell).
- Instrument (symbol).
- Original order identifier at the venue.

If you need to change these, you do so by canceling and replacing with a *new* logical order. Replaces may validly change price, quantity, or time-in-force, but even there you should move carefully and treat large, disruptive changes (e.g., doubling quantity) as a distinct risk decision.

Single State per Domain

At any point in time, an order must be in exactly one state within a given domain (strategy, gateway, venue interpretation). It cannot be simultaneously "Partially Filled" and "Canceled"; instead, it is "Partially Filled" until a cancel is confirmed, and then "Partially Filled, Canceled" as a terminal state with explicit tags for terminal cause.

From an implementation perspective this means:

- No overlapping state flags that can be true at the same time.
- State transitions are atomic in your internal models.

Idempotency and Duplicate Messages

Real-world networks drop, reorder, and duplicate messages. A safe order gateway assumes that any outbound or inbound message may be retried or replayed. Idempotency means that repeating the same logical request or processing the same event more than once has no additional effect beyond the first time.

Outbound Idempotency: Submits, Cancels, Replaces

For outbound messages, you must ensure that identical logical actions do not create new risk. Common mistakes include:

- Resending a new order after a timeout and ending up with two live orders instead of one.
- Re-sending a cancel for an order already canceled and misinterpreting the second confirmation.

Two tools are essential:

Client Order ID (ClOrdID).

Each logical order submission is assigned a unique client-side identifier at the strategy or gateway. Retries of the same logical order *reuse* this identifier so that the venue or broker can recognize duplicates and ignore or correctly relate them. For replaces, you typically use a chained series of ClOrdIDs, each referencing the previous one, so there is a clear lineage.

Idempotent state transitions.

Processing a "cancel confirmed" for an order that is already considered Canceled should have no additional side effect. The state remains Canceled, and a log entry confirms that a duplicate confirmation was seen.

Inbound Idempotency: Execution IDs and Drop Copies

For inbound messages, especially execution reports, you rely on identifiers such as:

- *OrderID*: the venue's order identifier.
- *ExecID*: a unique identifier per execution (fill, cancel, etc.).

Your gateway should keep a record of all seen ExecIDs for a session and ignore duplicates. The first time you see a given ExecID, you apply its effect (e.g., increase cumulative filled quantity). Subsequent arrivals are treated as resends and simply acknowledged in logs.

This logic must apply both on the primary order-entry channel and on any secondary / drop-copy feed. The same execution could reach you twice via different paths; idempotency prevents it from double-counting.

Correlation Keys and Stitching Fragmented Views

No single identifier is sufficient to track an order across strategy, gateway, broker, venue, and back-office systems. A robust design uses a small set of correlation keys, each with a specific role.

- **Internal Order ID.** Created by the strategy or gateway; never leaves your firm. Serves as the "anchor" for internal joins across databases and logs.

- **Client Order ID (ClOrdID).** Sent to broker/venue, visible on FIX or native messages; used for idempotency and tracing within and across sessions.
- **Venue Order ID (OrderID).** Assigned by the venue/broker; unique within that domain. This is what appears in exchange-level logs and sometimes in drop copies.
- **Execution ID (ExecID).** Unique per fill, cancel, or significant state change event from the venue.

Your state machine is really built around these keys. For each Internal Order ID, you maintain the canonical lifecycle, and you attach to it all ClOrdIDs, OrderIDs, and ExecIDs that refer to the same logical order. When you receive a message on any channel (primary, drop copy, back office), you can route it to the correct internal order state via these keys.

Reconciliation Boundaries

Even with a careful state machine, you must periodically stop and ask: "Does our view match the venue's?" Reconciliation boundaries define the points where you perform these checks systematically.

Intraday Real-Time Reconciliation

Intraday, you focus on questions such as:

- Do we have any orders that we think are Canceled but the venue still shows as live?
- Do we see executions in drop copy that are not reflected in the primary channel, or vice versa?
- Does our cumulative filled quantity per instrument match what the broker reports?

Practically, this means:

1. **Shadow books.** Maintain a "shadow" order and position book sourced from drop copy and venue status messages, separate from the strategy's internal book.
2. **Continuous comparison.** On a rolling basis, compare the internal canonical state (per Internal Order ID) to the shadow state assembled from external feeds.
3. **Defined tolerances and actions.** For example, any single stray live order (venue shows live, internal shows terminal) beyond a small tolerance may trigger an automated soft halt for that strategy or venue until the discrepancy is understood.

This real-time reconciliation builds directly on your state machine: discrepancies are always expressed as "our state is X, external state is Y," which is human-readable and amenable to alerting.

Session Restart and Book Rebuild

At session boundaries or after a connectivity failure, you may need to rebuild your internal view from venue or broker state. A typical procedure is:

1. Query the venue or broker for all open (live) orders at the start of the session.
2. For each open order:
   - Match it to an existing Internal Order ID via ClOrdID or OrderID.
   - If no match exists, create a "recovered" order entry tagged as external-originated (e.g., from manual trading or a previous system).
3. Set the internal state to Rested or Partially Filled as appropriate, then let normal message processing resume.

This ensures that your internal state machine starts from a ground truth that reflects actual live risk. From there, you can replay or ingest historical executions to reconstruct full fill histories.

End-of-Day and Back-Office Reconciliation

At end-of-day, the goal is that the sum of all order-level events matches:

- The official broker confirms.
- The clearing firm's positions.
- Your internal positions and P&L.

Because your order lifecycle is canonical and every fill is attached to a unique ExecID and Internal Order ID, you can roll up execution histories confidently. Any mismatch is immediately traceable to a specific order and state transition, not just a vague "position difference."

Handling Out-of-Order and Batched Messages

Finally, we must acknowledge that in real networks, messages can arrive out of order or in batches. Your state machine must tolerate, for example:

- Receiving a partial fill before an explicit acceptance message.
- Seeing multiple fills batched together after a delay.
- Receiving a cancel confirmation after you have already inferred a cancel from an expiration.

The design pattern is:

1. **Process by information content, not by strict sequence.** A fill implies that the order was accepted and working at the venue, even if you never saw the formal ack. Your state machine should move from New directly to Partially Filled when necessary.
2. **Allow "skipping" states while preserving invariants.** It is acceptable to move from New to Filled without ever explicitly visiting Rested in your internal logs, as long as quantity and immutability rules hold.

3. **Record unexpected transitions for investigation.** While the state machine permits them, you should flag anomalous sequences (e.g., fill after cancel confirmation) as potential venue or connectivity issues.

Designing your state machine to be *permissive* in processing but *strict* in invariants is the key. Messages may arrive late or out of order, but the final reconstructed lifecycle for each order is unique, self-consistent, and fully auditable.

From Lifecycle to Controls

The canonical order lifecycle is more than a bookkeeping device. It is the backbone for almost every safeguard discussed later in this chapter:

- Pre-trade limits rely on accurate counts of New and working orders.
- Session management and failover depend on being able to restart from a consistent set of Rested and Partially Filled orders.
- Throttling and flow control use state to decide which orders are candidates for cancellation or reprioritization.
- Drop-copy-driven alerts compare internal and external states to detect hidden risk.

By treating the order state machine as a first-class design artifact rather than an afterthought attached to protocol messages, you create a foundation where every share is traceable from initial intent to final fill or cancel, across sessions, venues, and failures.

4.2 Order Entry Protocols: FIX and Native

In the previous section we treated orders in an abstract, protocol-agnostic way: an order moved from New to Acknowledged to Rested,

Partially Filled, and eventually to a terminal state. We deliberately did not ask *how* those state changes traveled across the wire.

We now descend a level and look at the concrete order entry protocols that carry those messages between your gateway and the outside world. In practice you will almost always encounter two families:

- **FIX** (Financial Information eXchange): a widely adopted, text-based protocol that is broker and venue neutral.
- **Native exchange APIs**: venue-specific binary or compact protocols such as OUCH, BOE, iLink, and their cousins.

Both can express the same lifecycle events—new orders, cancels, replaces, fills, rejects—but they differ sharply in message semantics, latency, and operational complexity. This section compares them through the lens of the state machine you just learned, and equips you to choose and design around each style of gateway.

From States to Messages

Recall the canonical lifecycle: New, Acknowledged, Rested, Partially Filled, Filled, Pending Cancel/Replace, Canceled, Rejected, Expired. In any concrete protocol, you typically see these transitions expressed through a small set of core message types:

- **New Order** (often "New Order Single" in FIX): request to create a live order.
- **Cancel Request**: request to cancel the remaining quantity of an order.
- **Cancel/Replace (Modify) Request**: request to change price, quantity, or similar attributes.
- **Execution or Order Status Report**: reports about fills, partial fills, cancels, rejects, and other state changes.

The exact names vary, but conceptually:

- Outbound messages from you express *intent* (submit, cancel, modify).
- Inbound messages from the broker or venue confirm what actually happened and move you through the state machine.

What differs between FIX and native APIs is how those messages are structured, what extra information they carry, and how tightly they map to the venue's internal behavior.

FIX: The Neutral, Rich, and Verbose Workhorse

FIX was designed for interoperability. Instead of every firm and every venue inventing their own protocol, FIX provides a common language: a set of message types and fields (called "tags") that most participants understand. It is usually text-based (tag=value pairs separated by delimiters), human-readable with some effort, and highly extensible.

Session vs. Application Layers

A key characteristic of FIX is its division into two conceptual layers:

- **Session layer**: handles connectivity, logon/logoff, heartbeats, sequence numbers, and resends. Its job is to ensure a reliable, ordered stream of messages between you and your counterparty.
- **Application layer**: carries the business messages—orders, cancels, executions, quotes, allocations—that drive your order lifecycle.

From the perspective of your order state machine:

- The *session layer* ensures that you see each state change exactly once, in an identifiable sequence, and can request resends if you detect gaps.
- The *application layer* encodes the transitions themselves ("this order is now accepted / partially filled / canceled").

In this chapter we care mostly about the application layer, but you should keep in mind that FIX's robust session behavior is a major reason it is so common for high-value trading flows.

Core FIX Messages and Tags for Order Flow

Although the FIX standard defines many messages, a small subset covers most order entry:

- **New Order Single**: submits a new order. It includes tags for side, symbol, quantity, price, time-in-force, client order ID, and many others.
- **Order Cancel Request**: asks to cancel a live order, identified by client order ID and/or the broker's order ID.
- **Order Cancel/Replace Request**: asks to change parameters of an existing order.
- **Execution Report**: conveys almost every state change—acknowledgment, partial fill, full fill, cancel confirmation, reject.

Several application-layer tags are especially important for mapping FIX messages to your canonical lifecycle:

- **Client Order ID (ClOrdID)**: your own unique identifier for the order or request. This is how you tie responses back to your internal order objects and enforce outbound idempotency.
- **OrderID**: the broker or venue-assigned order identifier. This is your view into their world.
- **ExecID**: a unique identifier per execution event. You use this to detect and ignore duplicate execution reports.
- **OrdStatus**: FIX's order status field, which maps directly to your state machine (New, Partially Filled, Filled, Canceled, Rejected, Expired, etc.).
- **ExecType**: specifies what kind of event the execution report represents (new, trade, canceled, replaced, rejected, etc.).

At a conceptual level, you can think of each execution report as saying: "For the order you know as ClOrdID X / OrderID Y, its status is now Z, and here is any new trade or cancel information you should record." Your gateway translates that into a transition in your canonical state machine.

Semantics and Richness of FIX

Because FIX was designed for a broad range of asset classes and workflows, its execution reports often carry rich context:

- Detailed reasons for rejects (e.g., fat-finger checks, limit price outside venue thresholds).
- Flags indicating whether an event came from manual intervention, a self-match prevention system, or a venue-initiated cancel.
- Allocation and commission information, especially in post-trade flows.

This richness is valuable for:

- **Observability**: understanding *why* something happened, not just that it happened.
- **Control logic**: decisions to retry, reroute, or halt can be driven by precise reject codes.
- **Audit and compliance**: FIX messages and logs are often the primary evidence trail in post-mortems and regulatory inquiries.

The tradeoff is size and complexity: messages are larger than strictly necessary for execution, and both sides must agree on how to interpret many optional fields.

Latency and Overhead in FIX

FIX adds overhead along several dimensions:

- **Encoding**: text tag-value encoding, checksums, and parsing all add CPU cost and a bit of time, compared to fixed-layout binary messages.

- **Message size**: FIX messages are verbose. Larger messages mean more bytes on the wire, which can add microseconds on congested links.
- **Broker hops**: many firms connect to exchanges via brokers over FIX. The broker may then speak a native protocol to the venue. This extra hop adds latency and potential variability.

For most institutional strategies, this overhead is acceptable. When your holding periods are minutes to days, tens of microseconds of additional latency are not material. But for latency-sensitive or high-frequency strategies, these costs can be significant, especially if you already operate near the limits of venue speed.

Operational Complexity of FIX

Operationally, FIX has several advantages:

- It is widely understood; you can hire engineers, support staff, and vendors who already know how to work with it.
- Brokers provide managed FIX gateways, often with robust monitoring and risk controls.
- Upgrades and version changes are incremental; fields can be added without breaking the whole connection.

The main operational challenges are:

- Managing differing "dialects" of FIX: each broker and venue chooses which tags to support and how to interpret some of them.
- Maintaining multiple FIX sessions across brokers, each with its own configuration, sequence numbers, and failover rules.
- Controlling latency when features like compression, TLS, or heavy logging are layered on top.

In short, FIX gives you a rich and relatively uniform surface, at the cost of some latency and the need to curate configuration and compatibility.

Native Exchange APIs: Tight, Fast, and Venue-Specific

Native APIs, such as OUCH or BOE for some equity venues or iLink for certain futures venues, are designed from the inside out: they expose the venue's own native order model, often in a compact, binary encoding. There is usually little to no extra abstraction for brokers or diverse workflows.

Message Types and Semantics

Native APIs typically define a small, fixed set of messages:

- **New Order** messages with fields chosen by the venue (e.g., side, symbol ID, quantity, price, time-in-force, account).
- **Cancel** and **Modify** messages that usually reference a venue-assigned order ID or a client-chosen token.
- **Execution or Order Event** messages that report partial fills, full fills, cancels, expires, and rejects.

Compared to FIX, these messages:

- Use compact integer codes instead of text tags.
- Transmit only the fields considered essential by the venue.
- Mirror the venue's internal state transitions very closely.

For your order state machine, the mapping is straightforward but more tightly coupled: each native order event has a direct and unambiguous meaning in that venue's model. There is often less redundancy and fewer "optional extras" than in FIX.

Latency Characteristics

Native APIs are designed for speed:

- **Compact messages**: small, fixed-size messages require less bandwidth and are faster to encode/decode.

- **Simpler parsing**: fixed offsets and fields mean you avoid the cost of scanning tag-value pairs.
- **Direct connectivity**: you often connect directly to the exchange over a low-latency line, avoiding broker hops.

In high-frequency or latency-sensitive strategies, these differences can be decisive. Saving tens of microseconds per round-trip can change your queue position, reduce adverse selection, and improve realized edge.

However, native APIs do not magically eliminate all latency. You still face:

- Physical propagation delays.
- Queueing inside your own stack and the exchange.
- CPU and context-switch overhead.

The key point is that native APIs remove avoidable protocol overhead and intermediate hops, which is why they are standard in the fastest trading shops.

Operational Complexity and Coupling

The speed and simplicity of native APIs come with tradeoffs:

- **Venue specificity**: each exchange has its own native protocol. If you connect to five venues, you may have to support five different native stacks, each with different messages, life-cycle quirks, and upgrade cycles.
- **Version churn**: venues evolve their protocols. You must track release notes, test new versions rigorously, and perform cutovers on specific dates, sometimes under tight deadlines.
- **Less "hand-holding"**: brokers often provide FIX connectivity as a managed service. With native, you are usually closer to the metal and responsible for more of the reliability and risk-control logic yourself.

This complexity shows up in:

- Engineering: more protocol implementations, more testing, and more venue-specific edge cases.
- Operations: more runbooks, more monitoring integration, more coordination with each venue's operations team.
- Risk management: some protective features that brokers offer on FIX (e.g., global fat-finger limits, kill switches, credit checks) may be thinner or must be implemented entirely on your side.

For firms that trade many venues but are not ultra-latency-sensitive, this overhead may not be worth the marginal speed gains everywhere.

Comparing Message Semantics

From the perspective of your canonical state machine, both FIX and native APIs must answer the same questions:

- Has my order been accepted?
- What is my cumulative fill quantity and leaves quantity?
- Has my cancel/modify succeeded or failed?
- Is my order terminated (filled, canceled, rejected, expired)?

The main differences are in *how* they communicate these answers and how much extra information you receive.

Granularity of Events

FIX execution reports are often multi-purpose: the same message type carries both acknowledgments and fills, distinguished by status and type fields. Native APIs sometimes separate these more strictly:

- Separate "accepted" and "booked" messages, or
- Distinct message codes for partial fills vs. full fills vs. cancels.

In practice:

- FIX may give you richer, more standardized status codes, but you must understand the particular broker's usage.
- Native APIs give you a compact but venue-specific event vocabulary that often maps one-to-one to internal book events.

Error and Reject Information

FIX shines in expressiveness for rejects and errors. You typically receive:

- High-level reject type (e.g., order reject vs. cancel reject).
- One or more reason codes (e.g., price band violation, invalid symbol, insufficient permissions).
- Sometimes free-text descriptions for human consumption.

Native APIs may instead:

- Provide a short error code space with limited documented reasons.
- Bundle several failure causes into the same code.
- Expect participants to rely on out-of-band communication for detailed investigation.

If your focus is understanding and automating responses to a broad variety of failure modes, FIX's rich semantics are appealing. If you care more about lightning-fast, unambiguous "yes/no" responses, native APIs are usually adequate.

Latency: When Does It Matter?

Latency differences between FIX and native protocols matter most when:

- Your alpha decays quickly (e.g., microseconds to milliseconds).
- Queue position is critical to your edge.
- You frequently submit and cancel large bursts of orders.

In these settings:

- **Native** connectivity can reduce end-to-end round-trip time and jitter.
- **FIX** may introduce enough additional overhead to noticeably worsen your realized execution quality.

By contrast, if your strategy operates at human or macro time scales:

- The microsecond or even millisecond differences between FIX and native are negligible relative to decision times and market moves.
- Latency variation introduced by brokers or routing may be overshadowed by fundamental price uncertainty.

It is therefore not correct to say that native is "better" than FIX in an absolute sense. Each is better for certain latency profiles and business needs.

Operational Complexity and Support Tradeoffs

From an engineering management perspective, protocol choice is as much about human and organizational complexity as about bits and bytes.

Breadth of Coverage vs. Depth of Integration

FIX excels at breadth:

- **One protocol, many endpoints**: you can reach a wide array of brokers and venues with a single implementation and adaptors for differing field usage.

- **Leverage vendor tools**: many commercial and open-source tools support FIX logging, testing, monitoring, and certification.

Native APIs excel at depth:

- **Close mapping to venue behavior**: you often get fine-grained features earlier or exclusively via native.
- **Direct operational relationship**: you work more closely with the exchange's technical team, which can be helpful in diagnostics and performance tuning.

Maintaining multiple native gateways requires tighter discipline: more code, more integration tests, more staging environments, and better change management.

Risk Controls and Safeguards

Many brokers bundle pre-trade risk controls into their FIX gateways:

- Fat-finger checks on price and size.
- Per-account and per-instrument limits.
- Kill switches and circuit breakers.

Using broker FIX, you implicitly outsource some of your protection to their infrastructure. With native APIs, you may be responsible for implementing equivalent checks yourself at or before your gateway, and for convincing risk managers that they are as robust as what a broker would provide.

This difference interacts with the order lifecycle concepts from the previous section. For example, a reject at the broker's FIX gateway may happen before an order ever reaches the exchange's book, while a native reject may be purely venue-based. Your state machine and reconciliation logic must distinguish these if you rely on them for governance or reporting.

Design Patterns: Combining FIX and Native

Most professional trading firms use a mix of FIX and native APIs. A few common patterns emerge.

FIX for Broad Coverage, Native for Critical Venues

One widely used pattern is:

- **Default to FIX** for most venues and brokers, gaining ease of onboarding, standardized semantics, and rich monitoring.
- **Use native** only where the latency advantage or feature set has clear economic value, such as primary listing exchanges for your most profitable ultra-low-latency strategies.

To make this work, you design your internal gateway interface to the strategy layer to be *protocol-agnostic*. Strategies talk to a uniform abstraction:

- "Submit this order with these parameters."
- "Request cancel/replace."
- "Subscribe to state changes and fills."

Behind that abstraction:

- One adaptor speaks FIX to a broker, mapping internal lifecycle events to FIX messages and back.
- Another adaptor speaks a native protocol, mapping the same lifecycle to that venue's message types.

The canonical state machine from the previous section becomes the *unifying layer*. FIX-specific and native-specific details are translated into that common lifecycle so that:

- Strategy logic is written once.
- Risk controls and monitoring interpret states consistently.

- Drop-copy reconciliation can compare apples to apples across all connections.

FIX as Control Plane, Native as Data Plane

Another effective pattern is to use:

- **Native** for the raw, high-volume order and cancel traffic ("data plane").
- **FIX** for configuration, control, and lower-frequency flows ("control plane"), such as allocations, bulk cancels, and post-trade reporting.

This leverages the strengths of each:

- Native carries the time-critical, latency-sensitive traffic.
- FIX carries the richer, slower information needed for oversight, reconciliation, and back-office integration.

Once again, your state machine and correlation keys (Internal Order ID, ClOrdID, OrderID, ExecID) are the glue that holds everything together. They let you reconcile a fast, terse native execution with a more descriptive FIX confirmation of the same event.

Equipping Yourself to Choose

When deciding between FIX and native APIs for a given gateway, ask three sets of questions:

1. Latency and Strategy Profile

- How sensitive is the strategy's performance to tens of microseconds of additional latency?
- Does queue position at this venue materially affect your edge?
- Are you competing with other native-connected participants for speed?

If the answers point to high latency sensitivity, native is more attractive. Otherwise, FIX may be entirely sufficient.

2. Operational Scale and Team Capacity

- How many venues do you trade, and how many native protocols would that imply?
- Do you have the engineering and operations capacity to build, test, and maintain multiple native stacks?
- How comfortable is your risk team with taking on more direct responsibility for controls that brokers usually provide on FIX?

If you are bandwidth-constrained in engineering or operations, limiting native connectivity to a few critical venues can be prudent.

3. Semantics and Governance

- Do you need very detailed reject and error codes for automated decision-making and reporting?
- Does your regulatory environment or internal governance rely on standardized, well-understood message formats?
- How important is it to be able to onboard new brokers or markets quickly via a familiar protocol?

If governance, transparency, and flexibility across counterparties are central, FIX offers clear advantages.

Bringing It Back to the Lifecycle

The core message of this chapter is that the order state machine is your anchor. FIX, native APIs, and any other protocols are just different carriers of the same underlying concept: an order's progression from intent to final outcome.

If you design your system so that:

- All external messages—whether FIX or native—are translated into a common set of state transitions.

- All identifiers—ClOrdID, OrderID, ExecID, internal IDs—are carefully tracked and correlated.
- All reconciliation, risk checks, and monitoring interpret state in a protocol-agnostic way.

then you are free to evolve your connectivity mix over time. You can move a venue from FIX to native for latency reasons, or add a new broker, without rewriting your strategies or your risk logic. The complexity of each wire protocol is contained behind gateway adaptors, while the rest of your trading stack reasons in terms of the clean lifecycle model established earlier.

This separation of concerns—canonical lifecycle on the inside, diverse protocols on the outside—is the architectural pattern that allows your trading system to grow in scope and sophistication without losing control over risk and behavior.

4.3 Session Management, Sequencing, and Recovery

So far, we have treated orders and executions as if messages flow smoothly between your gateway and external venues. In reality, networks are imperfect. Packets are delayed, dropped, or delivered twice. Processes restart. Links flap. If you do not design explicitly for these conditions, small glitches can escalate into trading outages or, worse, silent mismatches between your internal books and the market.

This section introduces *sessions* and *sequencing* as the backbone of reliable order connectivity. A session is the long-lived logical conversation between your gateway and a counterparty (broker or exchange). Sequencing is the discipline that ensures both sides agree on exactly which messages were sent and received, and in what order.

We will:

- Distinguish session concerns from application-level order logic.
- Explain how sequence numbers and gap detection prevent double-processing and missed events.

- Walk through common failure modes and how robust gateways recover.
- Discuss hot, warm, and cold restarts, and how to rebuild a safe view of live risk.
- Emphasize cross-session consistency when you talk to multiple venues and brokers.

Throughout, keep in mind the canonical order lifecycle from earlier: if session handling fails, your state machine cannot be trusted. Session management is what keeps that lifecycle grounded in reality.

Session vs. Application: Two Intertwined Layers

It helps to separate two layers conceptually:

- **Application layer** carries business meaning: new orders, cancels, replaces, execution reports, order status. This is where your order state machine lives.
- **Session layer** carries control information that makes the stream of application messages reliable: logons, heartbeats, sequence numbers, resends, and disconnects.

The application layer answers questions like "Is my order partially filled?" The session layer answers questions like "Did I see every message exactly once?" You cannot safely interpret the first without confidence in the second.

Protocols like FIX make this split explicit: they define particular logon, heartbeat, test request, and logout messages for session management. Native exchange APIs often embed similar ideas (e.g., session IDs, sequence counters, heartbeat or "punch" messages), even if they are less standardized.

What Is a Trading Session?

A session is more than a TCP connection. It is a logical relationship defined by:

- Two endpoints (your gateway and a broker or venue).
- A direction (order entry, drop copy, drop cancel, etc.).
- A time span (from logon to logout, often within a trading day).
- A sequence number stream.

You might have multiple sessions to the same broker (for example, one for equities, one for options) and both primary and backup sessions to manage redundancy.

Within a session:

- Every message is assigned a strictly increasing *sequence number*.
- Both sides track the last sequence number they have sent and received.
- Any gap or duplication is detected and reconciled.

Your internal systems should treat the session as a first-class object: it has its own state (logged on, in recovery, logged off), metrics (latency, missed heartbeats), and runbooks for what to do when something goes wrong.

Sequence Numbers and At-Most-Once Processing

Sequence numbers serve two purposes:

- **Detecting missing messages** (sequence gaps).
- **Preventing duplicates from double-applying** effects.

When your gateway receives a message on a session, it compares the message's sequence number to the *next expected* number. Three broad cases occur:

- **Exactly the expected number**: This is the normal case. You process the message, advance your "last received" counter, and move on.

- **Higher than expected**: One or more messages are missing in between. You detect a *gap* and request resends for the missing range. You may hold the later message temporarily until the gap is filled, depending on your rules.
- **Lower than expected**: This message (or at least its sequence number) has been seen before. It is a resend or duplicate. You should *not* apply its business logic again, but you may log that you saw a duplicate for audit purposes.

On the send side, you number your outgoing messages similarly. If your counterparty sees a gap in your outbound sequence, they can ask you to resend. A well-behaved gateway keeps enough recent messages to respond to such requests, or at least provide gap-fill markers that say "you did not miss anything important here."

From the order lifecycle perspective, this mechanism protects you from:

- Losing an execution report that changes state from Rested to Partially Filled.
- Applying the same fill report twice and overstating your position.
- Missing a cancel confirmation and believing an order is still live when it is not.

Heartbeats and Liveness Detection

Sequence numbers help you know *what* has been exchanged; heartbeats help you know whether the session is *alive*.

Most protocols implement a periodic heartbeat or keep-alive:

- If no application messages are sent within a given interval, one side sends a heartbeat message.
- The other side responds either implicitly (by sending any message) or explicitly (by echoing a heartbeat or test response).

If a heartbeat or test message is not acknowledged within a configured timeout:

- The session may be marked as *suspect* or *down*.
- Your gateway may pause sending new orders and consider halting strategies that rely on that path.
- Recovery procedures are triggered (reconnect, failover, or controlled shutdown).

It is important to distinguish:

- A *quiet* but healthy session (low trading activity, heartbeats exchanged normally).
- A *frozen* session (no responses to heartbeats or test requests).

Monitoring these states and acting appropriately is a central part of stopping minor issues from becoming major outages.

Common Failure Modes and How Sequencing Helps

To make these ideas concrete, consider a few typical failure scenarios.

Scenario 1: Process Restart With Stale Sequence Numbers

Imagine your gateway process crashes and is restarted. If it simply reconnects and resumes sending messages starting from sequence number 1, your counterparty will see a large backward jump. They may disconnect you for protocol violation, or worse, try to treat the messages as duplicates of very old traffic.

To avoid this:

- You must *persist* the last sent and last received sequence numbers for each session.
- On restart, you restore these counters and either:

- Continue from the next number, or
- Negotiate a new starting point with the counterparty according to the protocol rules.

If you get this wrong, you can end up unable to reconnect, or in a state where neither side trusts the message stream. Meanwhile, your orders may still be working in the market, but your state machine is blind. Proper sequence management and restart logic prevent this.

Scenario 2: Network Partition and Delayed Executions

Suppose a transient network issue delays messages for a few seconds:

- You send several cancel requests.
- The exchange receives and processes them, but confirmations are delayed.
- During the delay, the orders may still trade or may already be removed from the book.

When the connection recovers:

- You receive a burst of execution reports and cancel confirmations.
- Sequence numbers allow your gateway to detect any missing messages in that burst and request them.
- Your state machine replays the events in correct order, even if they arrive close together.

Without strict sequencing and gap-filling, you might see only some of the cancels or some of the fills, ending up with an inconsistent view of what actually happened during the outage.

Scenario 3: Duplicate Resends During Recovery

During a recovery, it is common for one side to resend a range of messages to fill a detected gap. These resends are expected duplicates. They are necessary to ensure you did not miss anything, but they must not cause state to be applied twice.

Idempotent processing at the application layer builds on session sequencing:

- You track which sequence numbers and execution IDs have been processed.
- When a resend arrives, you recognize that it corresponds to already-applied business events.
- You acknowledge it at the session layer but skip its state changes.

If you confuse session-level recovery with new application events, you will overfill orders, double-cancel, or otherwise corrupt your state.

Resends, Gap Fills, and Recovery Mechanics

Let us look more systematically at how gaps are closed.

Gap Detection

Your gateway detects a missing message when:

- The next message's sequence number is higher than expected, or
- A heartbeat or test request times out, and you suspect recent messages have been lost.

The gateway then initiates a *resend request* for the missing sequence range, according to the protocol. This is analogous to requesting a missing page in a book: "Please send me pages 101–110; I have pages up to 100 and already received page 111."

Resend and Gap-Fill Responses

The counterparty may respond with:

- **Actual messages** for that range, if they are still available in their store.
- **Gap-fill markers** that state: "Nothing with business significance was sent in this range."

Gap fills are important for noise reduction. For example, some heartbeats or purely administrative messages may be considered safe to skip at the application level. However, execution reports, order acks, and cancels *must* be resent in full or reconstructed from another feed.

Your logic should:

- Treat gap-fill markers as session-level artifacts, not affecting order state.
- Apply actual resent application messages through your idempotent state machine.

Restart Strategies: Hot, Warm, and Cold

Even with good sequencing, there are times when you must restart components: planned maintenance, software deployment, or unplanned crashes. How you restart has a big impact on risk.

Hot Restart

In a hot restart:

- The process is briefly restarted, but session state is preserved in memory or quickly restored from persistent storage.
- Sequence numbers pick up where they left off.
- The system immediately requests any missing messages (if needed) and resumes normal operation.

Hot restarts are ideal for quick configuration changes or limited deployments, and they minimize trading interruption. However, they require careful engineering of state persistence and very fast recovery paths.

Warm Restart

In a warm restart:

- You deliberately drop and re-establish sessions.
- You reuse or renegotiate sequence numbers according to protocol rules.

- You rebuild your internal order book and risk view from a combination of:
  - Venue queries for all open orders.
  - Drop copy or back-office feeds for fills and cancels.

Warm restarts accept a brief pause in trading activity in exchange for a clean and reliable baseline. They are common after more substantial incidents, or when you suspect that in-memory state may be corrupted.

Cold Restart

In a cold restart:

- You treat the system as if it is starting from nothing.
- All sessions are freshly established, perhaps with re-initialized sequence numbers within protocol allowances.
- You perform comprehensive reconciliation: positions, live orders, and risk limits are rebuilt from external sources.

Cold restarts usually coincide with:

- Major outages.
- End-of-day transitions when carrying little or no overnight risk.
- Fundamental changes in configuration or topology.

They are the safest but also the most disruptive; during a cold restart, trading may be halted entirely until confidence in the reconstructed state is high.

When to Halt Trading vs. Attempt Automatic Recovery

A central design choice in session management is deciding when to let automated mechanisms try to heal the session and when to escalate to a controlled trading halt.

Some guidelines:

- **Short, isolated gaps or missed heartbeats** Attempt automatic recovery:
  - Request resends.
  - Wait a short, bounded amount of time for responses.
  - Continue trading if gaps are filled quickly and health metrics return to normal.
- **Persistent or repeated failures** Lean toward halting:
  - If resends repeatedly fail or produce inconsistent data, your view of order state is at risk.
  - If heartbeats or test requests are not answered in a timely fashion, you may be trading blind.

In ambiguous cases, good systems are biased toward safety: it is better to temporarily stop trading than to continue placing orders when you cannot trust connectivity or sequencing.

Cross-Session Consistency

Most real trading setups have *multiple* sessions:

- Several order entry sessions, sometimes across different venues or brokers.
- One or more drop copy sessions providing a second view of executions.
- Back-office or clearing sessions that confirm trades later.

Each session has its own sequence numbers and recovery procedures. Maintaining a coherent overall view requires careful coordination.

Aligning Order State Across Feeds

For a given order, you may see events on:

- The primary order-entry session.

- A drop copy session from the broker or exchange.
- A back-office confirmation channel.

These channels may be slightly out of sync in time. Session management per channel ensures each stream is internally consistent, but you still must *merge* them into a single canonical lifecycle.

This is where correlation keys from earlier sections (Internal Order ID, ClOrdID, OrderID, ExecID) come into play:

- You treat each event, from any session, as a candidate update to the canonical state of that order.
- You ignore duplicate events using ExecID and sequence logic.
- You resolve timing discrepancies using timestamps and well-defined rules (for example, treat drop copy as authoritative for fills if it disagrees with order entry).

If any session appears to be missing events that others show, you can target recovery efforts there instead of shutting down the entire system.

Failover Between Primary and Backup Sessions

Firms often maintain backup sessions or alternative paths (e.g., a secondary FIX session to the same broker, or a secondary data center). When failing over:

- You must ensure that sequence numbers on the active path start from a known, negotiated point.
- You must not send duplicate application messages that would create duplicate orders or cancels.
- You may need to re-request the current state of open orders and recent executions on the new session to synchronize.

Good design treats failover as a normal, rehearsed operation, not a last-minute improvisation. Regular testing in simulation and staging environments builds confidence that the state machine and session logic behave correctly under these transitions.

Monitoring, Alerts, and Runbooks

Session management is not purely technical; it is also operational. To prevent minor issues from becoming serious, you need:

- **Metrics**: sequence gap counts, resend volumes, heartbeat round-trip times, logon/logoff events, and error codes.
- **Alerts**: thresholds that trigger notifications or automated responses when metrics deviate from normal ranges.
- **Runbooks**: documented procedures for what to do when a session goes down, gaps cannot be filled, or failover is required.

For example, you might:

- Raise a "warning" when a small gap is detected but filled within a second.
- Raise a "critical" alert and halt affected strategies if more than a certain number of messages are missing or if resends fail repeatedly.
- Escalate to human operators for approval before performing a cold restart or large-scale failover.

These operational disciplines make session management predictable and auditable rather than ad hoc.

Connecting Back to Order Lifecycle and Protocol Choice

Session management, sequencing, and recovery are the invisible scaffolding underneath your order lifecycle and protocol usage:

- The canonical state machine for orders assumes that executions and confirmations arrive reliably and in a reconcilable order. Sequencing is what enforces that assumption.

- FIX and native APIs both expose session and sequence concepts, but with differing detail and tools. Your gateway must bridge these into a common internal model.
- Drop copy and back-office feeds rely on their own sessions; reconciling them with order-entry sessions depends on correct sequence handling across all channels.

When you design robust session handling and sequence control, you turn messy, failure-prone networks into something much closer to an idealized, ordered message stream. That, in turn, lets your order lifecycle model do its job: ensuring every share is traceable from intent to final fill or cancel, even in the face of restarts, network glitches, and partial outages.

4.4 Throttling, Flow Control, and Rate Limits

In the previous sections we assumed that if your sessions are healthy and your order lifecycle is well modeled, you can safely send whatever orders your strategy desires. Reality is less forgiving. Every exchange, broker, and internal system has limits on how many messages it will accept per second, how quickly it will process them, and how it behaves under overload.

If you ignore these limits, several bad outcomes become likely:

- You exceed an exchange's rate cap and get disconnected in the middle of trading.
- Your own gateway becomes overloaded, increasing latency or dropping messages.
- A single aggressive strategy starves others of bandwidth, distorting portfolio-level behavior.

This section develops the throttling and flow-control techniques that prevent such issues. The goal is twofold:

- **Respect external constraints** imposed by venues and brokers.
- **Protect internal infrastructure** while preserving low latency for the most important orders.

We proceed in layers: from understanding the types of limits you face, through basic rate-limiting algorithms, to trading-specific architectures that coordinate limits across strategies, symbols, and sessions.

The Landscape of Rate Limits

Before choosing algorithms, you must understand the different forms of rate and volume constraints in a real trading setup.

Venue-Imposed Limits

Most exchanges publish:

- **Messages-per-second caps**: maximum number of order, cancel, and modify messages per session or per member.
- **Order-per-second or volume caps**: constraints on how many new orders or how much traded volume you can generate in a period.
- **Burst limits**: tighter short-window caps (for example, per 100 milliseconds) to prevent micro-bursts that destabilize the market.

These may be enforced at the session, firm, or account level. Penalties range from soft throttling (the venue queues or slows your messages) to hard disconnections or trading suspensions.

Broker- and CCP-Level Limits

When you access venues through brokers or clearing firms, you often face additional *intermediate* limits:

- Broker gateway caps to protect their infrastructure.
- Clearing risk limits based on capital or credit exposures.
- Fairness policies that prevent any single client from consuming all of a shared resource.

These are sometimes stricter than the exchange's limits and can be less transparent. They may vary by time of day, product, or risk profile.

Internal Capacity Limits

Within your own environment, there are also finite resources:

- CPU and memory in the gateway, risk engines, and strategy servers.
- Network bandwidth on links to colocation facilities or brokers.
- Disk IO and logging throughput.

If your strategies generate more traffic than your systems can process with low latency, performance degrades non-linearly: queue lengths explode, garbage collection pauses become longer, and resends pile up during transient network issues.

You should therefore define *internal* limits that are stricter than external ones. Staying well inside the venue or broker caps gives you a safety buffer.

Separating "Hard" Limits from "Comfort" Thresholds

A practical design pattern is to distinguish:

- **Hard limits** Values that must not be exceeded, because doing so will trigger disconnection, regulatory issues, or loss of control.

- **Comfort thresholds** Softer targets that indicate "we are running hot" and should slow down or reprioritize traffic before any hard limit is approached.

For example:

- If a venue allows 10,000 messages per second, you might set a hard internal cap at 9,000 and a comfort threshold at 7,000.
- When the comfort threshold is crossed, low-priority strategies are throttled or paused, freeing capacity for higher-priority flows.

This separation is important because many anomalies-such as a runaway strategy or a flood of resends after a network hiccup-can push you from normal to overload very quickly. Comfort thresholds give you an early warning buffer.

Classical Rate-Limiting Algorithms

With the landscape and thresholds in mind, we now look at algorithms that control how many messages you send over time. These algorithms are not specific to finance, but we will interpret them in a trading context.

Fixed Window Counters

The simplest model is a fixed time window:

- Choose a window size (for example, one second).
- Count how many messages you send during that window.
- If the count exceeds a threshold, block or queue additional messages until the next window.

Advantages:

- Easy to understand and implement.

- Maps directly to limits expressed as "X messages per second."

Disadvantages:

- A burst at the end of one window and the start of the next can effectively produce a short-term rate almost double the limit.
- All messages within a window are treated equally; you cannot easily prioritize some over others.

Fixed windows work reasonably well for coarse-grained controls and reporting but are rarely sufficient as the only line of defense in fast markets.

Sliding Windows

A sliding window refines the fixed window idea:

- Instead of resetting the counter at fixed intervals, you maintain a log of timestamps for recent messages.
- For any new message, you count how many messages were sent in the last T milliseconds (for example, the last second).
- If that count exceeds the threshold, you delay or drop the new message.

Conceptually, the window "slides" with time, giving you a more accurate view of recent activity and avoiding the sharp resets of fixed windows.

In trading, sliding windows are useful for:

- Enforcing burst limits (e.g., no more than N messages in any 100 ms interval).
- Smoothing out aggressive order-modification behavior when markets move quickly.

The main tradeoff is computational cost-maintaining a dynamic log of timestamps can be heavier than a simple counter-but with careful implementation this is manageable.

Leaky Bucket

The leaky bucket algorithm imagines a bucket that:

- Receives water drops when messages are submitted.
- Leaks water at a constant rate (the allowed throughput).

If the bucket overflows, new messages must wait or be dropped. This model:

- Allows some burstiness, as the bucket can temporarily hold extra messages.
- Enforces a long-term average rate determined by the leak speed.

Applied to order flow:

- The leak rate corresponds to your target messages-per-second limit.
- The bucket size determines how much short-term bursting is allowed before you hit the cap.

Leaky bucket is intuitive and works well when you want to smooth out bursts while respecting an average rate.

Token Bucket

Token bucket is closely related but with a different emphasis. Instead of adding water, you add *tokens* at a fixed rate:

- Tokens accumulate in a bucket up to a maximum capacity
- Each message consumes one token (or more, if you weight messages differently).
- A message can only be sent if a token is available; otherwise, it must wait.

This has two desirable properties:

- **Burst handling**: If you have been idle, the bucket fills with tokens, allowing a future burst up to the bucket size.
- **Average rate control**: Over time, you cannot exceed the rate at which tokens are added.

For trading:

- Token bucket is a good mental model for "you can send at most X messages per second, but if you have been quiet, you can momentarily burst higher."
- You can have separate token buckets for different resources: per-venue, per-session, per-strategy.

Bringing Algorithms into a Trading Context

Classical algorithms are a starting point. To make them useful in trading, you must answer three practical questions:

- Which traffic should be counted against which limits?
- What should happen to messages that exceed a limit?
- How do we prioritize among competing flows?

Per-Venue, Per-Session, and Per-Strategy Limits

You will usually manage multiple layers of buckets and windows:

- **Per-venue limits** to match the exchange's and broker's caps.
- **Per-session limits** to avoid concentrating all activity on a single network link.
- **Per-strategy or per-portfolio limits** to prevent any single model from hogging capacity.

- **Per-symbol or per-instrument-group limits**, especially for illiquid names or products with special risk.

These can be conceptualized as a hierarchy. A message must pass every applicable check:

- The strategy bucket says, "you are under your strategy's rate limit."
- The venue bucket says, "you are under the exchange's rate limit."
- The global bucket says, "you are under our firm-wide comfort threshold."

Only then does the message go out. If any bucket is empty or any threshold is exceeded, the message is queued or suppressed according to policy.

What to Do with Excess Messages

When a limit is hit, you have three basic options:

- **Queue** Hold the message and send it later when capacity is available.
- **Drop** Discard the message and, ideally, notify the strategy.
- **Transform** Change the message into something else, such as:

- Coalescing multiple price updates into a single order replace.
- Replacing a flood of small orders with a single larger order.

Each choice has implications:

- **Queueing** preserves intent but increases latency, which can seriously degrade execution quality if delays are large or unpredictable.

- **Dropping** preserves latency for the messages that do go through but sacrifices some signals, which may break strategy assumptions if not expected.
- **Transforming** can be powerful but requires strategy awareness; not all strategies are compatible with coalescing or aggregation.

A common pattern is:

- Always honor critical actions (for example, cancels and risk-driven exits) if at all possible.
- Queue or drop less important actions (for example, micro-adjustments of passive quotes) when the system is under stress.

Prioritization and Fairness

When many strategies compete for limited capacity, you need a notion of *priority*. Some orders are more time-sensitive than others:

- Risk-reducing or stop-loss orders should be near the top of the priority list.
- Orders tied directly to strong, short-lived alpha signals should also rank highly.
- Housekeeping orders, rebalancing flows, and minor quote adjustments can be deprioritized.

Architecturally, this leads to:

- Priority queues at the gateway, where each message carries a priority label.
- Separate token buckets for high- and low-priority traffic, so that low-priority traffic cannot starve high-priority flows.

- Fair-share mechanisms (such as weighted fair queuing) that guarantee each strategy a minimum slice of capacity proportional to its importance or capital allocation.

Fairness matters not only from a governance perspective but also to prevent subtle biases in your portfolio. If one highly active strategy consistently crowds out others, portfolio-level risk and performance may drift away from the design.

Protecting the Gateway Under Stress

So far we have focused on external limits. Now we look inward: how throttling and flow control shield your gateway and order-handling infrastructure.

Back-Pressure and Queue Management

Your gateway sits between fast strategies and slower external venues. Under normal conditions, outbound queues are short, and messages flow freely. Under stress-say, an exchange slows down or starts to throttle you-those queues can grow.

Back-pressure is the discipline of:

- Measuring queue lengths, processing times, and error rates.
- Communicating “slow down” signals back up the stack to strategies.
- Enforcing hard caps on queue sizes to avoid unbounded memory use and latency.

Practically, this may involve:

- Rejecting or delaying new order submissions when outbound queues exceed a threshold.
- Providing explicit feedback to strategies (for example, a “gateway overloaded” status) so they can adapt behavior.

- Preferentially admitting high-priority or risk-reducing orders even when queues are long.

Without back-pressure, strategies will keep pushing messages into the gateway, which will either run out of resources or deliver hugely delayed orders-a silent killer of performance.

Handling Resends During Outages

Recall from the session management section that when connectivity blips, resends are often required. But resends are themselves messages that count toward rate limits and load the gateway.

A robust design:

- Allocates dedicated capacity for resends within the token buckets or rate limiters.
- Ensures that recovery traffic does not completely drown out new risk-reducing messages.
- Prioritizes resends of fills, cancels, and other high-impact state changes over lower-priority administrative messages.

The key is to treat recovery as a first-class workload with its own budgeting, rather than something that competes on equal footing with normal trading traffic.

Latency Preservation for Critical Paths

Under stress, average latency often increases. The goal of good flow control is to ensure that *critical* orders still see acceptable latency even if less important ones slow down.

Some techniques:

- **Separate processing lanes**: dedicate threads or processes to high-priority traffic, shielding them from load caused by low-priority orders.

- **Smaller, stricter queues** for critical orders, rejecting rather than queuing if overwhelmed, to avoid unpredictable delays.
- **Simpler risk and logging paths** for emergency risk-off actions, trading some richness of data for speed in extreme situations.

This mirrors approaches in other real-time systems (for example, emergency braking in vehicles), where critical functions are insulated from general traffic.

Testing and Tuning Throttles

Throttling and flow control are subtle. Overly aggressive throttles constrain alpha; overly permissive ones fail right when you need them most. Systematic testing and tuning are therefore essential.

Synthetic Traffic and Stress Tests

You should regularly subject your gateways to controlled overload scenarios:

- Generate synthetic order flows that exceed normal rates by a wide margin.
- Simulate exchange or broker slowdowns, including increased latency and sporadic throttling responses.
- Inject network faults that cause bursts of resends.

During these tests, measure:

- How close you come to external limits.
- How queue sizes, latencies, and drop/queue rates behave.
- Whether high-priority orders are still serviced promptly.

The aim is to verify that:

- Comfort thresholds trigger before hard limits.
- Strategies receive clear signals when throttling is in effect.
- The system degrades gracefully rather than catastrophically.

Production Monitoring and Feedback

Post-deployment, your monitoring should track:

- Message rates per venue, session, and strategy.
- Throttle activations: when and why limits were hit.
- Latency distributions, particularly tail latency (for example, 99th percentile).

Using these metrics, you can:

- Adjust bucket sizes and leak/token rates as market conditions change.
- Rebalance capacity between strategies based on their realized importance and performance.
- Detect pathological behaviors (such as strategies that constantly bump into throttles) and refine their design.

Throttling should be treated as a living part of your infrastructure, not a one-time configuration.

Putting It Together: An Architectural View

By this point, a picture emerges of how throttling, flow control, and rate limits fit into the broader chapter:

- The **order lifecycle and state machine** tell you exactly what each message *means* and how it affects risk.

- **Order entry protocols** (FIX and native) carry those messages with varying semantics and performance characteristics.
- **Session management and sequencing** ensure that messages are delivered reliably and in a reconcilable order.
- **Throttling and flow control** regulate the *volume and timing* of those messages, so the entire system operates within safe and efficient bounds.

Conceptually, you can view throttling as a set of gates through which all traffic must pass. These gates:

- Enforce external rules (venue and broker limits).
- Encode internal policy (priorities, fairness, risk preferences).
- Shield downstream components from overload.

Well-designed throttling and flow control transform a potentially chaotic stream of orders and cancels into something that respects constraints, preserves resources, and keeps latency low where it matters most. In the next section, when we discuss drop copy, real-time reconciliation, and alerts, you will see how monitoring the behavior of these gates in production becomes a powerful early warning system for hidden risk and looming capacity problems.

4.5 Drop Copy, Real-Time Reconciliation, and Alerts

Up to this point we have focused on the "forward" path: strategies generate orders, gateways translate them into protocol messages, sessions carry them to venues, and the order lifecycle tracks their states. If everything works perfectly, this is enough.

In real markets, however, components fail, sessions drift, and messages get lost or delayed. You cannot safely assume that your primary order-entry view always reflects reality. To close this gap, professional trading setups build *shadow books* and *alerting loops* driven by independent execution feeds, most notably *drop copy*.

In this section we design those secondary paths and show how they transform raw execution data into early warning systems for broken sessions and hidden risk.

What Is Drop Copy and Why Is It Needed?

A **drop copy** (sometimes called a mirror or post-trade feed) is an additional stream of order and execution messages provided by a broker or exchange:

- It typically carries confirmations of trades, cancels, and other significant state changes.
- It is logically separate from the primary order-entry session.
- It may lag slightly behind the primary path but is designed to be complete and reliable.

Think of it as a duplicate receipt printer in a store: even if the main till misprints a receipt or loses a log, the duplicate provides an independent record of sales.

In trading, drop copy is essential because:

- It gives you a second view of executions and order states.
- It can continue to function even if the primary order-entry session is impaired.
- It is often closer to the broker's or exchange's golden record used for clearing and risk.

By feeding drop copy into a *shadow order and position book*, and continuously comparing that with your internal strategy view, you can detect problems early:

- Orders that are live at the venue but invisible internally (stray risk).

- Fills that occurred but were never reflected in your strategies' positions.
- Cancel or replace requests that silently failed.

High-Level Architecture

Before going into details, it helps to visualize how the pieces connect: strategies, primary gateways, venues, drop copy feeds, shadow books, and an alerting engine.

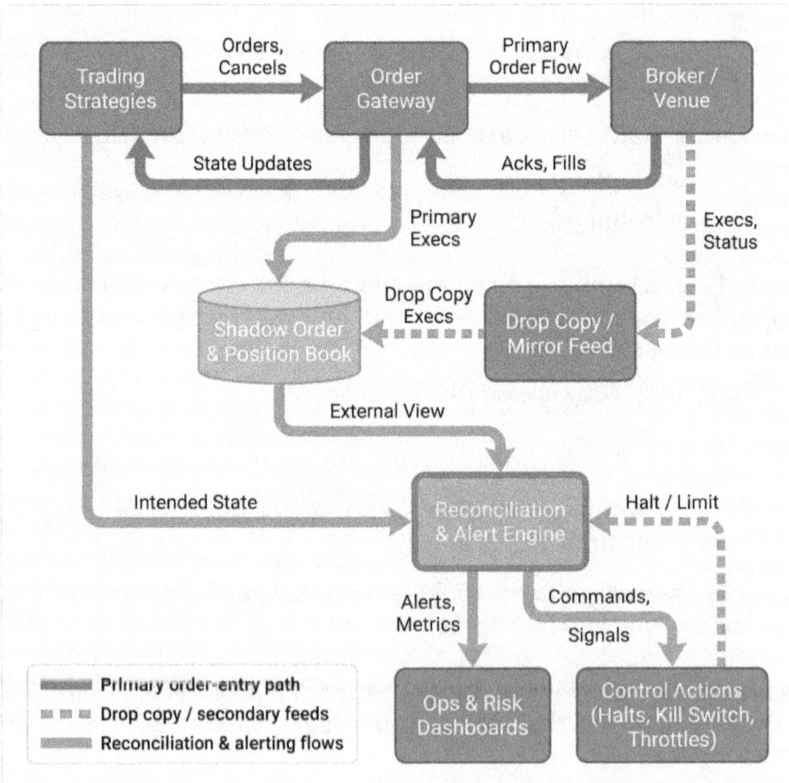

This architecture separates:

- The **forward path**: strategies $\rightarrow$ gateway $\rightarrow$ venue and back.
- The **shadow path**: venue $\rightarrow$ drop copy $\rightarrow$ shadow book.
- The **control loop**: reconciliation engine $\rightarrow$ alerts and automated responses.

We will now examine each part in more detail.

Building a Shadow Order and Position Book

The shadow book is a near-real-time reconstruction of your orders and positions using *only* external evidence: drop copy, broker reports, and, when needed, explicit queries to the venue.

Its job is to answer questions like:

- What does the venue believe our live orders and fills are right now?
- How does that compare to our internal strategy view?

Inputs and Correlation Keys

The shadow book typically ingests:

- Execution reports and order status messages from drop copy.
- Any late or corrected trades (busts, amendments).
- Occasionally, snapshots of open orders from venue queries.

To tie these events together and match them to internal orders, you rely on the correlation keys introduced earlier:

- **ClOrdID** (client order ID): your ID, which is often echoed on drop copy messages.

- **OrderID**: the broker or venue's order ID.
- **ExecID**: unique identifier for each execution event.
- **Internal Order ID**: your internal anchor, never sent on the wire but linked to ClOrdID and OrderID.

The shadow book maintains a mapping from each Internal Order ID (if known) or from a composite key (account, symbol, side, and OrderID) to its external lifecycle: cumulative fills, live/canceled status, average price, and so on.

State Model in the Shadow Book

The shadow book uses essentially the same canonical state machine as your main order book:

- New, Acknowledged, Partially Filled, Filled, Canceled, Rejected, Expired.

However, it has a stricter information diet:

- It does not directly see your intent to send an order; it only sees evidence that an order *exists* at the venue.
- It cannot know about purely internal cancels that never reached the market.

Thus, its lifecycle is derived entirely from:

- External acceptance messages (e.g., order accepted).
- Execution messages (new trades).
- Cancel/replace confirmations and rejects.
- Any venue-initiated events (mass cancels, expirations).

The invariants from the earlier lifecycle section apply here as well: cumulative fills never decrease, each ExecID is used once, and orders move monotonically toward terminal states.

Partial Visibility and Hybrid Sources

In many setups, drop copy does not provide a complete picture on its own:

- Some brokers only send fills, not explicit order acknowledgments or cancels.
- Certain exchanges may only support drop copy for specific products or sessions.

The shadow book must handle such partial visibility gracefully:

- For fills-only drop copy, the shadow book tracks only execution history and infers that any order with a fill must have been accepted and live for at least some time.
- For missing cancels, it may rely on:
  - End-of-day reports that list final open orders.
  - Active queries during incidents ("give me all open orders for this account right now").

In practice, well-run firms combine:

- Drop copy (streaming).
- Periodic snapshots or queries (point-in-time).
- Back-office confirms and clearing data (end-of-day).

to keep the shadow book as accurate as possible.

Reconciliation: Comparing Intended and External States

Once you have a shadow book, the next step is reconciliation: continuously comparing what your strategies *think* is true with what external feeds *say* is true.

Three Views of the World

For each order or position, you can identify three conceptually distinct views:

- **Strategy view**: What the strategy's internal book believes (based on its own state machine and primary gateway messages).
- **Gateway view**: What the gateway's canonical order state machine says (often closely aligned with the strategy view, but sometimes more conservative).
- **External view**: What the shadow book (from drop copy and snapshots) reconstructs.

Reconciliation logic compares these, using the gateway's canonical lifecycle as the reference. Typical checks include:

- Does the external view show any live orders that the gateway believes are terminal?
- Does the external view show fills that are not included in the strategy's P&L?
- Are there orders that the gateway considers live for which the external view has no record at all?

Reconciling Orders

For orders, reconciliation is often performed at multiple granularities:

- **Per-order** For each Internal Order ID:
  - Compare status: live vs. terminal, accepted vs. rejected.
  - Compare cumulative quantity: internal fills vs. shadow fills.
  - Compare key attributes: side, symbol, and (where possible) price and time-in-force.
- **Aggregate-by-dimension** For example:

- Total live buy quantity vs. total live sell quantity per symbol.
- Total notional exposure per account.

Per-order discrepancies reveal specific problem orders. Aggregate discrepancies catch cases where some orders are missing from both primary and shadow matching logic but show up in positions or back-office later.

Reconciling Positions

Because orders eventually roll up to positions, you should also reconcile:

- Net positions per instrument and account.
- Day's traded volume and average price.

Discrepancies can arise when:

- Small fills are missed or double-counted.
- Corporate actions or special events (e.g., stock splits) are mismodeled.
- Certain flows (manual trades, block trades, crosses) are processed outside your main gateway.

The reconciliation engine should be able to trace a position discrepancy back to:

- Specific unmatched ExecIDs or orders, or
- Explicit adjustments (such as manual bookings).

Classifying Discrepancies and Response Patterns

Not every mismatch means "stop everything." A practical system classifies discrepancies and maps them to appropriate responses.

Common Types of Discrepancy

Some examples:

- **Stale cancels**: Internal view: order canceled. External view: order still live. This implies hidden risk and usually warrants rapid action.
- **Missing fills**: Internal view: no fills. External view: one or more executions. Positions and P&L are understated.
- **Ghost orders**: External view: open orders with no corresponding Internal Order ID or ClOrdID. Often due to:
  - Manual trades entered by a human trader.
  - Legacy or test systems still active.
- **State drift**: Internal and external views agree on total filled quantity but disagree on final status (for example, internal says Partially Filled, external says Filled and Canceled).

Each type carries different risk implications.

Response Levels

A useful mental model is to define tiers of response:

- **Tier 1: Informational** Small, self-correcting discrepancies:
  - Slight timing differences (internal sees a cancel slightly before drop copy).
  - Temporary mismatch that resolves within a short timeout.

  Action: log and perhaps low-priority alerts for later review.
- **Tier 2: Warning** Discrepancies that persist past a timeout or exceed a small threshold:
  - One or two small missing fills.
  - A handful of ghost orders with small notional value.

Action: raise warnings on dashboards; possibly throttle affected strategies or venues; require manual acknowledgement.

- **Tier 3: Critical** Significant or growing mismatches:
  - Any live order externally that you believe is fully canceled.
  - Position differences larger than a configured notional limit.
  - Systemic issues (for example, all cancels appear stale across a venue).

  Action: automatic soft-halt of relevant strategies; trigger kill switches at the venue or broker; escalate to human operators immediately.

This tiered approach prevents the alert system from being either hysterical (halt trading on every minor blip) or complacent (ignore serious issues until too late).

Alert Hygiene: Making Alerts Actionable

An underrated challenge is *alert hygiene*. Poorly designed reconciliation alerts can overwhelm operators, produce noise, and eventually be ignored.

Reducing Noise

To reduce noise:

- Use **debouncing**: require a discrepancy to persist for a short period (e.g., several seconds or a number of reconciliation cycles) before raising an alert.
- Apply **thresholds**: ignore negligible mismatches below a dollar or share threshold that are operationally harmless.
- Aggregate related issues into a single alert, rather than emitting one per order. For example: "15 orders on Venue X show stale cancels; total exposure 120,000 shares."

Making Alerts Rich and Self-Contained

Good alerts contain enough context for an operator or on-call engineer to act quickly. For example:

- Affected strategies and symbols.
- Magnitude of the discrepancy (shares, notional, P&L impact).
- Relevant identifiers: ClOrdID, OrderID, ExecIDs.
- Links or references to supporting logs and dashboards.

Alerts should also suggest likely causes and next steps when possible:

- "Possible session outage between gateway and broker: cancels not acknowledged on primary, but drop copy shows fills continuing."
- "Manual orders detected outside gateway: 3 open orders on account XYZ not associated with any known strategy."

Closing the Loop

The reconciliation engine should not only raise alerts but also:

- Track whether they have been acknowledged and by whom.
- Monitor whether the underlying discrepancy has resolved.
- Escalate automatically (for example, from Tier 2 to Tier 3) if conditions worsen or remain unresolved.

This turns alerts into part of a controlled process rather than a stream of isolated messages.

Integrating with Session Management and Throttling

Drop-copy-driven reconciliation is most powerful when integrated with the session and throttling logic from earlier sections.

Detecting Broken Sessions Early

Because drop copy often runs on a different session or even a different physical link, it can reveal:

- That orders are still trading at the venue even though your primary session believes it is down.
- That drop copy itself has stalled while the primary path is active, indicating a problem in the oversight channel.

By comparing timings and content across sessions, the reconciliation engine can:

- Trigger targeted session recovery (e.g., restart or failover a specific drop copy session).
- Escalate to strategy halts if both primary and shadow channels are unreliable.

Feeding Back into Throttles and Safeguards

Reconciliation findings can also inform throttling and risk controls:

- If a venue repeatedly shows ghost orders or missing cancels, you may lower your internal rate limits or force more conservative usage of that venue.
- If position discrepancies spike during volatile periods, you may temporarily tighten volume caps or widen safety margins for certain products.

This creates a feedback loop:

- *Observation*: Reconciliation surfaces a pattern of issues.
- *Decision*: Risk and operations teams adjust throttles, limits, or routing preferences.
- *Effect*: Future trading on those paths becomes more controlled, reducing the chance of large unreconciled exposures.

Testing Reconciliation and Drop Copy Logic

Like any complex subsystem, the reconciliation and alerting pipeline must be tested under realistic conditions.

Replay and Simulation

Two practical tools are:

- **Log replay**: Feed historical primary and drop copy logs into a test instance of the reconciliation engine. Inject known anomalies (e.g., artificially drop some messages) and verify that appropriate alerts are raised.
- **Simulation**: Use simulation environments provided by brokers or venues that mimic real drop copy feeds. Introduce controlled discrepancies, such as:
  - Delayed cancel confirmations.
  - Randomly missing execution reports.
  - Extra “manual” orders created via test tools.

These tests help you validate both detection logic and alert volumes: you want to catch real problems without overwhelming operators.

End-to-End Drills

Beyond technical testing, conduct end-to-end drills:

- Trigger a scripted incident (for example, simulate a stuck cancel path).
- Observe:
  - How quickly reconciliation catches the issue.
  - What alerts are raised and who sees them.
  - How operators respond—do they follow runbooks, and is the process smooth?

These drills expose gaps in both tooling and human processes, which can then be addressed.

From Raw Feeds to Early-Warning Systems

Drop copy, by itself, is just another stream of messages. Its real value emerges when you:

- Build a reliable shadow book using canonical lifecycle logic and strong correlation keys.
- Continuously reconcile internal and external views at both order and position levels.
- Classify discrepancies and tie them to calibrated responses.
- Integrate alerts into your operational runbooks, session management, and throttling.

The result is an early-warning system for:

- Broken or degraded sessions.
- Hidden or stray risk not visible to strategies.
- Data and process quality problems that could compromise P&L and compliance.

In combination with the order lifecycle model, protocol abstractions, session control, and throttling techniques developed earlier in the chapter, drop-copy-driven reconciliation completes the loop from *intent* to *verification*. Every share is not only traceable from order to fill, but that trace is cross-checked against independent evidence in real time, turning your gateways from mere conduits into robust guardians of market risk.

Chapter 5

Risk Controls and Safeguards

Every profitable electronic strategy lives on a knife-edge between speed and disaster. This chapter shows how professional shops turn that edge into a safety rail: layering pre-trade checks, live exposure controls, self-trade defenses, and firmwide kill switches-independently verified through shadow paths-so that when something inevitably goes wrong, the damage is small, knowable, and quickly contained.

5.1 Pre-Trade Risk Controls and Fat-Finger Checks

In the previous chapter we described how strategies generate orders from signals and how those orders travel through your order-entry stack toward the exchange. In this section we insert a critical missing layer into that picture: the pre-trade risk controls that sit between the strategy and the market.

Pre-trade controls are the *first line of defense*. They filter dangerous or obviously erroneous intent before it ever leaves your infrastructure, long before regulators, brokers, or exchanges see the traffic. Properly designed, they reduce the probability of catastrophic loss, embarrassing technical incidents, and regulatory trouble—all while adding only microseconds to latency and minimal friction to normal fills.

This is not an optional add-on. In most jurisdictions, some form of pre-trade risk is legally required for any firm that accesses electronic markets, particularly if you connect via "sponsored access" or direct market access. But even if it were not required, any serious trading operation would still build it. Strategies, software, data, and humans all fail in sometimes surprising ways; the question is whether those failures can propagate unchecked into the market.

We will progressively build an intuition for what pre-trade risk controls are, how they work at a practical level, and how to calibrate them. We start with a high-level view of the order's journey, then examine the main categories of checks, then discuss implementation patterns and testing practices.

The Order's Journey: A Protective Membrane

Conceptually, you can think of the trading system as three broad layers:

1. **Strategy layer**: generates orders from signals, positions, and risk budgets.
2. **Gateway and risk layer**: validates and routes orders; this is where pre-trade checks live.
3. **External venues**: brokers, exchanges, and clearing infrastructure.

When a strategy decides to send an order, that intent should *never* flow directly to the exchange. Instead, the order passes through a protective membrane of checks: "Is this price reasonable? Is the size sane? Does it blow through our daily limit? Is it obviously a duplicate of something we just sent?" Only if it passes all relevant checks is it serialized into the exchange protocol and transmitted.

The key design challenge is balance. A risk layer that is too permissive can allow a single bug to create enormous exposure in milliseconds. A layer that is too restrictive or slow can cripple strategies: legitimate orders are throttled, rejected, or delayed, degrading execution quality and sometimes breaking the strategy's logic. The art is to design controls that are firm enough to block nonsense but thin enough to be nearly invisible during normal operation.

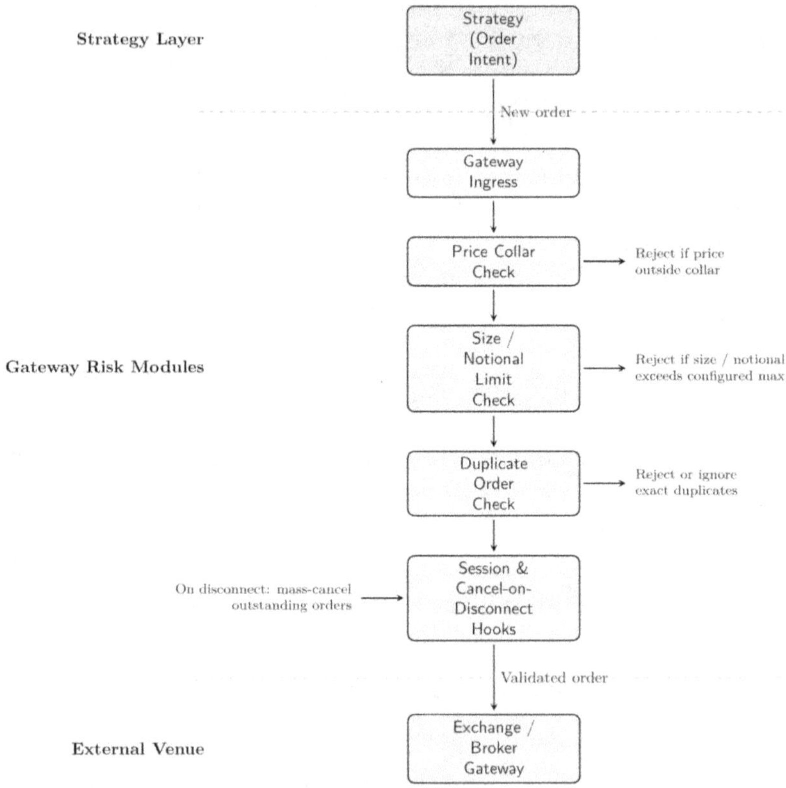

Canonical Pre-Trade Checks

While implementations differ from firm to firm, most pre-trade risk stacks share a common set of checks. Each addresses a specific class of failure:

- entering a wildly wrong price,
- entering an absurd size or notional,
- sending the same order many times,
- exceeding configured daily caps or other limits.

We will focus on four fundamental controls and how they manifest in real order flow: price collars, size and notional limits, duplicate order detection, and session-level safeguards such as cancel-on-disconnect.

Price Collars: Guardrails on Price Sanity

A price collar is a simple concept: for any order, you check whether its limit price is within a reasonable band around a reference price. If the price is too far away, you reject or adjust the order.

Intuitively, imagine a trader intending to buy 10,000 shares at $10.00 but mistypes $100.00. Without a price collar, the order could aggressively sweep the order book at prices far above fair value, causing instant and severe loss. With a collar, any price more than, say, a few percent away from the last traded price or mid-quote is blocked.

Choosing a reference price. A collar requires a reference:

- last trade price,
- best bid or offer,
- midpoint of the best bid and best offer,
- a slower-moving theoretical or fair value.

For highly liquid instruments, using the top-of-book midpoint is common. For less liquid assets, last trade may be more stable, while for derivatives you might use an implied fair value from the underlying.

Absolute vs relative bands. Collars may be specified as:

- a **relative band** (for example, no more than 5% away from reference price), or

- an **absolute band** (for example, no more than $0.50 away from reference).

For low-priced instruments, absolute bands prevent the relative band from being trivially small; for high-priced names, relative bands prevent the absolute band from being too wide. In practice, firms often mix both, for example: reject if outside the tighter of 5% or $1.00.

Behavior at the extremes. What happens if the reference data is stale or missing? If your market data feed lags or drops, your collar might mistakenly see valid prices as far from the stale reference and reject them. A robust design includes:

- "data freshness" checks: if the reference is older than a short threshold, switch to a more conservative mode or pause trading;
- safe fallbacks: for example, using the previous closing price if intraday data is missing, but with tighter size caps.

The key is that the collar should *fail safe*: if you cannot be confident in a price check, you should restrict or halt order entry rather than blindly trusting potentially corrupt references.

Maximum Order Size and Notional Limits

If price collars control *how far* you are willing to pay or receive, size and notional limits control *how much* you are willing to risk in a single shot.

Size limits. A size limit specifies the maximum number of units (shares, contracts, lots) allowed in one order for a given instrument or group of instruments. For example:

- no single equity order may exceed 50,000 shares;
- no single futures order may exceed 500 contracts in a given symbol;
- no single FX order may exceed 5 million units.

These limits address fat-finger cases where the quantity field is miskeyed (for example, 5,000,000 instead of 50,000) and also cap the damage that any one order can inflict.

Notional limits. Size alone can mislead when instrument prices differ by orders of magnitude. Buying 10,000 shares at $1.00 is very different from 10,000 shares at $1,000. A notional limit checks the product of price and size:

- total notional value of the order must not exceed some currency amount,
- often defined per symbol, per asset class, or per strategy.

By combining size and notional checks, you can catch both high-quantity and high-price fat fingers.

Calibrating thresholds. Thresholds must be chosen so that legitimate peak orders are not constantly hitting the ceiling, but still low enough to mitigate accidents. A common approach is:

- analyze historical orders and identify the 99th or 99.9th percentile order size and notional by symbol and strategy;
- set the limits somewhat above these percentiles (for example, 2–3 times the typical maximum) to leave breathing room for growth;
- review periodically as strategies evolve.

The aim is to block the truly outrageous while allowing rare but intentional large trades, possibly after additional human approval or with a slower path.

Per-Day and Per-Strategy Caps

Single-order limits are necessary but not sufficient. A strategy could send many moderately sized orders that together create an unacceptable exposure. To address that, most firms maintain running counters and caps:

- total daily notional traded per strategy and per firm;
- total daily volume (shares or contracts);
- sometimes total number of orders or messages.

When a new order arrives, the gateway checks whether adding the order's potential exposure would push any relevant counter beyond its configured maximum. If so, it rejects the order, or in some architectures, switches the strategy to a "read-only" mode where it may send cancels but not new orders.

These caps convert an abstract risk appetite ("strategy X should not trade more than 200 million notional per day") into hard, enforceable rules.

Duplicate Order Detection

Another common failure mode is "echoed" or repeated orders. This can occur when:

- a client system retries an order on network timeouts without realizing the first attempt succeeded;
- a bug resubmits the same order multiple times;
- a human operator double-clicks unintentionally.

From the market's perspective, multiple identical aggressive buy orders can create an unintended impact or inventory spike. From a regulatory perspective, accidental duplication can look like manipulative behavior.

Duplicate detection in the gateway usually works by maintaining a short-lived memory of recent orders keyed by some combination of:

- client or strategy identifier,
- instrument,
- side (buy or sell),
- price and quantity,
- sometimes a client order ID.

If a new order arrives that matches an existing record within a short time window, the gateway treats it as a duplicate. You then need a policy decision:

- *reject* suspected duplicates and report back to the client;
- or *silently drop* them and log an internal alert.

Rejecting is safer for transparency but can trigger cascades if the client keeps retrying on any non-fill response. Silently dropping can hide issues from the client. Most professional systems prefer explicit rejections and design their client logic not to retry blindly.

Session-Level and Cancel-on-Disconnect Safeguards

So far we have considered checks that look at individual orders. There is another layer that watches the *connection* itself.

Trading happens over persistent sessions (for example, a FIX session, or a native binary session). If that session disconnects unexpectedly while you have live orders in the market, you must decide what to do. Cancel-on-disconnect (CoD) is the policy that, upon detecting certain kinds of session failure, your system automatically sends cancels for all outstanding orders associated with that session or strategy.

You can consider this a pre-trade control in a broader sense: it prevents stale intent from surviving after you have lost control over it. In detail, you need to specify:

- which disconnect reasons trigger CoD (for example, only ungraceful drops, not deliberate restarts);
- the scope of cancels (per session, per strategy, per firm);
- how to ensure that the CoD logic is idempotent (re-running it does not cause errors) and auditable.

When combined with per-order checks, cancel-on-disconnect turns the gateway into a true risk membrane: orders cannot enter the market without passing checks, and they do not linger unmanaged if the connection breaks.

Fat-Finger Scenarios in Real Order Flow

To make these concepts concrete, consider a few typical fat-finger or failure scenarios and how the pre-trade layer responds.

Mis-Keyed Size. A trader intends to buy 20,000 shares but enters 2,000,000. The order enters the gateway:

1. Price collar: the price looks acceptable, so it passes.
2. Size limit: the configured maximum per order is 100,000 shares; the gateway rejects the order immediately.
3. The trader receives a rejection message that explicitly cites the size limit, prompting them to review and correct.

Without the size limit, the order could create a position impossible to manage within the strategy's risk budget.

Mis-Keyed Price. A strategy has a bug and sends a series of buy orders at a price ten times the current market level.

1. For each order, the gateway compares the limit price to the reference midquote.
2. Prices outside the collar are rejected.
3. The series of rejections can trigger an internal alert, causing operators to investigate the strategy.

The collar prevents the strategy from "lifting" the book at runaway prices.

Runaway Resubmission. A client retries any order that is not filled within one second, without checking whether the previous attempt is still working in the market. This creates a stream of identical orders.

1. The duplicate detection layer flags incoming orders as matching recent ones.
2. Policies either reject or drop the duplicates.
3. Counters tracking rejected-duplicate rates can alert risk staff to misbehaving clients or strategies.

This stops the runaway flow at the gateway, before it can flood the exchange.

Implementation Patterns: Where and How to Check

So far we have treated pre-trade risk as a black box. In practice, you must decide how to implement these checks relative to your order gateway. The main dimensions are:

- synchronous vs. asynchronous checks,
- shared vs. per-strategy limits,
- and degree of coupling to other systems.

Synchronous vs Asynchronous Checks

A **synchronous** check runs directly in the order path. The order is not forwarded to the exchange until the check passes. For example:

- verifying size and notional limits,
- checking price collars,
- confirming that daily caps are not exceeded.

This ensures strict control but adds to latency. In low-latency trading, the total budget for gateway processing may be on the order of microseconds, so each check must be carefully optimized.

An **asynchronous** check runs in parallel and does not block the order immediately. It is more like a monitor:

- analyzing patterns in orders, such as unusual activity spikes,
- computing richer exposure metrics that are too slow for inline checks.

Asynchronous logic can still enforce risk by, for example, switching a strategy to blocked mode if it detects a breach and then letting synchronous checks enforce that block on subsequent orders.

The general principle is: any rule that must be guaranteed for *every* single order (for example, "no order larger than X") should be synchronous. More complex or slower rules can run asynchronously and control subsequent flows.

Shared vs Per-Strategy Limits

Limits can be implemented at various scopes:

- per user or trader,
- per strategy instance,
- per desk or business unit,
- firmwide.

Technically, you can maintain a single shared set of counters and apply logic like "this strategy can send orders as long as the shared firmwide count is under the cap." This is simpler but can create unexpected interactions: one very active strategy might consume the entire firm's risk budget and starve others.

Alternatively, you can maintain per-strategy counters and caps and optionally roll them up to higher levels. For pre-trade checks, the key is that the gateway must be able to evaluate the relevant limits quickly. That means:

- the data structures holding counters must be in-memory and highly efficient;
- lock contention must be minimized in multi-threaded gateways;
- updates must be atomic enough to avoid race conditions that temporarily allow overage.

From a design perspective, per-strategy limits tend to produce clearer behavior and simpler incident analysis: you can see exactly how much each strategy was allowed and used.

Latency, Fill Quality, and the Cost of Protection

Every additional check you insert into the inline order path has a cost:

- in pure latency (time added before the order hits the exchange),
- in variability of latency (jitter),
- and sometimes in rejection rate or throttling under load.

At the same time, not having the check can be catastrophically expensive in terms of losses or regulatory penalties. Your task is to find the right tradeoff.

Measuring the overhead. You should empirically measure:

- the average and worst-case processing time per check,
- the cumulative cost of all checks,
- behavior under peak load (bursts of orders).

Often, careful engineering (using efficient data structures, avoiding remote calls, precomputing reference data) can bring the cost of robust checks down to an acceptable level.

Designing for graceful degradation. Under extreme conditions—for example, when market data becomes unstable or when you receive a surge of orders—naive implementations can "lock up," leading to timeouts and unbounded queuing. From the strategy's perspective, this looks like a sudden and unexplained degradation in fill quality.

To avoid this, you should:

- set clear internal timeouts: if a non-critical component becomes slow, fall back to a simpler but safe behavior rather than stalling;
- prioritize cancel and risk-reducing messages under congestion;
- monitor the health of the risk layer itself and treat abnormal delays as incidents.

Well-designed pre-trade risk should either operate normally or fail in a way that halts or sharply restricts new risk-taking. It should not grind slowly and silently, damaging alpha through unpredictable delays.

Testing and Tuning: Avoiding Two Failure Modes

Pre-trade risk is itself a potentially fragile system. Misconfiguration can create two opposite but equally dangerous failure modes:

1. **Over-permissive**: limits set so high or checks disabled so often that real fat-finger or runaway scenarios slip through.
2. **Over-restrictive or unstable**: limits too tight, or implementation so slow, that normal strategies are constantly throttled or rejected.

Robust testing and tuning must explicitly look for both.

Scenario-based testing. Before going live, you should construct a suite of test cases that simulate:

- extreme but plausible prices and sizes,
- duplicated and rapidly resubmitted orders,
- crossed and locked markets (where best bid exceeds best offer),
- stale or missing market data.

For each scenario, you define the expected gateway behavior: reject, accept with warning, or block further activity. Automated tests then verify that behavior across releases.

Shadow monitoring and post-trade analysis. In production, you can continue to validate and tune pre-trade risk by analyzing:

- distributions of rejected orders: which checks are firing and why;
- near-miss statistics: orders that passed but were close to limits;
- performance metrics: latencies introduced by the risk layer.

If you see a surge of rejections for legitimate orders, it may indicate that your thresholds are too tight or that strategy behavior has changed and your configuration needs updating. Conversely, if you *never* see certain checks fire, you may re-examine whether they are correctly wired.

Pre-trade risk controls and fat-finger checks turn an abstract risk policy into concrete, enforceable rules on every order. By putting price collars, size and notional limits, per-day caps, duplicate detection, and session safeguards directly in the gateway, you create a protective membrane between your strategies and the market.

Designing this membrane requires both technical care and risk judgment. Controls must be strong enough to block dangerous intent, yet light enough in latency and operational friction that strategies can trade effectively. In subsequent sections we will expand this picture from single-order checks to portfolio-level exposure management and firmwide limits, showing how pre-trade risk fits into a broader system of credit, position, and exposure control.

5.2 Credit, Position, and Exposure Limits

In the previous section we focused on *single-order* sanity checks: price collars, maximum order size, notional caps, and duplicate detection. Those controls are essential, but they answer only a narrow question: "Is this individual order obviously nonsensical or dangerous?"

Real trading risk is usually accumulated over many orders, fills, and partial fills across time. A strategy can stay within every per-order limit and still quietly build a large, concentrated position. At the firm level, several small strategies can each behave reasonably on their own yet, in combination, exceed what the firm wants to risk in a sector, a currency, or an entire exchange.

This is where **credit, position, and exposure limits** enter. They shift the focus from isolated messages to the *state* that those messages create: what you actually own or owe, how much directional or leveraged risk you carry, and how much of your balance sheet has been consumed.

The core idea is simple but powerful: you take an abstract statement like

> "Our US equity market-making desk should not lose more

> than X in a single day, and should not hold more than Y of unhedged exposure."

and you translate it into *concrete, real-time limits* that your systems can enforce automatically on each new order.

From Pre-Trade Checks to Portfolio-Level Control

Pre-trade fat-finger checks act as a gatekeeper for each message. Credit, position, and exposure limits operate at a higher level: they watch how all those messages add up.

A useful way to think about the relationship is:

- Pre-trade checks answer: "Is this order individually reasonable?"
- Exposure limits answer: "Can we afford to add this order to everything we already have?"

To enforce exposure limits, your systems must:

- maintain an up-to-date view of positions and outstanding orders,
- attach a *risk cost* to each new order, based on current prices and positions,
- compare the resulting exposure to configured limits, and
- take defined actions (warn, throttle, block, or de-risk) as limits are approached or breached.

We build these ideas step by step, beginning with definitions and then moving to implementation patterns.

Operational Definitions: Credit, Position, Exposure

These terms are often used loosely. Here we anchor them in concrete, operational meanings that can be implemented in systems.

Credit Limits

Credit in this context is your *capacity to trade*, usually expressed as a maximum amount of capital that a broker, clearing firm, or the firm's own risk committee is willing to put behind a given client, desk, or strategy.

Operationally, a credit limit is typically configured as:

- a maximum *gross notional* outstanding (sum of absolute market values of open positions and possibly working orders),
- sometimes a maximum *daily turnover* (total traded notional),
- sometimes a cap on margin consumed at the clearing house.

The gateway or risk engine monitors these quantities in real time. When a new order would cause the relevant quantity to exceed its cap, the order is blocked or the strategy is switched into a restricted mode.

You can think of credit as the outer envelope encompassing everything the client or strategy may do. It is a balance-sheet view: "How much are we willing to finance for this activity?"

Position Limits

A **position** is how much of each instrument you currently hold, long or short. Position limits control *inventory risk*: the exposure that comes purely from holding a given instrument, regardless of how you got there.

Position limits can be defined at multiple levels:

- per instrument (for example, no more than 200,000 shares long or 50,000 shares short in a single stock),
- per group (for example, total notional in all technology stocks),
- per side (for example, short-sales limits that differ from long limits),
- per strategy, desk, trader, and firm.

Because positions change only when fills occur (or when corporate actions like splits happen), your risk engine must continuously ingest fill reports and update per-instrument and aggregated positions as close to real time as possible.

Exposure Limits

Exposure is broader than raw position. It captures how sensitive your portfolio is to underlying risk factors.

Some examples:

- directional exposure (for example, total dollar amount that would be lost if a sector drops 1%),
- currency exposure (for example, how much you are effectively long or short each currency),
- volatility or gamma exposure in options portfolios,
- cross-asset exposures (for example, futures versus cash baskets).

Not all of these can be computed with the same speed and precision. For pre-trade enforcement, you often use simple but conservative approximations, such as:

- summing dollar values of long and short positions in related instruments,
- mapping instruments to buckets (for example, by sector or region) and limiting the total in each bucket,
- using exchange margin formulas as a proxy for risk.

More refined, model-based measures (such as full value-at-risk) can run slower and off the main path, informing limit calibration rather than being used directly in microsecond-level checks.

Real-Time Tracking: What Must the System Know?

To enforce limits in real time, your trading infrastructure must maintain, at a minimum, the following live state:

- **Current positions** by instrument, strategy, desk, and firm.
- **Working orders** (outstanding but not yet filled or canceled), including their sizes, sides, and prices.
- **Recent fills** and cancels, to keep positions and working-order views accurate.
- **Market prices** sufficient to value positions and approximate exposure.
- **Configuration of limits** at various levels and how they aggregate.

When a new order is proposed, the risk engine must be able to answer questions such as:

> "If this order were fully filled immediately, what would our position in this instrument become? What would that imply for our sector and firmwide limits? Would any of those exceed their caps?"

This "as if filled" reasoning is crucial. Waiting to see whether the order actually fills before checking limits would allow overshoots: you might send an order which, if fully filled, would break a limit, and then attempt to retroactively undo it.

In practice, the system treats each new order as if it were instantly and fully executed, adds this hypothetical change to the current state, and tests the result against limits. Only if the hypothetical post-trade state is still inside the envelope is the order allowed to leave.

Gross vs Net, and Simple Aggregation

Before you can configure limits, you must decide what exactly is being limited:

- **Gross exposure** is the sum of absolute positions or notionals. Long 1,000 and short 1,000 in two different stocks yields 2,000 gross.

- **Net exposure** is the algebraic sum of positions, allowing longs and shorts to offset. Long 1,000 and short 1,000 yields net zero.

Each has a role:

- Gross limits control total activity and gross leverage, regardless of direction or hedging.
- Net limits control directional risk, taking partial hedging into account.

For a simple market-making strategy, you might want:

- fairly tight *net* limits in each symbol, to avoid ending the day with an unwanted directional bet, and
- looser *gross* limits, since the strategy's job is to trade on both sides.

From the implementation side, aggregation works by assigning each instrument to one or more buckets (symbol, sector, asset class, currency) and then summing position or notional values within each bucket for each organizational level (strategy, desk, firm). These sums are maintained incrementally as fills occur, rather than re-computed from scratch each time.

Accounting for Hedges and Cross-Venue Fills

Modern strategies rarely trade a single instrument on a single venue. They may:

- hedge a cash equity position with index futures,
- trade the same symbol on several exchanges,
- use options or swaps to manage exposure.

To avoid either double-counting or ignoring important risks, your limit engine must handle cross-instrument and cross-venue aggregation.

Cross-Venue Consistency

If you trade the same stock on multiple venues, you still hold a single economic position in that stock. The risk engine should:

- maintain one consolidated position per instrument per strategy (and then roll up to desk and firm),
- ingest fills from all venues and brokers into the same position record,
- ensure that independent sessions (for example, separate gateways per venue) share a common view of limits.

This often motivates centralizing exposure logic in a shared service, or carefully replicating state across gateways with strong consistency guarantees.

Hedges and Offsetting Instruments

When hedging is involved, you face a design choice:

- *Simple view*: treat each instrument separately for limit purposes, perhaps with some coarse aggregation by asset class. This is conservative but may overstate risk and prevent efficient hedging.
- *Sophisticated view*: map each instrument to one or more risk factors (for example, sector index, currency, duration) and define limits on those factors, allowing partial offsets.

For example, if a strategy is long a basket of tech stocks and short an appropriate number of futures on a tech index, a sophisticated system may consider the net sector exposure relatively small, even though gross notionals are large. Limits can then be set differently on:

- sector-level gross exposure,
- net sector exposure after hedges,

- individual-name concentrations.

This richer treatment requires more inputs (for example, betas, correlations) and more computation. In many firms, a layered approach is used:

- inline pre-trade checks use simple, conservative aggregation (by name and sector),
- slower risk systems compute factor-based exposures and suggest calibrations and overrides,
- risk committees set and revise limits based on these analyses.

Soft and Hard Limits: What Happens at the Boundary?

Limits are not just numbers; they drive system behavior. When exposure approaches or breaches a threshold, your system must know what to do. It is useful to distinguish between:

- **Soft limits** levels where the system raises alerts or begins to gently slow activity, but does not outright block trading.
- **Hard limits** levels that must not be crossed; orders that would cross them are rejected or blocked.

For each limit, you might define, for example:

- a soft threshold at 80% of the maximum,
- a "warning" threshold at 90%,
- a hard ceiling at 100%.

System Behaviors Near Limits

As these levels are reached, behaviors can include:

- **Alerting**: sending notifications to traders, risk managers, and automated monitors when soft thresholds are crossed.
- **Auto-throttling**: slowing the rate of new orders or limiting certain types of trades (for example, disallowing inventory-building orders while still allowing risk-reducing closes).
- **Hard blocks**: rejecting new risk-increasing orders once the limit is at or above 100%.
- **Forced de-risking**: automatically guiding or forcing the strategy to reduce exposure, for example, by tightening quoting ranges or sending offsetting orders.

These behaviors should be carefully documented and tested. Traders need to understand how their strategies will be constrained as limits are approached; otherwise, a limit breach can look like a "mysterious system bug" from their point of view.

Limit Hierarchies: Strategy, Desk, Firm

Just as positions aggregate across instruments, limits aggregate across organizational levels.

A typical hierarchy might be:

- **Strategy-level limits**: tailored to each model's design, turnover, and typical risk.
- **Desk-level limits**: aggregating several related strategies under a common manager.
- **Firmwide limits**: set by senior risk management, often in consultation with the board and risk committee.

When a new order arrives, the risk engine evaluates it against all relevant levels:

- Would the strategy's own limits be exceeded?

- Would the desk's aggregate limits be exceeded?
- Would the firm's overall credit or exposure caps be breached?

If any of those answers is "yes," the order should be blocked. If different levels are in different states (for example, the strategy is healthy but the firm has hit its limit in a particular currency), the system still must refuse additional risk, even if the local strategy has room.

To keep this understandable, naming and reporting are crucial. Traders and risk managers should see clear dashboards explaining current consumption against limits at each level, so they can interpret rejections and tune their activity.

Handling Imperfect Inputs: Stale Data and Race Conditions

Exposure calculations rely on several data streams that can fail or lag: market data, fills and cancels, configuration updates. If these inputs are not handled carefully, your limit enforcement can become either too lax or too strict.

Stale or Missing Market Data

If price feeds are stale, computed notionals and exposures may be wrong. That can lead to:

- underestimation of exposure (dangerous),
- or overestimation that unnecessarily blocks trading (disruptive).

A robust design typically includes:

- freshness checks on all reference prices used in exposure calculation,
- a "degraded mode" where, if data becomes unreliable, the system either tightens limits or halts new risk-taking orders until prices are trustworthy again,
- logging and alerting whenever degradation occurs.

Race Conditions Between Trading and Risk Engines

If trading gateways and the central risk engine operate in parallel, you must address timing issues. A simple example:

- Gateway A sends an order that, when filled, pushes a strategy close to its limit.
- Before fills are fully processed and the central exposure state is updated, Gateway B for the same strategy sends another order, still thinking there is plenty of room.

To prevent this, firms use patterns such as:

- centralized limit checks via a shared real-time risk service that all gateways query synchronously before sending orders,
- or careful partitioning (for example, each strategy trades through a single gateway that maintains its own authoritative state, avoiding cross-gateway races).

Whatever pattern you choose, the guiding principle is that any two orders whose combined effect would break a limit should not both pass through unchecked simply because they happened to be evaluated against an outdated snapshot.

Designing Limits That Scale With the Business

As your strategy catalog grows, naïve limit setups can become unmanageable: too many overlapping thresholds, unclear interactions, and frequent false alarms.

To keep the system scalable and understandable:

- **Use simple, well-documented building blocks**: per-name, per-sector, and per-currency buckets; gross and net caps; clear soft and hard levels.
- **Align limits with how the business is actually managed**: if desks are organized by asset class, reflect that in the limit hierarchy.

- **Review limits regularly**: exposures that were aggressive when a strategy was small may be trivial once it scales, and vice versa.
- **Keep configuration coherent**: avoid random per-instrument exceptions that no one understands six months later.

Think of the limit framework as infrastructure, not a one-off patch. Good design up front will save you from confusing risk incidents later.

Bringing It Together: From Appetite to Guardrails

Ultimately, credit, position, and exposure limits are tools to translate human judgment into automated constraints. Risk committees and senior management express an *appetite* for how much, where, and in what form the firm is willing to take risk. Your job as system designer is to turn that appetite into:

- clear numerical limits,
- real-time state tracking,
- deterministic system behaviors when thresholds are approached or hit.

Combined with the pre-trade checks described earlier, these limits form a layered defense:

- individual orders are screened for basic sanity,
- the evolving portfolio is kept inside defined risk envelopes,
- breaches trigger predictable and auditable responses rather than ad hoc panic.

In the next section, we will zoom back down to the micro level and consider another subtle but important safeguard: how to prevent your own flow from accidentally trading against itself or echoing in the market, and how those controls interact with the exposure framework we have just built.

5.3 Self-Trade Prevention and Duplicate Order Controls

In the previous sections we built two layers of protection: first, per-order pre-trade checks (price collars, size and notional limits, cancel-on-disconnect), and second, portfolio-level credit, position, and exposure limits. Together they ensure that orders are individually sane and that the resulting positions remain within the firm's risk appetite.

There is a more subtle failure mode that these layers do not address on their own: your flow trading *against itself* or unintentionally echoing the same order many times. Even if all prices and sizes look reasonable and total exposure is within limits, you can still:

- incur unnecessary transaction costs because two of your own orders match,
- distort your apparent trading volume and footprint,
- and attract regulatory scrutiny for patterns that resemble manipulation or wash trading.

This section explains how firms prevent these problems with **self-trade prevention** (STP) and **duplicate order controls**. We will clarify the difference between the two, show how identifiers (firm, trader, strategy) are used to detect problematic interactions, and discuss practical policies and design choices that work under realistic market loads.

Why Trading With Yourself Is a Problem

At first glance, a self-trade can look harmless. If one of your systems posts a buy order and another posts a sell order in the same instrument at the same price, and they trade against each other, you end the event with:

- essentially the same net position you had before,
- but two sets of fees and spreads paid to the market.

Economically, this is almost pure leakage: you have paid the exchange, the clearinghouse, and possibly the broker, for no change in risk. The more competitive your strategy is, the less room you have for such waste.

Regulators care for a different reason. A pattern of trades where a party is effectively both the buyer and the seller is dangerously close to *wash trading*, which can artificially inflate reported volume or give a misleading impression of market interest. Most rulebooks explicitly prohibit wash trades except in narrowly defined circumstances. Modern regulations therefore often require that electronic access providers implement controls to prevent "self-match" scenarios where the firm is its own counterparty.

Finally, exchanges themselves may want to reduce self-trading because it consumes matching engine capacity, can complicate their surveillance, and may upset other participants who see odd patterns in the tape.

These motives together have driven the industry toward explicit self-trade prevention mechanisms at exchanges, brokers, and in-house gateways.

Self-Trade Prevention vs Duplicate Order Controls

Although they are related, STP and duplicate order controls address different failure patterns.

Self-trade prevention. STP aims to stop *opposite-side* orders from the same economic entity from matching against each other in the order book. For example:

- one strategy posts a buy limit at $10.00,
- another strategy (or the same one via another path) posts a sell limit at $10.00,
- without STP, if these are the best prices, they can cross and produce a trade where you are on both sides.

STP looks at the identities associated with each order (firm, trader, account, sometimes strategy) and intervenes when a potential match would be "internal."

Duplicate order controls. Duplicate controls address repeated *same-side* orders: for example, multiple identical or nearly identical buy orders sent in rapid succession. These can arise from:

- retry logic that blindly resends orders after a timeout,
- GUI double-clicks,
- software bugs that resubmit resting orders instead of modifying them.

Duplicate orders can lead to unintended position growth, unnecessary cancellations, and avoidable rejections from venues that enforce their own protections.

In short:

- STP is about *opposite sides crossing* within your own book.
- Duplicate controls are about *repeated, redundant intent* on the same side.

Both matter for your P&L, your operational stability, and your regulatory profile, and both need to fit cleanly into the pre-trade and exposure frameworks already established.

Identifying the Economic Entity: Firm, Trader, Strategy

To reason about self-trades, the system must decide what "*self*" means. This definition is encoded using identifiers on each order:

- **Firm or clearing account ID**: distinguishes your activity from that of other legal entities.
- **Trader or user ID**: identifies the individual or desk origin, useful for surveillance and policy.

- **Strategy or algorithm ID**: tags which model or component generated the order.
- **Session or gateway ID**: identifies the technical path taken (for example, which FIX connection).

Different levels of STP can then be defined:

- *Firm-level STP*: any orders from the same firm are considered "self" for prevention purposes, regardless of trader or strategy. This is the most conservative and most common from a regulatory perspective.
- *Desk-level or trader-level STP*: self-trade prevention applies within a desk or trader but allows crossing between different desks. This is sometimes used when separate desks are treated as economically distinct.
- *Strategy-level STP*: prevents a strategy from trading against itself, but not against other strategies at the firm.

In practice, most exchanges offer STP configuration keyed to a specific identifier (for example, a firm or account code), while firms may implement their own layers keyed to internal strategy or desk IDs. The key observation is that *you* decide, by tagging orders consistently, what the self-trade domain is.

Exchange-Side STP: Policies and Their Implications

Many modern exchanges offer built-in self-trade prevention mechanisms. When enabled, the matching engine detects when an incoming order would trade against a resting order with the same STP key and applies a chosen policy:

- **Cancel-newest**: The incoming order is canceled; the existing resting order remains in the book.
- **Cancel-oldest**: The resting order is canceled; the incoming order remains (and may then trade with other participants).

- **Reject-both**: Both orders (or the matching portions) are canceled, and no trade occurs.

Each policy has different consequences for queue position, inventory management, and the signals you send to the market.

Cancel-Newest

Cancel-newest preserves queue position. If you posted a passive buy order first and later a conflicting sell order arrives, the original passive order keeps its place; the later order is simply canceled or rejected.

This is generally favorable for market-making strategies that rely on queue priority: you do not want a defensive STP mechanism to sacrifice your earlier, potentially valuable resting interest.

However, cancel-newest has implications:

- If the incoming order was *intended* to flatten risk (for example, an urgent order to exit a position), canceling it may delay risk reduction.
- From a control perspective, orders with certain intent (like forced de-risking) may deserve different STP treatment than normal quoting flow.

Some firms therefore differentiate between order types or flags in their own logic, routing de-risking orders through paths where they are unlikely to collide with resting interest, or using cancel-oldest only for specific flows.

Cancel-Oldest

Cancel-oldest sacrifices queue position to honor the most recent intent. The idea is that the trader or strategy's latest action reflects its true desire; previous orders are treated as stale.

This behavior is convenient when your strategies frequently adjust their views and you do not want old quotes hanging around. However:

- throwing away queue position can increase slippage, because your new order starts from the back of the line,

- in highly competitive markets, repeatedly canceling and reposting may mean you rarely get filled at all.

Cancel-oldest can make sense when orders are more like discrete trades than continuous quotes, or when your primary concern is ensuring that inventory is aggressively managed rather than preserving priority.

Reject-Both

Reject-both is the strictest policy. If an incoming order would trade against a same-firm resting order, both sides (or their overlapping parts) are canceled, and no trade occurs.

This approach is the cleanest from a regulatory point of view: it eliminates internal matches rather than letting one side persist. It can simplify post-trade reporting and surveillance, since there is no trade to classify.

The cost is that you lose both the earlier and the later interest. In practice:

- this can be quite disruptive for high-frequency quoting strategies,
- risk managers may embrace it for particularly sensitive products or accounts where self-trading must be avoided at all costs.

Choosing a policy is about balancing regulatory comfort, economic efficiency, and implementation simplicity. Many firms select cancel-newest at the exchange, then add their own, richer logic on top.

Broker and In-House STP: Beyond the Exchange

Relying solely on exchange STP has two limitations:

- It only applies *within* that exchange; self-trades across venues are not prevented.
- It activates only when the match is about to occur; by then, you have already sent the problematic orders into the market.

Brokers and trading firms therefore often implement additional STP layers in their own gateways. These can:

- detect potential self-crosses before orders reach the street,
- coordinate behavior across venues,
- apply richer policies based on strategy, desk, and risk state.

An in-house STP engine typically maintains a view of:

- open buy and sell orders for each instrument,
- their prices, sizes, and owners (strategy, desk, firm),
- where they are resting (exchange A, exchange B, dark pool, and so on).

When a new order is proposed, the engine checks whether it would immediately cross any existing orders from the same self-trade domain, either on the same venue or across venues. Depending on firm policy, it may:

- modify or cancel the older interest to clear the way for the new order,
- reject or adjust the new order,
- route the order differently (for example, to a venue without conflicting interest).

Because this logic runs pre-trade, it can also take exposure limits into account: for instance, a new sell order that would internalize against your own bid might be blocked if it would just churn inventory without reducing net exposure.

Duplicate Order Controls: Keeping the Book Clean

While STP looks at the interaction between opposite sides, duplicate order controls focus on repeated orders on the *same* side and price.

Typical triggering patterns include:

- multiple identical new orders submitted within milliseconds,
- an order canceled and then immediately re-submitted with no change in parameters,
- a burst of new orders that differ only trivially in size.

These can result from:

- retry logic that does not inspect exchange acknowledgments carefully,
- misconfigured timeouts that encourage clients to resend orders prematurely,
- simple user interface errors.

The gateway can combat this by maintaining a short-term memory of recent orders per client or strategy and applying simple rules, such as:

- if an identical order arrives within a configured time window, reject it as a duplicate,
- if a near-identical order pattern suggests a bug (for example, dozens of near-identical orders in a second), temporarily block the client or require manual intervention.

Interplay With Quote-Heavy Strategies

For market makers and high-frequency strategies, duplicate control must be designed carefully. These strategies may:

- update quotes many times a second,

- send large bursts of orders when volatility rises,
- cancel and replace resting quotes with small price or size changes.

Naive duplicate detection can misinterpret these bursts as erroneous, causing widespread false positives and rejections. To avoid this:

- the definition of "duplicate" must be precise, often requiring an exact match on all order parameters and very short time windows,
- quote updates should use modify/replace semantics where possible, rather than cancel-and-new, making intent clearer,
- quote engines and gateways should be co-designed so that legitimate bursts are expected and tolerated, while truly accidental echoes still stand out.

The goal is to catch errors like misconfigured retries without penalizing normal high-frequency quoting.

Configuration Alignment: Avoiding Rejection Storms

Because STP and duplicate controls can exist at multiple layers-exchange, broker, in-house gateway-consistent configuration is essential. Misalignment can produce surprising behaviors.

Consider a scenario:

- Your in-house gateway implements its own STP and lets two opposite orders pass, trusting that they will not cross because of your logic.
- The exchange also has STP enabled with a different policy, canceling the newer order.
- Your client logic interprets any cancel or reject as a reason to resend.

This can lead to a "rejection storm," with the client repeatedly resending orders that the exchange promptly cancels for STP reasons. The market sees a barrage of ephemeral interest; you see strange cancellation metrics and possibly regulatory attention.

To avoid such feedback loops:

- explicitly document what each layer is responsible for (for example, broker handles cross-venue STP; exchanges handle local STP; in-house gateway coordinates behavior),
- align policies as much as practical (for example, choose cancel-newest consistently),
- ensure client and strategy code treats specific STP and duplicate rejection codes as *terminal*, not as triggers for blind retries.

Testing with exchange simulators and broker test environments is essential. You want to see, under stress, how the entire chain behaves when self-trade scenarios are forced.

Where Should STP Live? Architectural Choices

You must decide where to place the primary STP logic:

- **Exchange-only**: rely on venue-provided STP, keep your own code simpler.
- **Broker or sponsor**: if you access markets via a broker, they may implement STP on your behalf as part of regulatory obligations.
- **In-house gateway**: you own and operate STP logic as part of your risk controls.

There is no single right answer, but some general patterns emerge:

- High-frequency proprietary firms often implement STP in-house for fine-grained control and use exchange STP as a backstop.

- Buy-side firms connecting through brokers may rely more heavily on broker STP, but still add light in-house logic to catch obvious issues at the source.

When deciding, consider:

- **Latency**: in-house STP adds some processing time but can save trips to the exchange when orders are going to be blocked anyway.
- **Coverage**: only your own STP can coordinate across venues and strategy IDs the way you want.
- **Complexity**: each layer adds configuration and potential failure modes.

A layered but well-understood approach is often best: simple, low-latency checks in the gateway, coordinated with broker and venue capabilities.

Testing STP and Duplicate Controls Safely

Testing STP and duplicate logic is surprisingly tricky, because:

- you do not want to pollute production with artificial trades or order IDs,
- some behaviors only appear under real market load.

Practical testing techniques include:

- **Simulated environments**: run strategies against market simulators that mimic exchange matching and STP responses. Force scenarios where your own orders would cross or where retries run wild.
- **Replay testing**: feed historical order and market data into a test environment and observe how the STP logic would have behaved.

- **Shadow sessions**: in some setups, you can establish special test sessions to venues that do not interact with the live book, useful for protocol-level validation.

In all cases, expect to refine:

- which identifiers define the self-trade domain,
- how long potential duplicates remain in memory,
- how clients respond to different rejection codes.

As with pre-trade and exposure limits, monitoring in production is also crucial. Regularly review metrics like:

- number and share of STP-triggered cancels or rejects,
- patterns of duplicate order rejections,
- distribution across strategies and venues.

A surge in STP events or duplicates from a given strategy is often an early warning of misconfiguration or drift.

How STP Fits Into the Broader Risk Framework

Self-trade prevention and duplicate controls are part of the same philosophy that guided earlier sections:

- **Order-level sanity**: pre-trade checks prevent extreme values and obvious mistakes.
- **Portfolio-level discipline**: exposure limits keep the overall state within bounds.
- **Flow hygiene**: STP and duplicate controls keep your contribution to the market healthy and efficient.

Together, they protect P&L by avoiding unnecessary transaction costs and inventory churn, and they protect regulatory standing by reducing wash-trade patterns and noisy, error-prone order flow.

In the next section, we will consider the *last resort* layer of defense: firm-level kill switches and emergency procedures that come into play when, despite all of these safeguards, something goes seriously wrong and you need to stop the bleeding fast.

5.4 Firm-Level Kill Switches and Emergency Procedures

Up to this point we have focused on controls that operate during normal conditions: pre-trade checks that filter individual orders, exposure limits that keep portfolios within the firm's appetite, and self-trade and duplicate protections that keep your flow clean. All of these assume that the system is basically healthy and the market is functioning within expected bounds.

Real markets do not always behave that way. Models can blow up, data feeds can go bad, connectivity can partially fail, and external shocks can push prices and liquidity far outside the regime you calibrated for. In those moments, nuanced, finely tuned controls are not enough. You need blunt instruments that can *stop the bleeding fast.*

This is the role of **kill switches** and **emergency procedures**. They are the panic buttons, workflows, and playbooks that allow you to:

- halt or sharply reduce trading at different scopes (strategy, desk, firm, broker, or venue),
- cleanly cancel live orders and freeze new risk-taking,
- and then restart in a controlled way once you have assessed and repaired the problem.

In this section, we define what a kill switch really is, distinguish strategy-level stops from firmwide and external mechanisms, walk through typical incident scenarios, and discuss both the technical design and the human procedures that make these controls effective.

What Is a Kill Switch? Scope and Semantics

The term *kill switch* is often used loosely to mean "some big red button that stops trading." For system design, that is too vague. We need to specify:

- **Scope**: what exactly is being stopped? A single algorithm, a desk, the entire firm, or all activity through a particular broker or venue?
- **Actions**: what does "stop" mean? Block new orders, cancel working orders, disconnect sessions, or some combination?
- **Triggers**: who or what is allowed to activate it? Human operators, automated alerts, exchange or broker commands?
- **Duration and reversibility**: is it a toggle (on/off), a one-shot action, or a state that must be explicitly lifted?

At a high level, you can think in terms of escalating layers of control:

- **Strategy-level stop** disables a specific model or trading instance while leaving others unaffected.
- **Desk-level stop** applies to a group of related strategies supervised by one team or manager.
- **Firm-level kill switch** halts all proprietary trading across the firm's infrastructure.
- **Broker- or venue-level mass cancel / block** stops or cancels activity at a particular external access point, such as a sponsoring broker or a specific exchange.

Well-designed emergency controls make it easy to act at the smallest scope that resolves the problem, but they also provide a clear and tested path to more drastic actions when necessary.

Strategy vs Firmwide Actions: Granularity Matters

Before detailing the mechanics, it is helpful to see why granularity matters.

Suppose one strategy begins to behave erratically due to a bug or a data issue. If your only emergency control is a firmwide kill switch that stops *all* trading, you will be reluctant to use it. You might delay, hoping to fix the strategy in place, and valuable time is lost. Conversely, if you have only strategy-level controls and no firmwide mechanism, a broader infrastructure failure (for example, shared market data corruption) may leak through all strategies at once.

Therefore, most mature firms design a *hierarchy* of emergency actions, with clear semantics at each level:

- **Strategy-level stop**: prevents a particular strategy from sending new orders and often cancels its working orders, but leaves the rest of the firm unaffected.
- **Desk-level stop**: aggregates multiple related strategies; activated when an issue appears systemic within that business line.
- **Firm-level kill**: activated for broad incidents such as major data corruption, multiple strategies misbehaving, or large external market shocks.
- **Broker/venue mass cancel or block**: used when you suspect an issue specific to a particular external connection, or when a regulator or exchange requests immediate action.

These layers are not competing mechanisms but coordinated tools. The incident response process should guide operators in escalating from narrower to broader scopes as the situation demands.

Typical Emergency Scenarios

To ground the discussion, consider three categories of incidents where kill switches become relevant.

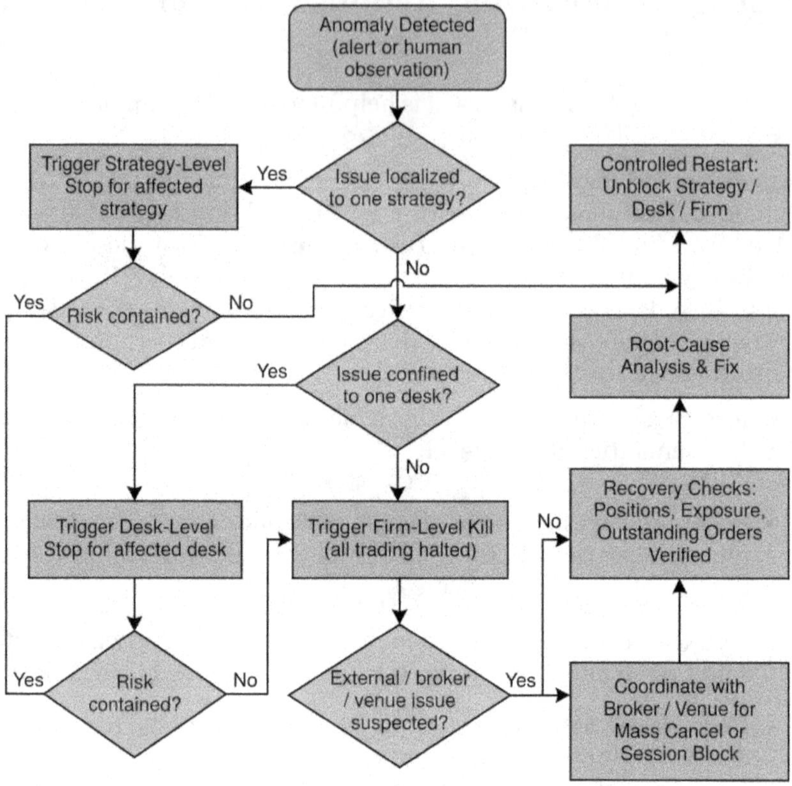

Runaway Strategy or Quoting Behavior

A common scenario is a strategy suddenly behaving in a way that was never seen in backtests or prior live behavior. Examples include:

- sending orders at an unusually high rate (message storm),
- placing orders at extreme prices that still pass basic pre-trade checks,
- rapidly accumulating inventory in a single name or sector.

Often, this is triggered by a bug, a change in input data, or unexpected market conditions. Early warning may come from:

- internal alerts (for example, "order rate above normal range," "limit breaches approaching," "STP/duplicate rejections spiking"),
- human observation on trading desks or risk dashboards,
- calls from a broker or exchange noticing odd behavior.

In such a case, the first line of emergency action is typically a **strategy-level stop**: block new orders from the misbehaving strategy and, depending on policy, either leave existing working orders alone or cancel them to freeze the situation.

Data-Feed Corruption or Infrastructure Failure

Another class of incident involves shared infrastructure going wrong:

- corrupted or delayed market data feeding multiple strategies,
- time synchronization failures leading to mis-ordered messages,
- widespread connectivity problems affecting several venues at once.

Here, the problem is systemic rather than confined to a single model. Multiple strategies may begin mispricing or misbehaving simultaneously because they are "seeing" a distorted view of the market.

In such cases, it can be pointless to stop one strategy at a time. Instead, the response may escalate quickly to:

- a **desk-level** stop for the affected asset class or region,
- or even a **firm-level** kill switch if the corrupted feed is used broadly.

External Market Shocks and Regulatory Requests

Finally, there are external events beyond your immediate control:

- abrupt regulatory announcements,
- exchange outages or trading halts in key names or indices,
- geopolitical shocks, flash crashes, or other extreme volatility spikes.

Exchanges or brokers may instruct participants to halt certain activities or close out positions in an orderly way. In addition, your internal risk committee may decide that continuing to trade in a particular product or region is unacceptable until more is understood.

In such cases, you may need to:

- coordinate with **broker- and venue-level** mass-cancel or block mechanisms,
- invoke firmwide or product-specific kill switches within your own infrastructure.

An effective emergency framework anticipates these possibilities and describes in advance who decides what, and how the technical mechanisms implement those decisions.

Technical Design of Kill Switches

Designing kill switches is more involved than simply adding a "disable" flag. To be reliable and auditable, they should have well-defined semantics and be implemented in ways that are:

- **idempotent**: triggering the same kill action multiple times has no harmful additional effect,
- **fast**: the time between decision and effective halt should be minimal,

- **consistent**: all relevant parts of the system interpret the state change the same way,
- **audited**: there is a clear record of what happened, when, and who or what initiated it.

Key elements include:

Blocking New Orders

The first and simplest effect of a kill switch is to stop new risk-taking orders from leaving the firm. This is usually accomplished by:

- maintaining a per-scope "enabled/disabled" state in the gateway or a central risk service,
- checking that state in the synchronous pre-trade path before any order is sent to a venue,
- rejecting or silently dropping orders when the state indicates a kill is in effect, with clear error codes and logs.

Because this check is applied at the same place as pre-trade and exposure checks, it can reuse that infrastructure and adds minimal additional latency.

Canceling Outstanding Orders

Stopping new orders is not enough if you already have a large book of working orders. A full kill operation typically includes a **mass-cancel** step:

- identify all live orders for the affected scope (strategy, desk, firm),
- send cancel requests to each venue where those orders reside,
- continue monitoring until confirmations indicate that the book is clear or that specific orders could not be canceled (for example, already filled).

This process needs to be robust to partial failures (some venues slower or unresponsive), and it must be possible to re-run it if confirmations are lost. That is where idempotence matters: repeated mass-cancel attempts should not introduce errors, but simply complete whatever cancellation remains.

Integration With Brokers and Venues

Some kill actions require cooperation from brokers or venues. For example:

- a sponsoring broker may have its own firm-level kill switch that halts all traffic from your market participant ID,
- an exchange may support mass-cancel commands that operate on all orders for a given account, session, or firm.

Your systems should be able to:

- invoke these external mechanisms when needed,
- detect when they have been invoked by others (for example, a broker activating a kill on your behalf),
- reconcile your internal view of working orders with the street's view after such actions.

This is where the shadow-path concepts in a later section become especially valuable: independent drop-copy or confirmation feeds help you verify that kill commands had their intended effect.

Procedures: Who May Hit Which Button, and How?

Technology alone does not produce an effective emergency response. You also need well-defined **procedures** that answer:

- Who is authorized to activate each type of kill switch?

- Under what conditions should they do so?
- How is the decision communicated and documented?

Authority and Documentation

A common pattern is to define tiers of authority:

- **Strategy-level stop**: front-line traders or designated quants operating the strategy may activate this directly, possibly with immediate notification to risk.
- **Desk-level stop**: requires approval from the desk head or designated deputy, plus risk or operations sign-off where feasible.
- **Firm-level kill**: reserved for senior management or a small incident-response group, often with at least two people approving (for example, a "four-eyes" principle).
- **Broker / venue mass cancel**: coordinated through named contacts at the broker or venue, often after internal firm-level decisions.

Every activation and deactivation should be logged with:

- time and scope,
- who initiated it,
- reason or incident ticket reference.

This not only supports regulatory accountability but also aids post-mortem analysis and process improvement.

Avoiding Accidental Activation

A kill switch should be easy to use under stress but hard to trigger accidentally. Practical design choices include:

- separate interfaces for live activation (for example, a secure internal web page or command-line tool) with strong authentication,
- explicit confirmation prompts stating the scope and impact ("You are about to halt all trading for Desk X. Proceed?"),
- different visual cues for strategy, desk, and firm-level actions to reduce confusion,
- training and drills so that operators are familiar with the tools and less likely to mis-click under pressure.

For automated triggers (for example, kill switches activated when exposure exceeds extreme thresholds), thresholds should be chosen conservatively and subjected to thorough testing, with clear alarms that these gates are near activation.

Recovery: Safely Restarting After a Panic Stop

Stopping trading is only half of the story. You must also be able to **restart safely**. Doing so prematurely or without proper checks can be more dangerous than not stopping at all.

A disciplined recovery process generally includes:

Sanity Checks Before Restart

Before lifting a kill switch, operators and risk managers should verify that:

- **Positions** are correctly reflected in internal systems, reconciled against broker or clearing data where possible.
- **Exposure** is understood and within acceptable bounds; any residual positions from partial fills during the incident are acknowledged.
- **Outstanding orders** are either canceled or clearly accounted for; there should be no uncertainty about what is still live in the market.

- **Underlying issues** that triggered the kill have been addressed (for example, bad data feeds fixed, problematic strategies patched or disabled).

These checks should be codified as a checklist, not left to ad hoc judgment in the moment.

Controlled Restart and Volume Ramping

When restarting, it is rarely wise to jump from zero to full size in a single step. A more controlled approach is:

- re-enable specific strategies or desks gradually,
- start with reduced limits or volumes,
- closely monitor behavior and exposures as trading resumes,
- only restore full capacities after a period of stable operation.

This staged approach ties back to deployment and volume-ramping practices discussed elsewhere in the book: after an incident, you effectively treat the restart as a fresh rollout that deserves extra caution.

Post-Mortem and Process Improvement

Finally, every significant kill event should be followed by a **post-mortem**:

- What exactly happened, and how was it detected?
- Were kill switches activated at the right time and scope?
- Did any technical or procedural weaknesses appear (for example, slow cancels, confusion over authority)?
- How can systems, limits, or training be improved to reduce the chance or impact of similar incidents?

The goal is not blame but learning. Over time, a healthy incident-review process will refine both technology and playbooks, making your firm more resilient.

Bringing It All Together

Firm-level kill switches and emergency procedures represent the final, most forceful layer in your risk-control stack. While pre-trade checks, exposure limits, and flow hygiene (STP and duplicate controls) are designed to prevent most problems, kill switches are designed for the cases where prevention fails or where external events move too fast for fine-grained measures.

Designing them well requires:

- clear definitions of scope and behavior,
- technically sound and auditable implementations,
- thoughtful procedures about who may act, when, and how,
- and disciplined recovery practices that restore trading safely.

In the final section of this chapter, we will add one more important layer: independent verification via shadow paths. That layer helps you confirm, even during and after emergencies, that your view of orders, fills, and risk matches what actually happened in the market—and that when you hit the kill switch, the bleeding really did stop.

5.5 Independent Verification via Shadow Paths

The previous sections of this chapter focused on *controlling* risk: pre-trade filters, exposure limits, self-trade prevention, and kill switches. All of these assume that your systems have an accurate picture of what is happening: which orders you have sent, which fills you have received, and what positions and exposures you currently hold.

In practice, that assumption is fragile. Messages can be dropped or duplicated, feeds can lag, bugs can corrupt internal state, and external parties (brokers, clearing firms, exchanges) can correct or adjust trades after the fact. If you rely on a single internal view of the world, you may not notice that it has quietly diverged from reality until a reconciliation hours later-or until a crisis exposes the gap.

Serious trading firms therefore build **shadow paths**: independent data flows, typically based on exchange drop-copy feeds, broker reports, or separate market data, that reconstruct orders, fills, and positions in parallel to the primary trading systems. These shadow paths continuously answer a blunt question:

> "Does the outside world see the same orders, trades, and risk that we think we have?"

This section explains how to design such paths, how to compare them to your primary view in real time, and how to use the resulting checks to strengthen every other control in your stack.

Why a Single Source of Truth Is Not Enough

At first glance, it is tempting to treat your main trading system as *the* source of truth. After all, every order originates there; every fill is ingested there; every risk calculation and dashboard is based on its state. If the system is reasonably engineered and the hardware reliable, why complicate things?

There are at least four reasons:

- **Software bugs and logic errors**. A subtle bug in reconciliation, order state transitions, or cancel handling can create discrepancies that are invisible internally but obvious in the external record.
- **Partial failures and message loss**. Network hiccups, session resets, or misconfigured gateways can cause missing or duplicated messages. Your system may think an order is canceled while the exchange still sees it as live, or vice versa.

- **External corrections**. Exchanges and clearing firms sometimes issue trade busts, price corrections, or post-trade adjustments. If your systems do not ingest these cleanly, internal records diverge.
- **Operational risk and oversight**. Risk managers, compliance, and auditors expect independent verification that internal books match what is on the street, not just promises from the trading engine itself.

Viewed this way, shadow paths are not a luxury but a form of **defense-in-depth**. If pre-trade controls are the membrane between intent and the market, shadow paths are the mirror that tells you whether that membrane is working as designed.

The Concept of a Shadow Path

A **shadow path** is any data flow that:

- runs *in parallel* to your primary trading and risk stack,
- is based on data sourced from outside the primary stack (or tapped at different points within it),
- reconstructs a view of orders, fills, and positions,
- and is used primarily to *verify* and *monitor*, not to drive new trading decisions directly.

The key idea is *independence*. If the shadow path is built from the same code, same database, and same message stream as the primary path, it will likely share the same blind spots and bugs. To be effective, it should differ along at least some dimensions:

- data sources (drop-copy feeds vs. primary order acknowledgments),
- processing code (separate implementation or at least separate configuration),

- operational ownership (for example, risk or middle office rather than front-office developers).

The goal is not to duplicate everything but to provide an independent cross-check that discrepancies will reveal.

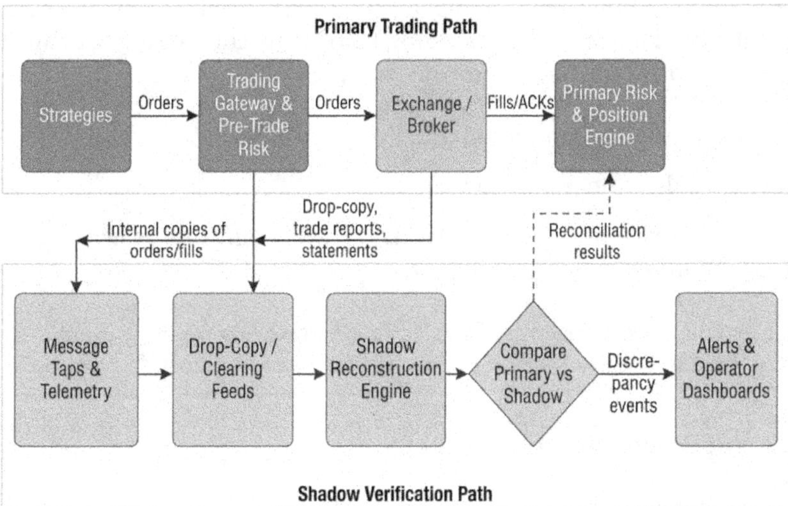

Common Shadow Data Sources

To construct a meaningful shadow view, you need data that reflects how the outside world sees your trading. The main sources are:

Exchange Drop-Copy Feeds

A drop-copy feed is a real-time stream of order and trade messages that mirrors your activity on the exchange. Unlike the primary order-entry session, it is:

- typically read-only,
- often delivered via a separate session or connection,
- designed explicitly for risk, surveillance, and monitoring use cases.

For each order you send, and each fill or cancel that occurs, the drop-copy stream carries a corresponding record. By consuming it in an independent process, you can reconstruct:

- all active and completed orders,
- all trades (including partial fills),
- sometimes additional metadata (for example, reason codes, matching information).

Because drop-copy is generated by the exchange's own systems, it reflects the exchange's authoritative view of your book on that venue.

Clearing Broker and CCP Feeds

Clearing brokers and central counterparties (CCPs) provide:

- intraday position and margin reports,
- end-of-day trade files,
- adjustment and correction notices.

While these are usually lower-frequency than exchange drop-copy, they represent the *settlement* view: what trades will actually clear, what positions will roll forward, and what cash movements will occur.

Feeding these into a shadow engine allows you to:

- confirm end-of-day positions and P&L,
- detect missing or misbooked trades,
- validate that exposure and credit limits were enforced as expected over the full day.

Independent Market Data

For some checks, you also want market data that does not depend solely on your primary feed. For example:

- independent top-of-book or consolidated feeds,
- delayed public data as a sanity reference,
- vendor or exchange reference prices used for valuation.

Shadow valuation processes can use this data to re-price your reconstructed positions and compare them to the P&L and exposures calculated in your primary risk engine.

Architectural Patterns for Shadow Paths

Once you know which data you will use, you must decide *where* and *how* to run your shadow computations. A few useful patterns:

Sidecar Process per Venue or Asset Class

In this pattern, each major venue or asset class has a dedicated *sidecar* service that:

- connects to the relevant drop-copy or risk feeds,
- ingests a subset of internal messages (for example, copies of orders as they leave the gateway),
- reconstructs a local book of orders and trades for that scope.

These sidecars can be developed and deployed somewhat independently from the main trading systems. They feed a central reconciliation and alerting engine that compares their view with the primary risk system.

Advantages:

- scalability across venues and products,
- fault isolation (a problem in one sidecar does not break others),
- natural alignment with how many firms already organize trading desks.

Central Shadow Risk Engine

Alternatively, you can build a single central shadow engine that:

- consumes all drop-copy, broker, and internal telemetry feeds,
- maintains a firmwide reconstructed view of orders, trades, and positions,
- performs reconciliations at multiple levels (per strategy, desk, and firm).

This approach simplifies some global checks (for example, firmwide exposure vs. clearing broker records) but requires careful scalability and robustness engineering.

Segregation from Production Trading

Whatever pattern you choose, it is critical that shadow infrastructure be *logically segregated* from production trading:

- it should not send orders itself,
- it should not be on the critical order-entry path,

- its failures should not directly halt trading, except where policy explicitly demands it (for example, "if reconciliation fails for more than N minutes, require human review before continuing high-risk strategies").

Segregation reduces the chance that a bug or outage in the verification system will itself cause trading outages. At the same time, the shadow path should be monitored and treated as important infrastructure: if it is down or lagging, you may want to proactively reduce risk until verification is restored.

Reconstructing Orders, Fills, and Positions

With drop-copy and related feeds in hand, the core task is to reconstruct the state of your orders and positions as the street sees them.

Order Lifecycle Reconstruction

For each order identifier seen in drop-copy or broker feeds, the shadow engine should track:

- its creation (new order messages),
- modifications (replacements, amendments),
- partial fills (trade messages with partial quantities),
- full fills,
- cancellations and expirations.

The result is an independent history of the order's life, including its final status and any intermediate states. This can be compared to the primary system's view:

- Does the primary system think the order is still working while the exchange has canceled it?

- Are there trades in drop-copy that the primary system never recorded?
- Are there internal orders that never appear externally (indicating they were blocked or dropped internally)?

Position and Exposure Reconstruction

Given reconstructed trades, the shadow engine can also:

- accumulate fills into positions per instrument,
- roll positions across days (accounting for corporate actions where possible),
- aggregate positions by strategy, desk, and firm, mirroring the limit hierarchies described earlier.

With access to independent market data, it can compute:

- approximate P&L,
- gross and net exposures,
- sector, currency, or factor exposures.

These can then be compared to the exposures and P&L calculated in the primary risk engine. Significant differences indicate a problem:

- missing or extra trades on one side,
- inconsistent mapping of instruments to buckets,
- failed or delayed ingestion of corrections.

Real-Time Comparison and Alerting

Reconstruction alone is not enough; you must actively *compare* the shadow view to the primary view and generate useful signals.

Levels of Comparison

Common comparison points include:

- **Per-order** status: internal state vs. drop-copy state.
- **Per-instrument position**: internal vs. shadow positions.
- **Aggregated exposure and P&L**: per strategy, desk, and firm.
- **Message counts and patterns**: for example, number of cancels or rejects by category.

Because exact equality is not always realistic (for example, due to timing or rounding), you typically define tolerances:

- acceptable timing gaps (for example, a small delay before shadow sees a trade that internal already recorded),
- acceptable numeric differences (for example, tiny P&L discrepancies due to different pricing sources),
- thresholds for alerting (for example, position differences above a certain size, or persistent stale orders).

Alert Design: Avoiding Noise

The hardest part of alerting is avoiding *noise*. If your operators are flooded with minor discrepancy alerts, they will learn to ignore them-defeating the point.

To keep the signal strong:

- focus alerts on **structural** discrepancies: orders that exist in one system but not the other, positions that differ by more than a tiny fraction, exposures that disagree materially,
- group related discrepancies into a single incident (for example, "all instruments in desk X show position mismatches" may indicate a shared feed issue),

- provide clear context in the alert: instrument, strategy, size and direction of difference, timestamps, and any related system health indicators.

In addition to real-time alerts, periodic summary reports are useful: for example, daily reconciliation summaries showing discrepancies found and resolved.

Using Shadow Paths to Validate Risk Controls

Shadow verification is not just about static reconciliation; it can directly support and strengthen the risk controls described in earlier sections.

Validating Pre-Trade Controls

Shadow paths can check whether pre-trade filters behaved as intended:

- Compare the population of *orders seen at the exchange* (drop-copy) to the population of *orders generated by strategies*. Orders blocked by pre-trade risk should appear only internally, never in drop-copy.
- Analyze rejected or throttled orders: do patterns in drop-copy and shadow data confirm that limits and price collars are correctly filtering out extreme or erroneous requests?

When discrepancies appear-such as an obviously bad order that somehow reached the exchange-they are strong signals that your pre-trade membrane has a hole.

Confirming Exposure Limits and Kill Switches

Similarly, you can use shadow data to verify:

- that exposure limits truly bounded the risk seen externally (for example, shadow positions never exceeded configured caps),

- that, when kill switches or strategy stops were activated, no further new risk-increasing orders appear in drop-copy after the activation time,
- that mass-cancel operations actually removed live orders from the exchange's book.

These checks are especially important after incidents. They allow you to answer, with evidence, whether the designed safeguards worked on the street, not just in your own logs.

Operational Considerations and Governance

Designing shadow paths is not purely a technical exercise; it has organizational and governance implications.

Ownership and Independence

Decide explicitly:

- which team owns and maintains the shadow infrastructure (for example, risk technology, middle office, or a joint function),
- how independent it should be from front-office development (for example, separate code repositories or at least separate review and deployment processes),
- how discrepancies are triaged and resolved (for example, a runbook specifying when to escalate to trading, operations, or the broker).

A healthy pattern is to give risk and operations strong visibility and influence over the shadow design and its alerts, since they are the primary consumers of its outputs.

Performance and Resilience

While shadow systems are not on the critical trade path, they still need to be:

- **timely**: near real-time where possible, so that large discrepancies are caught quickly rather than hours later,
- **reliable**: designed with redundancy and failover, since outages here reduce your visibility,
- **transparent**: with clear monitoring and metrics, so you know when the shadow view is stale or incomplete.

You may choose different service-level targets for different horizons: for example, sub-second for key order-state checks, and end-of-day for full clearing reconciliation.

Putting It All Together

Independent verification via shadow paths closes the loop on your risk-control architecture:

- Pre-trade controls and exposure limits define what *should* reach the market and what risk *should* be taken.
- Kill switches and emergency procedures define how to *stop* trading when things go wrong.
- Shadow paths, built on drop-copy, clearing, and telemetry feeds, tell you whether what *actually* happened on the street matches your internal narrative.

By reconstructing orders, fills, and positions in parallel, and by continuously comparing that reconstruction to your primary state, you greatly reduce the chance that silent discrepancies will build up unnoticed. You equip risk managers, operations, and developers with concrete evidence that the gateways, safeguards, and cutover practices described throughout this book are not only well-designed in theory, but effective in the live complexity of electronic markets.

Chapter 6

Reliability and Testing for Production Readiness

Before a single live order leaves your gateway, markets will assume your system already behaves like a seasoned participant: always available, precisely observable, and resistant to chaos. This chapter shows how to earn that trust-not with hope or heroics, but with a disciplined reliability and testing stack that makes failure predictable, contained, and boring.

6.1 Logging, Metrics, Tracing, and Audit Trails

Production readiness in electronic markets is not only about fast code and clever strategies; it is about being able to explain, after the fact, *exactly* what happened and why. When your system sends or refuses an order, when an exchange rejects or partially fills it, when a risk limit stops a runaway strategy—you must be able to reconstruct that story, step by step, from durable evidence.

This section describes how to build that evidence. We will work with four complementary pillars:

- **Structured logging**: detailed event records about what the software did and saw.
- **Metrics**: aggregated, numeric views of system health and performance over time.
- **Distributed tracing**: end-to-end flow records for individual requests, across services.
- **Audit trails**: immutable, long-lived records designed to satisfy regulators and internal control requirements.

Together they create a richly instrumented, time-synchronized view of your trading stack. The goal is not "more data" for its own sake, but *actionable observability*: the ability to answer concrete questions quickly and reliably:

- Why did this specific order get rejected at 09:30:02.153?
- Did we stop trading within our prescribed risk limits during the spike at 09:31?
- Are we gradually getting slower to acknowledge client orders this week?
- Can we demonstrate, a year from now, that we followed our stated controls?

To keep the discussion grounded, assume a simplified but realistic architecture: a client or strategy connects to an *order gateway*, which talks to a *pre-trade risk engine*, a *router or smart order router*, and then one or more venues (via FIX or native protocols) over well-defined market sessions. Market data, reference data, and external risk systems feed into these components. Everything runs in a latency-sensitive, highly parallel environment.

After outlining the four pillars, we will walk through concrete design choices: what to log, how to structure identifiers, how to avoid under-

and over-logging, which metrics to capture, how to design traces that match real market workflows, and how to build audit trails that meet regulatory expectations. Throughout, we will emphasize a simple but critical discipline: **design observability at the same time as business logic**, not as an afterthought.

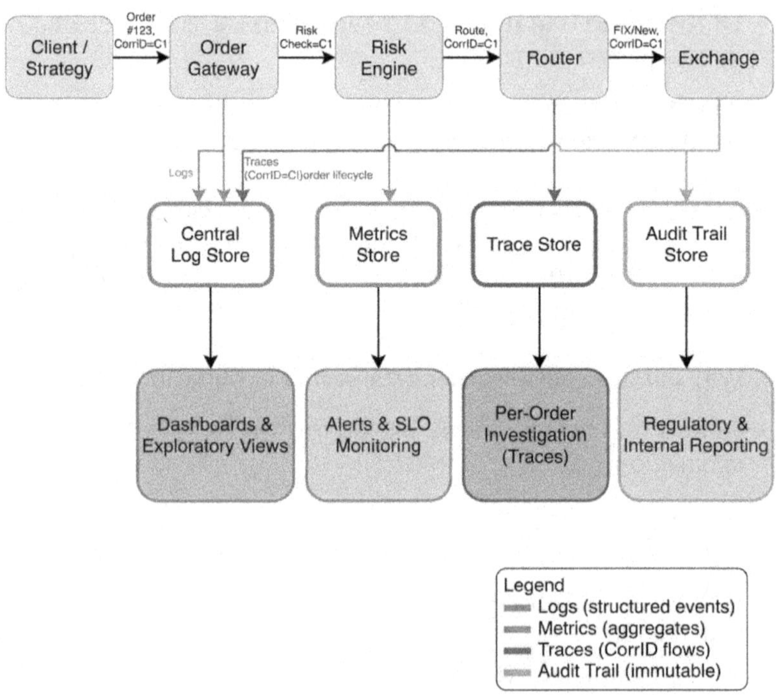

Structured Logging: Events You Can Reason About

Most systems start with simple, free-form text logs: lines written to standard output with a few pieces of information. In a modern trading stack that is not enough. You need **structured logs**: machine-readable records with consistent fields, so that you can search, filter, and aggregate them at scale.

A useful mental shift is to stop thinking about logs as "debug printouts" and to treat them instead as *event records*. Each log line should answer three questions:

1. **When** did this happen?
2. **What** happened (which event, which state transition)?
3. **Who / which object** did it happen to (which order, which session, which client)?

Core fields and identifiers. At minimum, every log entry in a trading system should contain:

- A precise **timestamp**, including timezone and preferably in a single standard (for example, UTC).
- A **log level**: info, warn, error, debug, and so on.
- A **component name**: gateway, risk-engine, router, market-data, etc.
- A **message or event name**: for example, ClientOrderReceived, PreTradeRiskCheckPassed, ExchangeAckReceived.
- **Correlation identifiers** that tie events together:
  - an internal order ID,
  - the client's order ID, if applicable,
  - the chosen correlation ID for tracing across services, and
  - venue order IDs and execution IDs once known.

These IDs are the threads that let you reconstruct a story. If a client complains that order #ABC123 was rejected, you can search for it using either their ID, your internal ID, or the venue ID, and reliably find all related events across services.

Market-aware content. Beyond generic fields, you need log fields that reflect market microstructure and order semantics. Examples include:

- instrument identifier (symbol, ISIN, or venue-specific code),
- side (buy/sell),
- order type, time-in-force, and any special instructions (for example, IOC, FOK, hidden),
- limit price, quantity, and minimum quantity constraints,
- risk limit identifiers (which credit or volume limit was checked),
- session identifiers (which FIX session, which native session, which trading phase).

When a venue rejects an order, you want to see in one place both the exact parameters you sent and the exact text and code of the rejection. That makes it possible to distinguish between a bug in your translation of strategy intent into protocol fields versus a genuine business rule violation at the venue.

Avoiding under- and over-logging. Under-logging means you do not have enough detail to understand a failure; over-logging means you drown in noise, consume too much storage, or slow the system.

A pragmatic way to balance this is:

- **Log every state transition** in an order's lifecycle at info level: received, accepted, routed, acknowledged, partially filled, filled, cancelled, rejected, expired.
- **Log every error** that affects a client or your risk posture at error level, with enough context to explain it.
- Use **debug-level logs** sparingly in hot paths; they should be turned on only for investigations, not in the default production config for low-latency components.
- **Batch noisy detail** where possible: for example, instead of logging every heartbeat as a separate info message, aggregate heartbeats into a periodic summary metric.

A good discipline is to ask, for any log you add: "In what scenario would this log help me make a decision or answer a specific question?" If you cannot answer that, consider omitting or lowering the level.

Time synchronization in logs. Timestamps are only useful if they are consistent across services. In a market event that unfolds over a few milliseconds, a clock drift of even one millisecond between two machines can lead you to completely wrong conclusions about the order of events.

Production systems typically use a combination of:

- a network time protocol (NTP) infrastructure with monitoring of offset and jitter, or
- hardware clock synchronization like PTP (Precision Time Protocol) for sub-microsecond alignment where needed.

You should monitor clock offsets as a metric and treat large offsets as a reliability issue, not a minor operational nuisance. In some regimes, regulators explicitly require evidence of clock synchronization within defined bounds.

Metrics: Seeing Health and Performance at a Glance

If logs tell individual stories, metrics describe the *crowd*. A metric is simply a numeric time series: a value measured repeatedly over time. In trading systems, useful metrics typically describe:

- **Volume and throughput**: orders per second, cancels per second, messages per second to each venue.
- **Latency**: time from client send to gateway acknowledge; from gateway to exchange ack; from exchange execution to client fill notification.
- **Error and rejection rates**: proportion of orders rejected by you (risk or validation) versus rejected by the venue.

- **Resource usage**: CPU, memory, garbage collection pauses (for managed languages), network utilization, queue depths.
- **Exchange-specific health**: heartbeat statuses, sequence gap events, session disconnects and reconnects.

Capturing latency shape, not just averages. Average latency can be misleading. For client experience and market impact, the *tail* of the distribution matters: the worst 1% or 0.1% of events.

To capture this, aim to record:

- median latency (50th percentile),
- high-percentile latencies (for example, 95th, 99th, 99.9th),
- counts of outliers beyond your stated service objectives.

For example, if your internal objective is that client orders receive an initial acknowledgement within 5 milliseconds, you might track: "Number of orders per minute with ack latency greater than 5 ms." Persistent breaches of that objective are a sign of performance or overload problems, even if the average still looks fine.

Business-aligned alerting. Metrics enable automated alerts, but you must choose thresholds that relate to business risk, not random round numbers.

Instead of alerting when CPU exceeds 80%, you might:

- alert when *both* CPU and order ack latency percentiles degrade,
- alert when venue reject rate exceeds a normal band for that instrument or client,
- alert when risk checks per order spike unexpectedly (perhaps due to a misconfigured strategy generating excessive modifications).

The best alerts are those that clearly imply an action. For example: "If median latency doubles and queue depth stays high for more than 5 minutes, consider temporarily throttling low-priority flow or failing over to additional capacity."

Distributed Tracing: Following a Single Order End-to-End

Logs and metrics make it possible to reconstruct stories if you are willing to search and correlate by hand. Distributed tracing makes that correlation explicit and automatic.

The idea is simple: when a client order enters your system, you assign it a **trace ID**. Every service that touches that order includes the trace ID in its logs and sends structured trace events to a central store. Later, you can retrieve the entire chain of events for that order as a single trace:

- client request received by gateway,
- gateway calls pre-trade risk engine,
- risk engine queries risk data store,
- risk decision returned,
- gateway routes to exchange via router,
- exchange acknowledges or rejects,
- fills arrive and are propagated back to the client.

Each "span" in a trace corresponds to a step in this flow, with its own start and end times, outcomes, and attributes.

Designing spans for trading workflows. For trading systems, natural span boundaries often line up with:

- layer crossings (client → gateway, gateway → risk, gateway → router),
- protocol boundaries (FIX session, native session, internal RPC from gateway to risk engine),
- risk and state transitions (pre-trade check, post-trade check, credit update).

It is useful to include, as attributes on each span:

- order identifiers (internal and client),
- instrument and side,
- whether this is a new order, cancel, or modify,
- relevant risk flags (for example, near limit, limit exceeded, fat-finger triggered),
- venue and session identifiers.

This allows you to filter traces for patterns, such as “orders for symbol X that failed risk” or “orders to venue Y with unusually slow acknowledgement.”

Tracing and performance. In low-latency code, adding more work per order matters. To keep tracing overhead acceptable:

- keep span objects light, avoiding heavy string formatting in hot paths,
- use sampling for very high-volume paths (for example, trace fully for a fraction of orders, but always trace orders that end in errors),
- offload trace export to background threads or sidecar processes where possible.

Even with sampling, you get a valuable view into end-to-end behavior, especially for failure cases and rare anomalies.

Tying traces back to logs and metrics. Trace IDs should appear in your structured logs as fields. That way, when you inspect a problematic metric (for example, a spike in 99th-percentile latency), you can:

1. drill down to example time windows and orders,
2. fetch representative traces that fall into the slow or error category,
3. use the traces to identify which service or step is adding latency or failing.

This is where the earlier insistence on consistent identifiers pays off. A single correlation ID connects: log lines, trace spans, metric dimensions (for example, per client or per venue), and, in some cases, audit trail entries.

Audit Trails: Evidence That Stands Up to Scrutiny

Operational logs and traces are primarily for engineers and on-call staff. **Audit trails** serve a broader audience: risk managers, compliance officers, internal and external auditors, and regulators. Their questions are more formal:

- What orders did you send on behalf of client X on date D?
- Did you respect the client's instructions and your own documented policies?
- Can you prove that you did not alter historical records after the fact?

This leads to different design requirements.

Content and scope. An electronic trading audit trail typically includes, at a minimum:

- the full lifecycle of every client order you handle: every new, modify, cancel, and the responses from venues,
- the internal decisions that affected those orders: risk checks, credit holds, fat-finger triggers and overrides,
- timestamps for when requests were received, processed, and forwarded,
- identifiers linking to counterparties, desks, traders, and any algorithm identifiers.

In many jurisdictions, there are explicit regulatory specifications for what must be captured and for how long. Even where not mandated, it is wise to be conservative: discarding audit data prematurely is hard to justify in hindsight.

Immutability and access control. Unlike day-to-day logs, audit trail records are not meant to be edited or deleted casually. Typical patterns include:

- writing audit records to append-only stores,
- applying cryptographic integrity checks to detect tampering,
- restricting access so that only specific roles can query or export data, with their own actions audited.

It is also essential to keep audit trails logically separate from normal operational logs. You may compress, archive, or eventually discard portions of operational logs, but audit trails should be governed by clear retention policies aligned with regulation and internal risk appetite.

Reconstruction and replay. A practical test of your audit trail design is: "Can we, using only audit data, reconstruct the lifecycle of an arbitrary order a year from now?" That includes:

- when and how the order entered the system,
- all changes made (who requested them, when they were forwarded),
- all outcomes at venues (executions, cancels, busts),
- any overrides, manual interventions, or exceptional workflows.

If the answer is no, examine the gaps: perhaps certain state transitions, error conditions, or manual actions are not being written to the audit store. Filling these gaps early pays off when the first real investigation arrives.

Designing for Idempotent Replay and Investigation

A well-instrumented system should not just let you read the past; it should let you *replay* it safely for analysis. That is, you should be able to take a sequence of historical events—orders, market data, risk limit changes—and feed them into a test environment to see how the system behaves. This is especially powerful when debugging complex failures or validating new versions of the code.

To support this:

- Ensure that order processing is **idempotent**: re-processing the same event with the same identifiers should not produce a different external effect or corrupt state.
- Make sure your logs and audit trails contain enough information to reconstruct the event stream, including external inputs like reference data snapshots at the time decisions were made.
- Avoid hidden state that is not reflected anywhere in your observable records (for example, in-memory counters that influence risk limits but are not persisted or logged).

This is closely related to later topics in the chapter on high availability and failover: the same event logs and identifiers that enable smooth takeover by a new node also enable faithful post-mortem analysis.

Building Observability In, Not Bolting It On

Finally, a process point. Many teams treat logging, metrics, and tracing as optional extras to be tidied up near go-live. In a trading environment, that is too late. Observability is part of the design.

A few concrete practices help:

- When you define a new feature (for example, a new order type or risk check), explicitly specify: *What will we log? Which metrics will we expose? How will traces for this feature look?*
- Treat missing or low-quality observability as a defect. If an incident occurs and the team cannot explain what happened due to gaps in logging or metrics, fix those gaps as part of the post-incident work.

- Keep configuration of log levels and metric collection under version control, reviewed and tested like code.

- Regularly rehearse investigations using your observability stack: pick a known corner case (for example, a venue reject), and have an engineer find and explain it using only dashboards, logs, and traces.

The payoff is tangible. When the market is volatile or an exchange is misbehaving, you will be under pressure from clients, risk managers, and possibly regulators. The only way to respond calmly and credibly is to base your statements on solid, time-synchronized evidence. A well-designed combination of structured logs, rigorous metrics, coherent tracing, and robust audit trails turns your trading system from an opaque black box into something you can understand, debug, and trust when it matters most.

6.2 Automated and Performance Testing Frameworks

In the previous section we focused on *seeing* your production system clearly: logs, metrics, traces, and audit trails that let you reconstruct what happened and why. Observability answers the question, "What is my system doing now, or what did it do before?"

This section addresses a different but related question: *"How do I know that my system will behave correctly and fast enough when the next change goes live?"* Markets evolve, venues change their protocols, strategies are refined, and infrastructure is patched. A one-off test campaign before first go-live is not nearly enough. You need a **multi-layered, automated test harness** that runs every day, every release, and in some cases every commit.

We will build this idea from the bottom up:

- Unit tests that validate small pieces of logic, like pricing and risk checks, with millisecond runtime.

- Integration tests that exercise boundaries between components, such as FIX gateways and risk engines.
- System and end-to-end tests that drive the full stack with realistic order flows and market data.
- Performance and capacity tests that stress latency, throughput, and resource usage under market-like conditions.

These layers form a **test pyramid**: many fast, cheap tests at the bottom; fewer, more expensive tests at the top. As in a physical pyramid, the stability of the structure depends on broad, solid foundations. The goal is not to chase some abstract notion of test coverage, but to continuously produce credible evidence that your trading system is *correct enough* and *fast enough* for the flows it will face.

The Test Pyramid as a Reliability Argument

Before diving into each layer, it is useful to understand the *logic* behind the pyramid.

Consider a simple but realistic trading bug: a new risk rule is coded incorrectly, and under specific conditions it mistakenly approves child orders that should be blocked. If you rely only on a handful of manual end-to-end tests, this bug might slip into production and only emerge under unusual market patterns.

A robust pyramid would give you multiple chances to catch it:

- A **unit test** on the risk function would check that given particular prices and quantities, the function returns "reject" instead of "approve".
- An **integration test** would feed a sample order through the gateway–risk–router pipeline and verify that the risk decision is enforced and logged correctly.
- A **system test** with recorded market data might simulate the same pattern that caused the bug in production, producing a regression test for the full stack.

- A **performance test** would ensure that the additional risk logic does not slow down order acknowledgements beyond acceptable limits, even under load.

The idea is not redundancy for its own sake. Each layer provides a different type of evidence:

- Unit tests say: "Individual decisions are correct, in isolation."
- Integration tests say: "Components agree on protocols and state transitions."
- System tests say: "The whole trading workflow behaves sensibly under realistic scenarios."
- Performance tests say: "The system is fast and stable enough at expected and peak loads."

When stakeholders—risk, compliance, or a venue—ask, "How do you know your changes are safe?", this layered evidence is your answer.

Unit Tests: Fast, Deterministic Checks of Core Logic

Unit tests are the foundation. They are small, fast, and numerous. In trading systems, good candidates for unit testing include:

- pricing and valuation routines,
- pre-trade risk checks (fat-finger checks, credit limits, volume caps),
- order state machines (how an order moves from New to Working to Filled, Cancelled, or Rejected),
- routing decisions based on simple rules (for example, primary vs alternate venue selection, before smart routing logic is layered on).

Determinism and realistic fixtures. A unit test should give the same result every time it runs. That means:

- no reliance on live market data feeds,
- no hidden dependence on current time (unless time is injected as a controlled parameter),
- no external network or database calls.

However, "deterministic" does not mean "unrealistic". One of the common mistakes in trading-unit tests is to use simplistic or artificial data that ignores real market conditions. Instead, build **fixtures**—small snapshots of plausible market data and order books—that capture:

- normal markets: tight spreads, moderate depth,
- stressed markets: wide or inverted spreads, thin depth,
- special conditions: halts, auctions, indicative prices, trading status changes.

For pre-trade risk, write tests that simulate edge cases:

- orders that are just inside and just outside limits,
- large notional values at low prices and vice versa,
- rapid-fire cancels and replaces that count toward message or volume limits.

These tests are cheap to run and can be executed on every commit. When a developer modifies the risk logic, the unit tests provide immediate feedback about unintended changes.

Integration Tests: Checking the Seams Between Components

Unit tests live inside individual components. Integration tests live at the boundaries: where your order gateway talks FIX to a broker, where it calls the risk engine, or where it writes to a database.

In an electronic trading context, typical integration test targets are:

- **FIX / native protocol adapters**: mapping of internal fields to protocol fields, session logon/logoff behavior, heartbeat handling, sequence number management.
- **Market data consumers**: decoding of ITCH or similar feeds, handling of out-of-order or duplicate messages, session recovery.
- **Persistence layers**: storage of orders, executions, and positions; replay of events on restart; transaction boundaries.
- **Risk engine adapters**: request/response contracts between the gateway and risk service, including timeout and error handling.

Protocol correctness and sequence handling. For order entry protocols like FIX or OUCH, integration tests should validate:

- that required tags are present and valid for each message type,
- that optional tags are handled correctly when present or absent,
- that messages are rejected locally when they cannot possibly be accepted by the venue,
- that sequence gaps, resend requests, and recovery behavior follow the venue specification.

This often means building a *fake venue* for testing: a simple piece of software that speaks FIX or the native protocol, echoes or rejects orders according to a small script, and checks that your adapter behaves like a well-mannered client.

State and failure modes. Good integration tests do not only check happy paths. They also cover:

- loss of network connectivity and reconnection behavior,
- database unavailability and fallback procedures,

- risk engine timeouts and degraded modes (for example, hard block vs soft fail with reduced functionality).

For example, if the risk engine is temporarily unavailable, your gateway may be configured to reject all new orders with a clear error message. An integration test can simulate the risk engine going offline and verify that the gateway behaves accordingly, logs the right information, and recovers automatically when the risk engine returns.

System and End-to-End Tests: Rehearsing Real Market Scenarios

System tests drive the *entire* trading stack in a controlled environment: from client entry to order gateway, through risk and routing, out to a simulated exchange, and back. Where unit and integration tests focus on pieces, system tests focus on *stories*.

Examples of such stories include:

- a client logs in before the open, sends a wave of limit orders, sees some executed at the open auction, and cancels the rest,
- a strategy adjusts its quotes during a fast market, with many cancels and replaces, hitting cancel-throttle limits at the venue,
- a venue disconnects mid-session, your routing logic detects the outage, automatically fails over to an alternate venue where possible, and later recovers.

Synthetic vs recorded market feeds. To drive realistic system tests, you need market data. There are two broad approaches:

- **Synthetic feeds**, generated according to a script or model. These are useful when you want to control specific patterns, such as a sudden spike in volatility or an instrument halt at a predetermined time.
- **Recorded feeds** from production or a realistic paper trading environment. When replayed at the original or scaled timing, they can reveal how your system behaves under historic stresses.

A powerful pattern is to combine the two: use recorded data for the background market, while overlaying synthetic events to explore edge conditions that you have not yet encountered in the wild.

Order lifecycle validation. In system tests, you care not only that individual decisions are correct, but that the *lifecycle* of each order makes sense across components. Using the observability tools discussed earlier, a system test can automatically verify that:

- each client order has a coherent trail of states: received, checked, routed, acknowledged, executed or cancelled,
- risk limits are enforced consistently across instruments and venues,
- logs and traces contain the expected entries, with correct correlation IDs.

In other words, system tests are an opportunity to test not only your trading logic but also your logging and tracing logic. After all, in production you will rely on those to understand what happened.

Throttling and safeguards. System tests are also where you validate safeguards that depend on overall behavior rather than single events, such as:

- per-client or per-strategy message rate limits,
- maximum open orders per instrument,
- circuit breakers that halt trading when loss or volume thresholds are breached.

By simulating bursts of orders and specific P&L patterns, you can check that these controls trip when expected and that the system responds gracefully—for example, by rejecting further orders with clear reasons and notifying operators.

Performance and Capacity Testing: Latency, Throughput, and Saturation

Even a perfectly correct trading system is unacceptable if it is too slow under load. Performance and capacity testing answer questions such as:

- How many orders per second can we handle while keeping client acknowledgements below our latency targets?
- What happens during the opening and closing auctions when message rates spike?
- Which resource becomes a bottleneck first: CPU, memory, network, or disk?

Workloads that mimic the market. A simple "hammer the system with random orders" test is rarely informative. Instead, construct scenarios that resemble distinct trading phases:

- **Pre-open and opening auction**: many orders arriving in a short window, concentrated in liquid instruments, with no immediate executions until the auction uncrosses.
- **Midday continuous trading**: steadier flow, more cancels and replaces as strategies manage their queues.
- **Closing auction**: similar to the open, but often even more intense for index constituents and ETF baskets.

For each scenario, vary both the total volume and the concurrency (how many independent clients or strategies send messages at once). Use these workloads to generate latency distributions, as illustrated in the inset histogram of the figure. Focus on:

- median latency (typical client experience),
- high-percentile latency (worst-case client experience),
- error rates and timeouts under stress.

Seeing inflection points. A well-designed performance test helps reveal *inflection points*: where a small increase in load causes a disproportionate increase in latency or error rates. Often this corresponds to:

- CPU saturation on critical threads,
- garbage collection pauses in managed runtimes,
- network interface card (NIC) queues overflowing,
- kernel or OS limits being hit (for example, file descriptors, sockets).

By gradually ramping up throughput and plotting latency percentiles against load, you can see where microseconds become milliseconds. That is usually the point at which you should set your operational limits and alerts: in production, avoid running the system in the "red zone" where small load changes risk large degradations.

End-to-end and component-level profiling. Performance tests operate at two levels:

- **End-to-end**: measure time from client send to venue response and back. This is what clients care about and what often drives business commitments.
- **Component-level**: measure time spent in individual services and functions (gateway, risk, router, protocol adapters). This helps locate bottlenecks and prioritize optimization work.

The distributed tracing infrastructure discussed earlier is invaluable here. Under load, you can aggregate traces to see, for example, that 70% of added latency comes from risk checks, not network transmission, and focus your tuning effort accordingly.

Embedding Tests in CI/CD: Continuous Evidence, Not One-Off Campaigns

A powerful test harness is of limited value if it is only run manually before major releases. In modern trading technology, changes are frequent: exchange upgrades, new instruments, updated risk policies, and strategy tweaks. To stay ahead of this, tests should be **embedded in your continuous integration and deployment (CI/CD) pipeline**.

A simple but effective pattern is:

- Run **unit tests** on every commit or merge request. They are fast and provide immediate feedback to developers.
- Run a curated set of **integration tests** as part of a standard build pipeline. These may run on every commit to the main branch or on every proposed release candidate.
- Schedule **system tests** to run automatically at least daily or on every significant gateway or risk-engine change, using a stable test environment with access to synthetic or recorded feeds.
- Trigger **performance test suites** on demand for major changes, or regularly (for example, weekly) to detect gradual regressions in latency or capacity.

Each stage in the CI/CD pipeline should have clear **acceptance gates**. For example:

- No merge to the main branch if unit or critical integration tests fail.
- No promotion from test to staging environment unless system tests pass and key latency metrics are within bounds.
- No production release if performance tests show regression beyond agreed thresholds, unless explicitly waived by stakeholders with documented rationale.

This structure turns tests into more than a technical artifact. They become part of your organization's risk management: a formal, repeatable process that reduces the chance of surprises in live markets.

Maintaining and Evolving the Test Suite

Markets and systems change. A test suite that once was comprehensive can become stale, no longer reflecting current strategies, venues, or regulatory requirements. To keep your tests relevant:

- Treat tests as **first-class assets**. When you design a new feature or onboard a new venue, define the tests it requires alongside the implementation plan.
- Use **production incidents** as fuel for new tests. After any significant failure or near-miss, ask: "What test would have caught this earlier?" Then add that test to the appropriate layer.
- Periodically review and prune tests that are redundant, flaky, or no longer relevant. A noisy or brittle test suite undermines confidence and encourages people to ignore failures.
- Keep **market fixtures** up to date. For example, refresh recorded feeds used in system tests to include recent periods of stress or structural change.

Over time, your test harness becomes a living record of your collective learning about how the system should behave. It encodes not only technical expectations, but also the risk tolerances and business commitments of your firm.

From Backtest to Live: Tests as a Bridge

Finally, connect this back to the broader theme of the book: moving from backtest to live execution. Backtests and simulations validate a strategy in an idealized world. The multi-layered testing framework described here validates the *machinery* that carries that strategy into the real market.

When both are strong, you can move from research to production with confidence:

- The strategy has been stress-tested on historical and synthetic data.

- The trading stack has been tested, component by component and end-to-end, for correctness, latency, and capacity.
- Observability is in place to monitor live behavior and to feed findings back into new tests.

In the next sections, we will build on this foundation to explore high availability, failover, and disaster recovery: how to keep the system running and safe even when individual components fail or entire sites go dark. Automated and performance tests remain central in those discussions as well, because only by exercising your resilience mechanisms regularly can you trust them when the market is moving fast and the stakes are high.

6.3 High Availability, Failover, and Stateless Design

The previous sections have focused on *correctness* (via tests) and *observability* (via logging and metrics). Both assume that your trading system is up and running. In live markets, however, you must also plan for the moments when it is not.

Servers fail, processes crash, network links flap, and software needs to be upgraded. None of these are exceptional events; they are the normal background noise of running systems at scale. What distinguishes a production-ready trading platform is not the absence of failures, but the ability to **survive** them without:

- dropping orders,
- violating risk limits or sending duplicate messages,
- confusing or surprising exchanges and brokers,
- creating unexplained gaps in your audit trail.

To achieve this, we design trading services to be *highly available*. That means they continue to perform their essential functions—accepting, risk-checking, routing, and acknowledging orders—even when individual components are taken away or replaced. The central pattern we will explore is the combination of:

- **active-active clusters** of gateways and risk engines,
- **stateless service instances** that can be added or removed at will,
- **external, replicated state stores** that preserve order and risk state across failures,
- **automated failover and health checks** that isolate bad nodes quickly.

We will build this step by step, starting from business-level availability goals and moving down to technical mechanisms such as idempotency keys, sequence numbers, and brownout handling.

From Business Availability to Technical Objectives

Availability targets should not be plucked from thin air as "five nines" or similar slogans. They must be grounded in market structure and client expectations.

For example:

- During the continuous trading session of a major equity venue, any unplanned outage of your primary gateway that lasts more than a few seconds can cause missed fills, client dissatisfaction, and regulatory questions.
- In pre-open or post-close periods, short maintenance windows may be acceptable, provided all in-force orders are preserved and ready for the next session.
- For risk and credit systems, a fail-closed behavior (rejecting orders when risk cannot be checked) may be acceptable for a short time but not for extended periods, as it effectively locks clients out of the market.

Translate these business statements into more specific technical objectives, such as:

- No single machine failure should interrupt order flow for more than a few seconds.
- Loss of any one gateway instance must not cause loss or duplication of in-flight orders.
- Planned software upgrades must be possible during trading hours without a full outage (via rolling or blue-green deployments).

These objectives guide architectural choices: how many instances to run, how to distribute traffic, how to persist state, and how to design failover behaviors.

Active-Active Clusters and Stateless Services

A traditional, fragile architecture might run a single "primary" gateway with a "standby" instance that only takes over after manual intervention. In modern electronic trading, this is rarely sufficient. Instead, we aim for **active-active** clusters:

- Multiple gateway instances are all live, all accepting traffic, and all considered peers.
- Traffic is distributed across them by a load balancer or client-side logic.
- If one instance fails, others automatically pick up its load.

To make this robust, we strive to keep each instance as **stateless** as possible. Here, "stateless" does not mean that the system as a whole has no state. Orders, risk limits, positions, and session status are state. Rather, it means:

> *No single gateway instance is the sole owner of critical state. Any instance can, in principle, process any incoming message if it has access to external state.*

Practically, this leads to an architecture where:

- Gateways and risk services maintain only transient, in-memory caches.
- Durable state (order books, positions, risk limits, session metadata) lives in replicated databases, event logs, or distributed caches.
- When an instance fails, another can reconstruct the necessary state from those shared sources.

Immediately after we introduce this idea, it is helpful to visualize it.

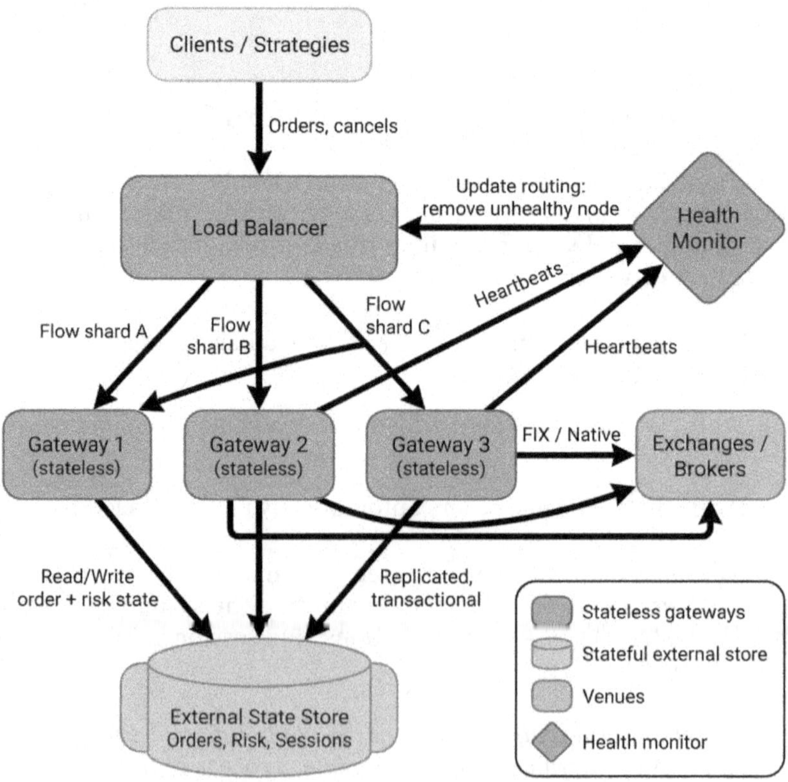

In this design, the load balancer and health monitor jointly ensure that:

- traffic is distributed across healthy gateways;
- if one gateway stops responding to health checks, it is removed from rotation;
- clients need not know which specific instance serves which order.

However, stateless design on its own does not solve all problems. We must now consider how to maintain consistency of orders and risk across failures.

Externalized State, Idempotency, and Sequence Numbers

From an exchange's point of view, your gateway is a single logical participant. Whether messages come from Gateway 1 or Gateway 3 is irrelevant; what matters is that:

- you do not send duplicate new orders or cancels,
- you respect sequence and session rules,
- you do not lose track of outstanding orders after a failure.

To align this logical view with a distributed implementation, three concepts are essential: **externalized state**, **idempotency**, and **sequence management**.

Externalized state. Key pieces of state should reside in shared, durable stores:

- a replicated order store or event log that records each order's lifecycle,
- a risk state store that tracks current exposures, credit usage, and limits,
- a session store that records venue logon status, sequence numbers, and capabilities.

Gateway instances act more like *stateless processors* that read from and write to these stores, rather than hoarding knowledge locally. When a gateway crashes:

- another instance can consult the shared state to determine which orders are live, which cancels are pending, and what risk headroom remains;
- upon restart, the crashed instance can rebuild its in-memory view by replaying the external event log.

Idempotency keys and order identifiers. Idempotency means that if you repeat the same operation with the same identifier, the effect is the same as doing it once. In trading:

- Each incoming client order, cancel, or replace is assigned a stable internal identifier (and often a separate client-supplied ID).
- When the gateway sends a message to the venue, it includes a unique key (or a combination of fields) that allows your system to recognize duplicates upon replay or retry.

If a gateway crashes after sending a cancel but before logging the response, the replacement gateway may be tempted to send another cancel. With idempotency keys and a consistent external order store, it can detect that a cancel has already been requested or applied, and avoid double-sending.

Sequence numbers and replayable logs. Many order entry protocols, including FIX, use sequence numbers to ensure ordered delivery. Your cluster must manage these as if it were a single logical sender:

- Sequence numbers and related session state are stored centrally, not tied to one machine.
- Only one gateway instance at a time is authorized to send messages on a given physical session, or the cluster coordinates sequence use carefully.
- If that instance fails, a takeover procedure selects a new sender, which resumes with the correct next sequence.

An event log—ordered, append-only records of outbound and inbound messages—is invaluable. It allows:

- reconstruction of what was sent and when,
- comparison against exchange views in case of dispute,
- safe replay into a replacement instance to re-establish in-memory state.

The combination of externalized state, idempotency, and sequence-aware replay ensures that failover is not only rapid, but also *logically correct* in the eyes of the exchange and clients.

Health Checks, Circuit Breakers, and Fast Isolation

High availability is as much about *removing* unhealthy components quickly as it is about adding new ones. Two practical tools here are health checks and circuit breakers.

Health checks. A health check is a small probe that asks, "Is this instance able to do its job?"

Examples include:

- a simple HTTP or RPC endpoint that reports internal status,
- deeper checks that verify connectivity to the state store and risk engine,
- self-assessment of error rates or queue backlogs.

Load balancers and cluster managers use health checks to:

- remove instances from rotation when they stop responding or report critical problems,
- avoid routing new traffic to nodes that are overwhelmed or degraded.

Health checks must be carefully designed so they represent *real* readiness. For example, a gateway that can respond to a trivial ping but has lost connectivity to the risk engine is not truly healthy: it cannot safely accept new orders.

Circuit breakers. Circuit breakers are patterns that prevent repeated attempts to use a failing dependency. For example:

- If a venue session is repeatedly rejecting logons or dropping connections, the gateway can "open the circuit" for that destination and stop routing new orders there, instead failing them fast with a clear reason or routing to an alternate venue where allowed.
- If the risk service is not responding, rather than letting calling threads pile up and time out, the gateway can temporarily stop sending risk requests and instead reject client orders immediately, preserving overall stability.

In both cases, observability plays a key role: metrics and logs must show when a circuit is open, why, and when it recovers. Later sections on chaos engineering will describe how to test these behaviors deliberately.

Brownout Handling: Degrading Gracefully Under Stress

Not all functionality is equally critical. During market stress or partial outages, you may prefer to *degrade* non-essential features in order to keep core trading alive. This controlled degradation is sometimes called a **brownout**, by analogy with reduced-voltage situations in power grids.

In trading systems, examples of brownout policies include:

- Temporarily disabling low-priority analytics or enrichment (such as optional tagging or complex pre-trade analytics) when CPU usage is high.
- Pausing acceptance of new algorithmic strategies or non-essential order types while continuing to process simple limit and market orders.

- Reducing logging verbosity in hot paths (while keeping critical audit trails intact) to prevent I/O saturation.

To implement brownout cleanly:

- Define, in advance, which features are core and which are optional.
- Expose configuration "switches" that can be toggled automatically when metrics cross thresholds or manually by operators.
- Ensure clients receive clear feedback (for example, well-defined error or rejection codes) when features are temporarily unavailable.

Brownout strategies should be rehearsed in system tests. For example, you can simulate a CPU-intensive load and observe whether the system correctly sheds non-critical work while preserving order acknowledgements and risk checks.

Safe Deployment: Blue-Green and Canary Releases

High availability is not only about reacting to unexpected failures. Planned changes—software releases, configuration updates, protocol upgrades—are themselves a major source of incidents. The goal is to be able to evolve your system while it remains live, especially when exchanges and clients expect continuous access.

Two practical deployment patterns are particularly relevant: **blue-green** and **canary** releases.

Blue-green deployments. In a blue-green setup:

- You maintain two production-like environments: Blue (current) and Green (new).
- You deploy and warm up the new version in Green while all live traffic still goes to Blue.

- Once Green has passed health checks and smoke tests, you switch traffic over—often by changing load balancer configuration or DNS.
- If problems appear, you can quickly revert by routing traffic back to Blue.

For trading systems, care must be taken with state:

- Both Blue and Green must see a consistent view of orders, risk, and sessions (often via shared external stores).
- You may temporarily restrict which functions run in Green during the cutover (for example, read-only operations first, then write operations).

Day boundaries and session resets can be convenient times for major blue-green switches, as exchange state is naturally reinitialized. However, with careful design, smaller upgrades can also be done intra-day.

Canary releases and volume ramping. Canary releases introduce a new version to a small slice of traffic first:

- Start by routing only a few clients or a low percentage of orders through the new version.
- Compare behavior, latency, and error rates between old and new, using your metrics and traces.
- If the canary remains healthy, gradually ramp up the proportion of traffic.

This staged approach is particularly valuable when you modify risk logic, routing algorithms, or protocol adapters, where subtle bugs could have material financial impact.

Again, the stateless, active-active architecture makes this easier. You can run both old and new gateway versions side by side, all reading from the same external state stores, while directing slices of traffic to each.

Designing for Routine Failure

A useful mindset shift is to treat node failures, restarts, and network hiccups as *routine*, not exceptional. Ask, for each component:

- What happens if this machine disappears right now?
- How do in-flight orders complete, fail, or get retried?
- How long until another instance takes over, and what state does it need?
- What do clients, venues, and internal operators see during and after the event?

Your earlier work on testing and observability supports this mindset:

- System and performance tests can simulate restart and failover scenarios repeatedly.
- Logs, metrics, and traces show whether the transition was smooth, whether any messages were lost or duplicated, and how long it took.

By incorporating failure drills into regular practice, you ensure that failover paths are not only designed on paper but also proven in action.

Putting It All Together

Designing for high availability in electronic markets is not about building an indestructible system. It is about:

- accepting that components will fail,
- arranging them so that failures are contained and quickly compensated,
- externalizing and protecting the state that really matters (orders, risk, sessions),

- ensuring that exchanges and clients see a consistent, predictable participant.

Stateless service instances, active-active clusters, external state stores, idempotent order processing, careful sequence management, health checks, circuit breakers, brownout handling, and safe deployment patterns all work together toward this goal.

With these foundations, the next sections on disaster recovery and business continuity will expand our scope further, from surviving individual host or process failures to enduring entire data center or regional outages—always with the same guiding principle: keep control of your orders, your risk, and your narrative, even when the infrastructure beneath you is shifting.

6.4 Disaster Recovery and Business Continuity

The previous sections treated failures at the scale of *nodes* and *services*: a gateway crashes, a risk engine times out, a venue disconnects. We designed high availability and failover so that such events are absorbed with minimal disruption, often invisible to clients.

Disaster recovery and business continuity extend that thinking to a harsher world. Here we plan for incidents that may remove:

- an entire data center or cloud region,
- a shared storage system that underpins multiple services,
- connectivity to a critical exchange or clearing broker,
- key operational functions such as the trading desk itself.

In these situations, no amount of local redundancy within a single site is enough. The question shifts from "How do we keep this server cluster healthy?" to:

How do we keep the firm able to control orders, manage risk, and meet its obligations when a primary site or shared dependency is severely impaired?

To make this tractable, we will:

- Introduce the language of **Recovery Time Objective (RTO)** and **Recovery Point Objective (RPO)** and relate them to trading-specific risks.
- Describe common **second-site architectures** (warm standby and active-active) and how they influence achievable RTO/RPO.
- Treat **runbooks and drills** as first-class artifacts: who does what, in which order, under pressure.
- Connect these designs to **regulatory and client expectations** that increasingly require evidence, not just good intentions.

Throughout, we will assume you already have strong observability, automated tests, and high-availability patterns in a single site. Disaster recovery (DR) builds on, but does not replace, those foundations.

RTO and RPO: Putting Numbers on Pain

RTO and RPO are simple concepts that force you to quantify what is otherwise hand-waving about "acceptable downtime" and "tolerable data loss."

Recovery Time Objective (RTO). RTO is the *maximum acceptable duration* between the onset of a disruptive incident and the point at which critical services are restored to an acceptable level.

In trading terms, examples might be:

- "For our primary equities DMA gateway, we must be able to resume order entry and cancellation within 15 minutes of a primary-site loss."
- "Post-trade reporting to regulator X must resume within 4 hours after the incident."

RTO is not the same as a guarantee; it is a design target. If your architecture cannot plausibly meet the RTO, the design is inadequate for your obligations.

Recovery Point Objective (RPO). RPO is the *maximum acceptable amount of data loss*, often expressed as a time window. It answers: "How far back in time can our systems be rolled without causing unacceptable risk or regulatory breach?"

Examples:

- "We can tolerate at most one second of order and execution data loss for live trading systems."
- "For historical analytics that do not drive live risk, an RPO of one hour is acceptable."

For live trading, RPO is tightly connected to your ability to:

- know which orders are currently live at the exchange,
- reconcile your positions and P&L,
- demonstrate complete and accurate audit trails.

A cavalier RPO—for example, "we may lose a few minutes of orders"—is usually unacceptable for order-routing infrastructure, both from a risk and regulatory standpoint.

Linking RTO/RPO to concrete risks. RTO and RPO are not abstract technology metrics; they are proxies for business harms:

- A long RTO for order gateways means clients cannot adjust or cancel orders during a disruption. They may incur losses and seek compensation.
- A weak RPO for positions can lead to incorrect risk views. You may believe you are flat when you are not, or vice versa.
- Incomplete audit trails can expose the firm to regulatory fines or legal challenges.

When setting RTO/RPO, therefore, involve multiple stakeholders: trading, risk, technology, operations, compliance, and legal. Their joint input determines what must be treated as "mission critical" and what can recover more slowly.

What Disasters Look Like in Electronic Markets

Before selecting architectures, it is useful to name the types of incidents for which DR and business continuity planning are intended. Typical scenarios include:

- **Data center loss:** power, cooling, or physical access incident makes a facility unavailable.
- **Network partition:** a fiber cut or routing failure isolates a region from key venues or from your own backup site.
- **Shared service failure:** a storage array, message bus, or managed database cluster fails in a way that affects many systems at once.
- **Extensive security incident:** you may decide to take a site offline proactively, to contain suspected compromise.
- **People and process disruption:** events that prevent key staff from physically reaching an office or primary control room.

High availability techniques—multiple servers, health checks, failover within a cluster—help for smaller-scale technical failures. Disasters cross *blast-radius* boundaries: they take out entire silos of redundancy at once.

Your second-site architecture and runbooks must be designed with those wider blast radii in mind.

Second-Site Architectures: Warm Standby vs Active-Active

At a high level, you have two main options for a secondary site: **warm standby** and **active-active**. Each trades cost, complexity, RTO, and

RPO differently.

Warm Standby

In a warm standby design:

- The primary site handles all normal production traffic.
- The DR site runs a smaller or partially dormant set of services, kept ready but not generally in use.
- Data from primary is replicated to DR, often with a small lag.
- In a disaster, traffic is redirected to the DR site and services are scaled up to handle full load.

Warm standby tends to be:

- *Cheaper*, because you are not running two full-size production environments.
- *Simpler* from a business flow perspective: there is only one "active" place for live orders.

But it typically implies:

- A non-zero RTO, because the DR site must be promoted and possibly scaled.
- Some RPO exposure, depending on replication frequency and how much in-flight data is buffered only in the primary site.

In trading, warm standby is sometimes used for functions where brief unavailability is tolerable, or where volumes are moderate enough that scaling from warm to full capacity can be done quickly.

Active-Active Regional Deployment

In an active-active design:

- Two or more sites are fully capable of handling production traffic.

- Under normal conditions, traffic is balanced between them (for example, by geography or client segment).
- Data is replicated in near real time between sites.
- If one site fails, the other can take over its share of traffic with minimal manual intervention.

Active-active offers:

- Very low achievable RTO (potentially seconds).
- Tight RPO (approaching real-time if replication is synchronous or near-synchronous).

But it also introduces:

- Higher *cost*, as you effectively run multiple full-scale production environments.
- More *complexity*, especially around data consistency, routing rules, and operational procedures.

For core order-routing and risk systems, where RTO and RPO tolerances are narrow, active-active is increasingly the norm. It also dovetails well with the stateless, external-state architecture discussed earlier: if both sites share replicated state stores and consistent order identifiers, they can act as a single logical entity from the point of view of exchanges and clients.

Data Replication: Orders, Positions, and Risk Limits

Whatever topology you choose, the heart of DR is **data replication**. In trading systems, certain datasets are particularly sensitive:

- **Order state:** all open and historical orders, including their lifecycle events.

- **Executions and trades:** fills as reported by venues and counterparties.
- **Positions and P&L:** current holdings and their valuations.
- **Risk limits and configurations:** credit lines, volume caps, kill-switch states, algorithmic guardrails.
- **Audit trails:** immutable logs of activity for regulatory and internal use.

The replication strategy for each may differ:

- For live order and execution data, **low-latency, near-synchronous replication** is usually required to meet tight RPO.
- For historical analytics or non-critical reference data, **asynchronous replication** with higher lag may be acceptable.

Key design questions include:

- Are you using database-level replication, application-level event streaming, or both?
- How do you handle replication lag during a disaster? For example, if the DR site is a few seconds behind, how do you reconcile open orders with exchanges?
- How do you avoid "split-brain" situations where both sites believe they are primary and diverge in their state?

One robust pattern is to treat your event log of inbound and outbound messages as a *system of record* and replicate it in near real time. In a failover, the DR site uses the event stream to reconstruct state as of the last committed point, while any subsequent uncertainty is resolved through reconciliation with exchanges and clearing houses.

Runbooks: Turning Architecture into Action

A DR architecture, no matter how elegant, is useless if nobody knows how to operate it under pressure. This is where **runbooks** come in.

A runbook is a structured, step-by-step guide that answers: "If scenario X happens, what exactly do we do? Who does it? In what order? Using which tools?" Good runbooks are:

- **Specific**: tailored to particular incident types (for example, "Primary site network isolation" vs "Corrupted database cluster").
- **Actionable**: written in operational language, with concrete commands or system names, not vague statements.
- **Role-aware**: clearly assign responsibilities to teams and individuals: trading desk, operations, infrastructure, application support, compliance, communications.

For a primary-site loss affecting the main equities gateway, a runbook might include sections such as:

- **Detection and initial assessment**

- How is the incident detected (monitoring alerts, venue notifications, client reports)?
- Who is the incident commander?

- **Immediate risk controls**

- Confirm whether existing orders can still be cancelled via backup channels.
- If not, escalate to venues or brokers to request cancel-on-disconnect or other emergency procedures.

- **Failover steps**

- Actions to promote the DR site (for example, updating DNS or routing configurations).

- Verification steps: confirming that order paths, risk checks, and logging are functional.

- **Client and venue communication**

- Templates for notifying clients about temporary limitations and restoration of service.
- Points of contact at key venues and brokers.

- **Post-incident reconciliation**

- Procedures to match orders and executions across sites and venues.
- Checks to ensure audit trails are complete.

Runbooks should not remain theoretical documents. They must be **rehearsed**, refined, and kept in sync with system evolution.

DR Drills: Practicing Under Safe Conditions

Just as you would not trust untested code in production, you should not trust an unpracticed DR plan. Regular **DR exercises** are essential. Their aim is twofold:

- **Technical validation**: does the architecture behave as expected under failover?
- **Human validation**: can the people involved execute the runbook correctly under stress?

Effective DR drills have a few common characteristics:

Realistic but safe. Use production-like data and traffic patterns *without* risking real capital. Techniques include:

- Conducting drills in a fully separate environment that mirrors production configuration and data as closely as possible.

- Using replayed market data and order flows from historical periods of stress.
- For more advanced organizations, conducting "live" drills outside market hours, with careful safeguards.

Clear scope and success criteria. Define for each exercise:

- which failure scenario you are simulating (for example, full primary-site loss vs partial service degradation),
- what RTO and RPO targets you are testing,
- what observable outcomes will be used to judge success (for example, time to restore order entry, completeness of audit logs, absence of duplicate orders to venues).

Structured debriefing. After each drill:

- review what went well and what did not, both technically and procedurally,
- capture findings as updates to runbooks, system configuration, and, where applicable, automated tests,
- store evidence of the drill and its outcomes; this is valuable for internal governance and often for regulators.

Over time, drills should become more challenging: starting with simple scenarios and progressing to complex, multi-fault situations. The goal is not to "pass a test" once, but to build organizational muscle memory.

Regulatory and Client Expectations

Many jurisdictions now explicitly require financial institutions to maintain, document, and *test* their disaster recovery and business continuity capabilities. Even where not legally mandated, institutional clients increasingly ask detailed questions before entrusting you with order flow.

From a regulatory and client perspective, key themes include:

- **Documentation**: written DR and business continuity plans, including RTO/RPO targets, architectures, and runbooks.
- **Evidence of testing**: records of DR drills, their outcomes, and subsequent improvements.
- **Clarity on partial outages**: policies for when you restrict or halt trading in specific products or venues due to DR events.
- **Communication protocols**: how and when clients will be informed about incidents, limitations, and restoration of service.

Your observability and audit trail infrastructure from earlier sections is central here. It provides:

- timestamps and sequence-of-events for the incident,
- proof that you adhered to your procedures,
- data for post-incident reports and reviews.

A robust DR strategy is therefore both a technological capability and a *governance* asset. It enables you to demonstrate to regulators and clients that you take resilience seriously and can back those claims with evidence.

Avoiding "DR in Name Only"

A common anti-pattern is the "paper DR plan": a secondary site exists, perhaps with some replicated data, but in practice:

- its software versions lag behind production,
- configuration drifts over time and is not rigorously managed,
- connectivity to venues and brokers is untested or limited,
- operational staff are unfamiliar with how to promote it.

In a real incident, such a DR site proves unusable, forcing the firm into improvised, risky measures.

To avoid this, treat the DR environment as:

- **A peer to primary** in terms of code, configuration, and data schema. Use the same deployment pipelines and configuration management, so changes propagate consistently.
- **A regular participant** in your testing. System and performance tests should run there as well, not only in the primary site.
- **A visible asset** in monitoring. Metrics and logs from DR should be available in the same dashboards, with clear indication of its current role (standby, partial active, full active).

In active-active designs, DR ceases to be a separate environment at all; both sites are always "live." Even in warm standby, strive to minimize divergence from primary, so promotion is a modest step, not a leap into the unknown.

From Resilient Components to Resilient Enterprise

Taken together, disaster recovery and business continuity planning shift perspective from individual systems to the *enterprise as a whole.* They ask:

- Not just "Can my gateway survive a server failure?", but "Can my firm keep control of its orders if a building goes dark?"
- Not just "Is my risk engine highly available?", but "Can I still produce accurate risk and regulatory reports after a major outage?"

The tools and concepts we have developed so far—observability, automated testing, stateless design, active-active clustering—are building blocks. DR and business continuity add:

- explicit RTO/RPO targets rooted in business and regulatory needs,

- multi-site architectures with thought-through data replication,
- rehearsed runbooks that coordinate technology, trading, operations, and compliance.

In the next sections, we will see how external parties such as exchanges formalize some aspects of reliability via certification and conformance testing, and how internal practices like chaos engineering can be used to continuously probe and strengthen the DR and HA mechanisms you have designed. The overarching aim remains the same: to ensure that from backtest to live execution, your systems not only perform well in fair weather, but remain controlled, explainable, and operable when the environment turns hostile.

6.5 Exchange Certification and Conformance Testing

Up to this point we have focused on *your* readiness: observability, automated testing, high availability, and disaster recovery. In live markets, however, you are not the only party whose confidence matters. Every exchange, alternative trading system, and broker-sponsored access platform has its own view of what "safe and correct" behavior looks like. Before you are allowed to send live flow, they insist on verifying your implementation.

This is the role of **exchange certification and conformance testing**. It is an external safety gate between your internal readiness and live trading. Certification answers questions such as:

- Does your gateway speak the venue's protocol correctly—field-by-field, message-by-message?
- Does your state machine for orders, cancels, and replaces align with the venue's rules?
- Do you behave safely under stress and failure scenarios (disconnects, sequence resets, rejects)?

- Can you produce evidence—logs, message captures, reports—to demonstrate what happened in a test session?

This section explains how to navigate that process in a disciplined way, and how to turn certification from a one-off hurdle into a continuing source of test cases and assurance.

Why Certification Matters in Practice

Venue certification is sometimes treated as a bureaucratic obligation: fill in a form, do a few scripted tests, collect an approval email, move on. That mindset is risky.

From a venue's point of view, your gateway is an unknown participant that could:

- send malformed messages that break their systems,
- mis-handle rejects or disconnects in ways that create runaway order flows,
- misunderstand order semantics, leading to unintended market impact,
- fail to honor risk and throttling rules, exposing the venue and other participants to excessive volatility.

Certification is their opportunity to ensure that your system is a well-behaved citizen of their market. For you, it is a chance to:

- validate your implementation against the definitive reference (the venue itself),
- uncover mismatches between your assumptions and their actual behavior,
- gather realistic test cases and transcripts for future regression testing.

Seen this way, certification is an extension of your own reliability and testing discipline, just operated by an external party with their own requirements.

Typical Certification Workflow

Most venues follow a broadly similar sequence, even if the details differ:

1. **Registration and documentation**
    - You apply for access, describing your role (broker, prop firm, vendor), order types, and expected volumes.
    - You receive protocol specifications, certification guides, and test case descriptions.
    - You are issued test credentials (session IDs, passwords, IP addresses, ports).
2. **Connectivity and handshake tests**
    - You establish test sessions (FIX, binary native, or both), perform logon/logoff, and verify heartbeats.
    - The venue verifies that you connect from approved IPs and respect session-level rules.
3. **Functional and semantic tests**
    - You execute scripted scenarios covering new orders, cancels, replaces, time-in-force, special order types, and basic recovery.
    - The venue checks that your messages conform to field rules and that your behavior matches their expected outcomes.
4. **Robustness and recovery tests**
    - The venue may simulate disconnects, resend requests, sequence resets, and rate-limiting conditions.
    - You must demonstrate that you handle these situations gracefully and consistently.
5. **Approval and ongoing obligations**
    - If tests pass, the venue issues an approval or certificate for production connection.

- You may be required to re-certify after major protocol changes or material modifications to your gateway or risk logic.

The rest of this section explores how to approach these stages systematically so they strengthen, rather than bypass, your internal quality bar.

Building an Internal Certification Harness

A common failure pattern is to drive certification by hand: engineers manually key in orders, watch the venue's test GUI, and adjust the gateway until the venue is satisfied. This may be workable once, but it is nearly impossible to repeat consistently, especially as venues or your own systems evolve.

A better approach is to build an **internal certification harness**: an automated layer that can:

- connect to the venue's test environment with the same gateways and risk engines used in production,
- drive the specified test scenarios as sequences of requests,
- capture all relevant outputs: venue responses, internal logs, protocol captures, and traces,
- produce an evidence pack that you can share with the venue and archive for internal audit.

Conceptually, the harness sits "above" your gateway, acting like a smart test client. For each venue test case (for example, "submit a day limit buy order, receive partial fill, then cancel remainder"), the harness:

- sends the appropriate API request to your gateway,
- monitors responses and state transitions,
- verifies that the sequence of outbound and inbound venue messages matches expectations.

By automating this, you gain several advantages:

- **Repeatability**: you can re-run the same tests after code changes or venue upgrades.
- **Coverage**: you can systematically cover corner cases that are easy to forget in manual testing.
- **Speed**: you can complete certification campaigns faster and with fewer human errors.

Crucially, the harness reuses your *existing* observability, test fixtures, and configuration management. It becomes another layer in your testing pyramid, not a separate throwaway effort.

Protocol Compliance: Field-Level Correctness

At the heart of certification is protocol correctness. For FIX or native binary protocols, this involves more than simply "sending syntactically valid messages." The venue will validate:

- **Required fields**: Are all mandatory tags present for each message type? Are their values in allowed ranges and formats?
- **Conditional rules**: When you specify a particular order type or time-in-force, are you including all dependent fields the venue expects?
- **Enumerations and codes**: Do you use the venue's codes correctly for sides, ord types, rejects, and execution types?
- **Versioning**: Are you using the correct protocol version, with up-to-date extensions or custom tags?

Many venues provide a certification script that lists test cases such as:

- Send a day limit order and receive an "accepted" acknowledgment.

- Send an order with an invalid price and receive a reject with error code X.
- Send a cancel request for an already filled order and receive a specific reject.

Your certification harness should encode these as assertions about both:

- your gateway's outbound messages (do they match the expected FIX fields or native fields?), and
- the venue's responses (do you parse and interpret them correctly?).

This is not just about passing certification. Protocol mismatches are a common source of subtle production bugs. Encoding the venue's rules into automated tests gives you a robust defense against regression when your mapping logic changes.

State Machines and Order Semantics

Beyond individual messages, venues care that your **order state machine** aligns with theirs. For a given scenario, they expect a particular sequence of states and transitions.

Consider a simple example:

1. You submit a new order: it moves from "New" to "Working" when acknowledged by the venue.
2. A partial execution arrives: the order moves to "Partially Filled" with updated remaining quantity.
3. You submit a cancel request: the order moves to "Pending Cancel" locally.
4. The venue confirms the cancel: the order moves to "Cancelled" with final quantities.

Certification tests will check that:

- you do not prematurely mark orders as filled or cancelled,
- you handle partials without losing track of remaining volume,
- you respond to rejects by reverting to appropriate states (for example, if a cancel is rejected because the order is already filled).

Touchpoints include:

- your internal in-memory state,
- your persistent order store,
- the audit trail you keep for regulatory purposes,
- what you expose to upstream clients or strategies.

Well-designed certification harnesses cross-check all of these views. If your internal state machine allows a transition that the venue never produces (for example, a direct jump from "New" to "Filled" without acknowledgments), that is a red flag to investigate, whether or not the venue's scripted tests surface it directly.

Recovery, Disconnects, and Sequence Handling

A key part of conformance is how you behave when things go wrong. Venues take seriously the risk that a participant mismanages:

- dropped TCP connections,
- missed heartbeats,
- gaps in sequence numbers,
- session logon/logoff transitions,
- failover from one session or physical connection to another.

Certification tests in this area may include steps like:

- Abruptly closing the connection mid-session and requiring you to reconnect and resynchronize sequences.
- Sending a "resend request" and verifying that you replay messages correctly.
- Introducing duplicate or out-of-order messages and observing whether you handle them according to specification.

For your architecture, already designed with externalized state and active-active services, these tests are important validation that:

- your replayable event logs and sequence stores behave as intended under real venue behavior,
- failover between gateway instances does not confuse the venue or violate session rules,
- your cancel-on-disconnect or kill-switch mechanisms are understood and honored by the venue where supported.

Carefully captured logs and protocol traces from these scenarios are extremely valuable. They help you refine your runbooks for live incidents and test your high-availability mechanisms under venue-supervised conditions.

Evidence Packs: Logs, Captures, and Screenshots

Venues often ask you to provide **evidence** of what occurred during certification: not only their own records, but also artifacts from your side. Typical elements of an evidence pack include:

- **Gateway logs**: structured records showing internal state changes, risk checks, and message sends/receives.
- **Protocol captures**: raw message streams captured as packet traces (pcap) or binary logs.
- **Screenshots or reports**: views of your internal monitoring or client-facing interfaces for selected test cases.

- **Summary tables**: mapping test case IDs to timestamps, order IDs, and outcomes.

If you have invested in strong observability, generating such packs becomes relatively straightforward:

- Use correlation IDs and consistent order identifiers so all evidence lines up cleanly.
- Establish standard log filters or queries that extract the relevant events for each test.
- Automate as much of the evidence assembly as possible in your certification harness.

These evidence packs serve not only the venue, but also your internal audit and compliance functions. They show, concretely, that you tested key behaviors before go-live, and how.

Re-Certification Triggers and Lifecycle Planning

Certification is not a one-time affair. Over the life of a gateway, you will likely need to re-certify several times. Common triggers include:

- **Venue protocol changes**: new message fields, deprecation of old versions, new order types or time-in-force options.
- **Material internal changes**: major rewrites of gateway code, risk logic changes, or new routing algorithms.
- **Scope expansion**: onboarding new asset classes, markets, or special access models (for example, co-location or certain low-latency programs)

A mature program therefore:

- Maintains a **certification calendar**, tracking upcoming venue changes and their deadlines.

- Links internal change management to certification requirements: a change that impacts protocol behavior or risk semantics cannot be promoted to production until relevant certification is done.
- Uses versioned configuration and infrastructure so that certification environments mirror the intended production state.

Your internal harness shines here: re-running updated certification suites becomes primarily an engineering exercise, not an organizational scramble.

Using Certification to Strengthen Internal Regression Suites

If you treat certification solely as a hurdle, you risk throwing away valuable knowledge once approval is obtained. A more productive approach is to **harvest certification scenarios as internal regression tests**.

For each venue test case:

- Encode it as an automated test in your harness, runnable against simulation environments without the venue's direct involvement.
- Capture the venue's expected behavior (message sequences, state transitions) as assertions.
- Add local variations that the venue did not explicitly require, but which are plausible in real trading (for example, different order sizes, subtle timing variations).

Over time, your internal suite will become richer than the venue's official script, while still anchored to it. When you change your gateway, risk logic, or infrastructure, you can run this suite to catch regressions early, long before the next formal certification.

This approach also supports multi-venue strategies. Although each venue has its own quirks, many behavioral themes repeat: handling partial fills, respecting cancel/replace rules, managing sequence resets. You can abstract shared testing patterns while preserving venue-specific details where necessary.

Collaboration with Venues and Brokers

Certification is a technical process, but it is also a relationship. Constructive collaboration with venue support teams yields benefits long beyond initial approval.

Practices that help:

- **Clear point of contact**: designate engineers who are responsible for day-to-day technical communication with the venue during certification and beyond.
- **Shared understanding of test coverage**: maintain a mapping between the venue's test cases and your internal requirements or risk controls. This clarifies what is, and is not, validated externally.
- **Feedback loops**: when a test uncovers an ambiguity or a documentation gap, engage with the venue to clarify and feed that knowledge back into your internal documentation and tests.

In some cases, venues may be willing to run additional ad-hoc tests to validate particular behaviors important to your strategies, such as specialized order types or unusual recovery patterns. It is easier to request and conduct such tests when you have already demonstrated diligence and preparedness.

Certification as Part of Your Reliability Story

Ultimately, exchange certification and conformance testing sit alongside your own reliability measures:

- **Your tests** ensure that the implementation behaves according to your intent and risk policies.

- **Your observability** ensures that you can see and explain live behavior.
- **Your high-availability and DR designs** ensure that behavior remains controlled across failures.
- **Venue certification** ensures that this behavior is compatible with the market's own rules and expectations.

When all four align, you have a robust foundation for going live:

- You can show regulators and clients that every gateway has passed both internal and external checks.
- You can trace any future incident back through logs, traces, and certification artifacts to determine root causes.
- You can adapt to evolving venue protocols and products without starting from scratch each time.

In the next section, we will look at chaos engineering and fault injection, which close the loop by deliberately inducing failures—including some that mimic venue behavior—to validate that your entire stack, from code to certification, behaves as expected under stress.

6.6 Chaos Engineering and Fault Injection

By this point in the chapter we have built a trading platform that, on paper, is robust: it is observable, thoroughly tested, highly available within and across sites, and certified by venues. Yet all of those assurances are based on *assumptions*:

- that health checks will notice failing components quickly enough,
- that circuit breakers will trip before an overload becomes a meltdown,
- that failover paths will really carry the load under stress,

- that DR runbooks will be followed correctly when a whole site is impaired.

Chaos engineering and fault injection are about **testing those assumptions in a disciplined way**. Rather than waiting for real markets and real incidents to reveal hidden weaknesses, you deliberately introduce controlled failures into your systems and observe what happens. When done well, this practice turns rare, high-impact events into something you have rehearsed.

In this section, we will:

- Define chaos experiments as structured tests, not random breakage.
- Identify typical fault scenarios for trading systems: network partitions, time skew, dependency outages, venue misbehavior.
- Describe how to design safe experiments in non-production and, later, in production with tight guardrails.
- Show how observability, HA patterns, and DR runbooks from earlier sections become key tools in planning and evaluating these experiments.
- Explain how to turn the findings into lasting improvements: new tests, alerts, and operational procedures.

Chaos Engineering as Hypothesis-Driven Testing

Chaos engineering is sometimes caricatured as "pulling plugs at random." That is not helpful or accurate, especially in finance. In a trading context, chaos experiments must be:

- **hypothesis-driven**,
- **controlled and observable**,
- **reversible**, with clear abort conditions.

A simple template for an experiment is:

- 1. Define steady state. Identify measurable signals that represent "normal" behavior for the system. For example:
  - order acceptance rate for a given test client,
  - median and 99th-percentile end-to-end latency,
  - error and reject rates,
  - risk limit enforcement (e.g., no orders beyond a limit).
- 2. Formulate a hypothesis. For a chosen failure mode, state what you *expect* to happen. For example:

  > "If a single gateway instance fails, then overall order acceptance rate remains within 5% of baseline, and no duplicate or dropped orders occur, as measured by audit trails and venue views."
- 3. Inject the fault. Introduce the failure in a controlled way:
  - kill a process,
  - add latency or packet loss on a network link,
  - simulate a stalled risk service,
  - skew clocks between components.
- 4. Observe and compare. Use your logging, metrics, and tracing to see whether the system's behavior matches the hypothesis:
  - did the right health checks and circuit breakers activate?
  - did failover paths and DR mechanisms work as designed?
  - what was the impact on latency, errors, and user-visible behavior?
- 5. Learn and improve. If reality diverges from the hypothesis, identify why and fix the gaps: code, configuration, alerts, or runbooks. Then add automated tests where possible.

In other words, chaos engineering is an extension of the testing pyramid introduced earlier, but focused on complex, emergent behaviors that only show up when multiple components fail or interact in surprising ways.

Choosing Failure Scenarios for Trading Systems

Not all failures are equally interesting. For trading infrastructure, you want to focus on faults that:

- are realistic given your hardware, software, and network architecture,
- can materially affect order flow, risk management, or regulatory obligations,
- test the specific safeguards you have built: high availability, circuit breakers, DR procedures.

Several classes of faults stand out.

Network Partitions and Degradations

Trading systems are distributed by nature: gateways, risk engines, state stores, market data handlers, and venues are connected by networks that can fail in partial, asymmetric ways.

Faults to consider include:

- **Gateway–venue link degradation:** increased latency, packet loss, or intermittent disconnects between a gateway and an exchange.
- **Intra-site partition:** a subset of application servers loses access to shared state stores or message buses.
- **Inter-site partition:** the DR site loses real-time replication from the primary site, or a geo-balancing mechanism starts routing clients to a site that has stale data.

Hypotheses might be:

- If latency and packet loss between gateway and venue exceed threshold X, the circuit breaker should declare the venue unhealthy, route new orders elsewhere where allowed, and fail others fast with clear rejects.

- If a gateway instance cannot reach the central order state store, it should remove itself from service rather than continuing to accept orders it cannot persist.

Time Skew and Clock Failures

Earlier we emphasized precise, synchronized clocks for logging and latency measurement. But what happens if that synchronization breaks?

Possible experiments:

- Intentionally skew the clock on one gateway instance by a small but non-trivial amount (e.g., several milliseconds) and observe:
  - Are health checks monitoring clock offset and flagging this instance?
  - Do its timestamps cause apparent out-of-order events that confuse your tracing and monitoring?
- Skew the clock of a risk engine relative to gateways and see:
  - Does time-based risk logic (e.g., per-minute limits) misbehave?
  - Do audit trails remain coherent when reconstructed later?

The goal is not to accept large clock drift as normal, but to verify that drifts are detected and that diagnostic tools remain usable when they occur.

Dependency Failures: Risk, Reference Data, and State Stores

Your gateways depend on several internal services:

- pre-trade risk engines,
- credit and limits services,
- reference data services (instruments, symbols, trading status),
- central state stores and databases.

Chaos scenarios here include:

- **Risk engine stall:** simulate extreme slowness or failure of risk checks.
- **Reference data unavailability:** make symbol lookup calls fail or return delayed results.
- **State store degradation:** add latency to writes, or temporarily make the primary database read-only.

Your hypotheses might be:

- If the risk engine does not respond within Y milliseconds, the gateway should reject new orders with a specific error, rather than hanging clients.
- If reference data is unavailable, the system should either:
  - fail fast with explicit "instrument unknown" errors, or
  - continue trading only for instruments whose configuration is already safely cached and validated.
- If the order state database cannot be written to, gateways should stop accepting new orders rather than trading "blind."

These experiments stress your brownout policies: which functions are allowed to degrade, and which must fail closed to protect the firm and clients.

Venue and Market-Data Anomalies

Faults outside your own infrastructure are also worth testing, especially if you can simulate them without involving the actual venue:

- **Market data gaps or bursts:** delayed, dropped, or duplicated price updates from simulated feeds.
- **Unexpected rejects:** a higher-than-normal rate of order rejections from fake venues to stress your reject-handling and backoff logic.

- **Session behavior anomalies:** simulated sequence gaps, out-of-order execution reports, or late cancel/replace responses.

Here, your hypotheses might involve:

- ensuring your strategies do not assume perfect, gapless market data,
- confirming that gateways and routers interpret venue responses correctly under stress,
- verifying that your observability stack highlights these anomalies clearly for operators.

Starting Safely: Non-Production Experiments

Financial markets are unforgiving; you cannot start by "pulling cables" in your live environment. Instead, build your practice in non-production settings and gradually increase realism.

Key principles for early-stage chaos work:

Use production-like environments. Your test or staging environments should:

- run the same code versions as production,
- use comparable configurations and topologies (e.g., number of gateways, clustering patterns),
- connect to test venues or simulated exchanges, not production sessions.

Without this similarity, your experiments may give a false sense of security.

Replay realistic traffic. To see meaningful effects, drive these environments with:

- recorded production order flows and market data (appropriately anonymized and time-shifted), or

- synthetic workloads calibrated to match the volume and patterns of your real strategies.

This aligns with the system and performance tests described earlier; chaos experiments can piggyback on those harnesses, adding fault scenarios during test runs.

Automate fault injection. Instead of ad-hoc manual interventions, use tools or scripts that can:

- introduce network latency or packet loss on defined links,
- restart or kill particular processes,
- toggle feature flags or configuration switches (e.g., disabling a service),
- alter clock offsets within a controlled range on selected hosts.

Automation ensures repeatability and avoids human error during the experiments.

Graduating to Controlled Production Experiments

Once you have confidence in your mechanisms and procedures in test environments, you may consider limited chaos experiments in production. This is not obligatory, and many firms choose to stay entirely in non-production. If you do proceed, additional safeguards are essential.

Narrow scope. Limit production experiments to:

- a small subset of hosts or instances,
- services that you have designed to fail over seamlessly (e.g., a single gateway in a large active-active cluster),
- off-peak periods where trading volumes and risk are lower.

Strict abort conditions. Define in advance:

- thresholds on key metrics (latency, error rates, order rejections) that will immediately halt the experiment,

- human oversight requirements: someone with authority to abort must be watching,
- clear rollback steps (e.g., re-enabling instances, restoring normal routing).

Stakeholder sign-off. Involve risk management, trading desks, and operations:

- explain the proposed experiment, its scope, and its safeguards,
- agree on what constitutes unacceptable impact,
- schedule the experiment so critical clients or strategies can adjust if needed.

Even with these controls, production chaos should be approached cautiously and iteratively. The goal is not to be adventurous, but to gradually increase confidence that your protections behave correctly in the exact environment that matters most.

Measuring and Interpreting Impact

Chaos experiments are only as useful as your ability to *measure* their effects. This is where observability—logs, metrics, traces, and audit trails—returns to center stage.

During and after each experiment, you will want to analyze:

- **Latency and throughput**: Did median and tail latencies stay within agreed bounds? Did throughput drop more than expected?
- **Error and reject patterns**: Did error rates spike? Were rejects consistent with the failure mode (e.g., "risk engine unavailable")?
- **Failover behavior**: How long did it take for health checks and circuit breakers to react? Did traffic redistribute as intended?
- **Order and risk integrity**: Did any orders get lost, duplicated, or routed in violation of limits? Do audit trails and venue records reconcile?

End-to-end traces are particularly valuable. They let you see:

- exactly where additional latency was introduced,
- whether retries and timeouts behaved correctly,
- whether unexpected dependencies were dragged into the failure's blast radius.

If your experimental results match your hypotheses closely, that increases confidence that your resilience designs are functioning. If they diverge, the discrepancies tell you where your mental model of the system was wrong.

Feeding Learnings Back into Tests and Runbooks

Each chaos experiment should leave the system in a slightly better state than before, even if the experiment itself "failed" by exposing problems. To achieve that, institutionalize a feedback process:

Post-experiment review. Just like a post-incident review, conduct a structured debrief:

- Did the system behave exactly as expected? If not, why?
- Were alerts triggered appropriately—not too early, not too late, and not excessively noisy?
- Did on-call engineers or operators have the right tools and information to interpret what they saw?

Concrete actions. From this review, derive specific follow-ups:

- **Code changes**: fix bugs in health checks, timeouts, retry logic, or state management uncovered by the experiment.
- **Configuration updates**: adjust circuit breaker thresholds, routing rules, or brownout policies.
- **New tests**: add unit, integration, or system tests that simulate the observed failure mode without requiring full chaos infrastructure.

- **Runbook revisions**: update DR and incident-handling procedures with what you learned.

Documentation and evidence. Record the experiment and its outcomes:

- parameters and hypotheses,
- metrics and traces collected,
- issues discovered and how they were addressed.

These records are useful not only for internal learning but also for demonstrating to regulators and clients that your reliability claims are backed by empirical testing.

Integrating Chaos Engineering into Regular Practice

Finally, chaos engineering should not be an occasional spectacle. Its value multiplies when integrated into routine reliability practice:

- Schedule **regular experiments**, even if small, as part of your reliability calendar: for example, monthly non-production drills and quarterly broader scenarios.
- Align experiments with **change cycles**: after major architectural changes (new HA design, new DR topology, new risk engine), design specific chaos tests to validate them.
- Coordinate with **DR drills**: combine site-level failover exercises with more focused fault injections to see how local and global mechanisms interact.
- Use **metrics and error budgets** (from earlier sections) to inform where to focus: systems or venues consuming most of your error budget are good candidates for targeted chaos work.

Over time, this practice changes the culture around failure. Instead of being surprising, rare, and paralyzing, failures—at least in their common forms—become familiar and rehearsed. The organization gains a realistic understanding of its resilience strengths and weaknesses, grounded not in slideware but in observed behavior.

From Assumptions to Evidence

Chaos engineering and fault injection close the loop on everything discussed in this chapter:

- Observability provides the eyes and ears to see how faults propagate.
- Automated tests give you a stable baseline and isolate smaller logic errors.
- High availability and DR architectures supply the mechanisms that are being tested.
- Exchange certification ensures your gateway behaves well from a venue's perspective, while chaos ensures it behaves well under stress and failure.

In modern electronic markets, it is not enough to say "our system should survive a host failure" or "our DR site should take over in 15 minutes." You must be able to say: *"We have repeatedly tested those scenarios under controlled conditions, observed the outcomes, and corrected weaknesses. Here is the evidence."*

Chaos engineering, applied thoughtfully, turns that aspiration into something concrete. It shifts your reliability story from belief to measured fact, reinforcing the central theme of this book: that the journey from backtest to live execution must be anchored not only in models and code, but in hard-won operational understanding of how those systems behave when the market and the environment push them to their limits.

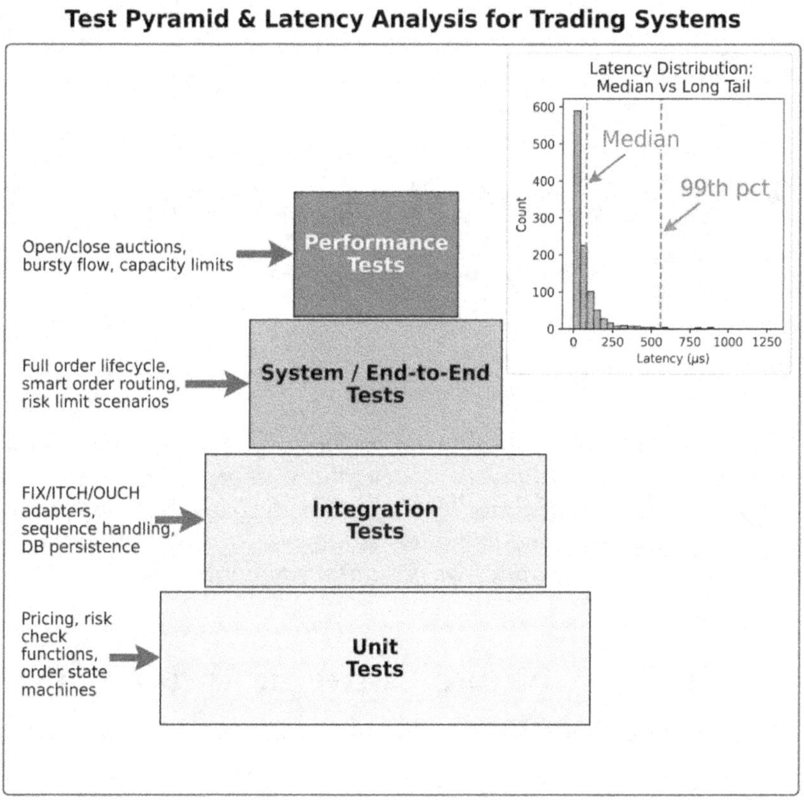

Figure 6.1: The automated test pyramid for trading systems, annotated with typical examples at each layer and an inset showing why latency tests must focus on the long tail, not only the median.

Chapter 7

Deployment, Cutover, and Governance

A trading strategy is only as good as the way it is changed in production. This chapter shows how disciplined deployment, staged cutover, and robust governance turn fragile code drops into repeatable, auditable upgrades-so your models can evolve quickly without ever losing control of risk, capital, or regulatory obligations.

7.1 CI/CD, Change Control, and Segregation of Duties

In earlier chapters we focused on how to design, backtest, and validate trading strategies so that they are statistically sound and operationally realistic. We now turn to a different question: once you have a strategy that appears ready, how do you move it from a developer's laptop into the exchange matching engine in a way that is repeatable, controlled, and auditable?

In electronic markets, the move from source code to live binaries is not a mere technicality. A broken build, a misconfigured risk limit, or an unreviewed bug fix can immediately translate into rejected orders, missed fills, or, in the worst case, uncontrolled trading and regulatory breaches. A production-grade continuous integration and continuous delivery (CI/CD) pipeline is the mechanism that connects your research work to the live market, while enforcing the risk controls and governance standards regulators expect from algorithmic trading firms.

At a high level, a CI/CD pipeline for trading systems defines a *single, standard path* that every change must follow:

1. A developer commits a change to version control.

2. Automated systems build the code and run tests (unit, integration, replay, simulation).

3. If all checks pass, a deployable artifact (binary, container image) is published.

4. The change is linked to a tracked ticket, reviewed, approved, and promoted through environments (development, test, UAT, production).

5. Each promotion step is gated by explicit approvals, logs, and, where required, sign-off from risk and compliance.

The rest of this section makes this flow concrete, and shows how it embeds three key ideas: robust automation (CI/CD), formal change control, and segregation of duties.

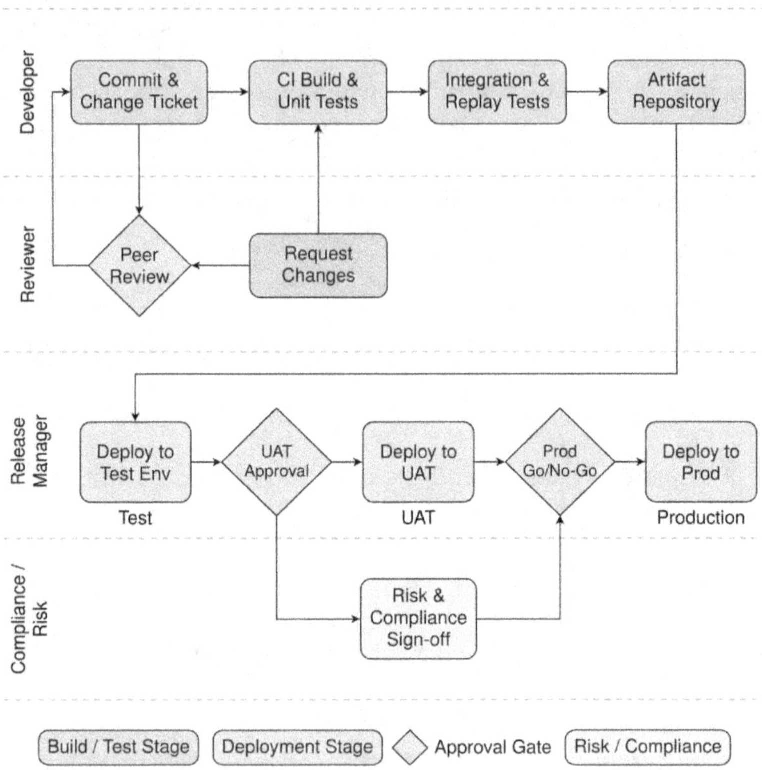

From Source Control to Reproducible Artifacts

The foundation of any CI/CD pipeline is reliable version control. In a trading context, this is more than a collaboration tool; it is a legal and operational record of exactly which code produced which orders.

Version tagging and traceability.

Every change that might affect trading—strategy logic, risk checks, order-routing rules, connectivity adapters—must live in a source repository with:

- Unique commit identifiers, so you can say "this particular hash was running when we sent these orders."

- Branching policies that distinguish stable branches (used for releases) from feature branches (used for research and experimentation).
- Release tags that mark the specific commit associated with each production deployment.

In an incident investigation, you should be able to take an order ID, look up which application instance handled it, see which artifact it was running, and follow a chain of references back to a tagged commit in version control and an associated change ticket.

Reproducible builds.

A reproducible build means that if you build the same version again, with the same configuration, you get an identical binary or container. This matters because regulators and internal audit may ask you to rerun a previous version to explain behaviour. To achieve this:

- Automate builds on CI servers rather than building on individual laptops.
- Fix dependency versions (libraries, compilers, runtimes) or bundle them into containers.
- Store build metadata: commit hash, build time, CI job ID, build parameters.

The output of this process is a versioned artifact (for example, a container image or executable package) in a central artifact repository. No one should ever "sneak" a hand-built binary into production; if it did not come through the pipeline, it does not run.

Automated Test Stages: Unit, Integration, Replay, Simulation

After a change is committed, the CI pipeline acts as your first line of defence, rejecting bad changes automatically. In trading, you typically layer several kinds of tests, each catching different classes of error.

Unit tests: correctness of small pieces.

Unit tests check individual functions or components in isolation. For example:

- Does the order sizing function compute the correct clip size given volatility and target participation?
- Does the risk check reject orders that exceed a symbol's maximum notional limit?
- Does the parser correctly interpret a FIX message and populate internal fields?

Unit tests are fast and run on every commit. They protect you from many simple logic errors that could otherwise leak into higher environments.

Integration tests: components working together.

Integration tests check that multiple components interact correctly. In a trading stack, this may include:

- The strategy engine sending an order through the risk gateway to a simulated exchange gateway.
- The OMS and market data feed handler staying in sync across restarts.
- The translation between internal order objects and external FIX or native protocol messages.

Integration tests are slower than unit tests, but they reveal class of issues that only appear when systems talk to each other: mismatched field formats, wrong message sequencing, or unexpected timeouts.

Replay tests: behaviour on historical tapes.

Replay tests feed recorded market data and historical events into the system to see how the new version behaves compared with a known-good baseline. Typical questions include:

- Does the new strategy version produce materially different orders under the same historical conditions?

- Are there new spikes in order cancellations or rejects?
- Does the new code path remain within expected latency bounds?

Replay testing is particularly powerful because it exercises the system under realistic market microstructure: auctions, halts, bursts of activity after news.

Simulation suites: end-to-end scenarios.

Simulation takes replay a step further by modelling both the market and your P&L. For example:

- Simulate a morning with a major economic release and see whether the new strategy respects risk limits and position caps.
- Simulate a deteriorating network and see how the system degrades and recovers.

These suites run less frequently (for example, nightly or on release candidates) but provide the deepest assurance that a configuration is safe to move forward.

A production-grade pipeline orders these stages so that cheap tests run first and expensive tests run only after earlier checks pass. The result is an automated "funnel" that filters out most unsafe changes long before humans need to intervene.

Formal Change Management: Tickets, Reviews, and Approvals

Automation alone is not enough. Regulators and exchanges expect firms to demonstrate that they know *who* changed *what*, *why*, and *when*, and that those changes were approved by appropriate people. This is the role of formal change management.

Change tickets as the spine of control.

A change ticket is a record in a tracking system (for example, an internal change-management tool or issue tracker) that describes:

- The purpose of the change (bug fix, new feature, parameter adjustment).

- The systems and instruments affected.
- The associated risks and expected impact.
- Links to code commits, test results, and deployment logs.

Every code change that could touch production must be linked to a ticket. In turn, the CI/CD pipeline is configured to require a valid ticket identifier before accepting a merge or a deployment. This linkage between code and ticket is what makes the pipeline auditable.

Peer review and code ownership.

Before a change is allowed to progress, it should undergo peer review by someone other than its author. In practice:

- Merge requests (or pull requests) are required for all changes to protected branches.
- Each merge request must be approved by at least one designated reviewer.
- Code ownership rules define which teams or individuals are authorized to review specific areas (for example, only the risk team can approve changes to pre-trade checks).

Peer review is not just a quality practice; in trading, it is also a fraud and error control. A second set of eyes can catch not only mistakes but also any unauthorized attempts to weaken safeguards.

Sign-off matrices and environment promotions.

A sign-off matrix defines which roles must approve which types of changes at which stages. For example:

- A minor UI change for a monitoring dashboard might require approval only from technology.
- A new order type or strategy change affecting client flow might require approvals from technology, trading desk leadership, and compliance.
- Any change that affects regulatory reporting fields may additionally need sign-off from operations and regulatory reporting teams.

The CI/CD tooling enforces this matrix by preventing promotion to the next environment unless required approvals are present. For instance, a build could be deployed automatically to a test environment after automated tests, but moving to user acceptance testing (UAT) might require sign-off from trading, while moving from UAT to production demands both trading and risk/compliance approvals.

Segregation of Duties: Who May Do What

Segregation of duties (SoD) is the principle that critical functions should be split across different people or teams so that no single individual can unilaterally cause (or hide) a serious problem. In trading, SoD is both a best practice and a regulatory expectation.

Separating strategy research from production operations.

Researchers and quantitative developers are incentivized to experiment quickly. Production operations is incentivized to keep the system stable. A healthy pipeline respects both:

- Researchers can freely commit to feature branches, run backtests, and experiment in isolated environments.
- Only release managers or designated operations engineers can approve and execute deployments to production.

This means a researcher cannot directly push a new strategy version to the live system; their work must pass through review, testing, and promotion steps controlled by other roles.

Separating development from release management.

Even within technology, you typically distinguish:

- **Developers**, who write and submit changes.
- **Reviewers**, often senior engineers or domain owners, who review and approve changes.
- **Release managers** or **production engineers**, who control deployments to shared environments, particularly production.

Tooling enforces these distinctions by:

- Restricting who may merge into release or main branches.
- Restricting who may trigger or approve a production deployment.
- Logging every such action with user identity, timestamp, and associated ticket.

If your pipeline relies on informal agreements ("we usually ask Bob before deploying"), you do not yet have real segregation of duties.

Segregation across business functions.

Beyond technology, other functions must be involved:

- **Trading and business owners**: accountable for the commercial rationale and risk of strategy changes.
- **Risk management**: accountable for ensuring pre-trade and post-trade controls remain effective.
- **Compliance**: accountable for ensuring alignment with algorithmic-trading and market-abuse regulations.

For high-impact changes, SoD means that trading cannot approve its own changes in isolation. Compliance or independent risk must have defined approval steps, and their approvals must be required by the pipeline before deployment.

Encoding Governance in CI/CD Tooling

A key theme is that governance rules should not live only in policy documents; they must be encoded into the tools that engineers and traders use every day. This reduces reliance on memory and goodwill, and provides a hard technical barrier against non-compliant behaviour.

Protected branches.

Protected branches are main or release branches where:

- Direct pushes are forbidden; all changes must come through merge requests.
- Specific status checks (test suites) must pass before merging.
- Required reviewers are enforced by the platform; merges without their approval are blocked.

For example, you might require that any change touching a risk module must:

1. Pass all unit and integration tests.
2. Pass replay tests for a set of stressed days.
3. Receive approval from a risk-module code owner.

The platform simply will not allow merging otherwise.

Mandatory code owners.

Code-owner rules map directories or files to designated owners. When a change affects those paths, the CI/CD system automatically requests their review. This prevents situations where someone outside the risk team silently changes a risk limit or bypasses a pre-trade check.

Audit logs and observability of change.

Every action in the pipeline should leave a durable trace:

- Who authored and reviewed each change.
- Which tests ran, when, and with what outcomes.
- When a specific artifact was deployed to each environment, by whom, and under which ticket.

These logs are invaluable in three situations:

1. **Incident response**: tracing which change caused a problem and whether to roll back.
2. **Regulatory inquiries**: demonstrating that you have disciplined control over algorithm changes.
3. **Internal audit**: proving that policies (for example, SoD, review requirements) are not just written but enforced.

Balancing Speed and Control

A natural tension arises: quants want quick iteration to adapt to market conditions; governance wants careful review and stability. A well-designed pipeline accommodates both, by separating where you move fast from where you move carefully.

Fast loops in non-production environments.

In research and early testing environments:

- CI runs core unit tests on every commit to catch basic errors quickly.
- Integration and replay tests may be scheduled more flexibly, for example triggered by developers or run nightly.
- Branch protection can be lighter, allowing rapid experimentation.

This supports creativity and responsiveness without exposing the firm to live-market risk.

Strict gates near production.

As changes approach production:

- Branches become more protected; only release candidates pass into UAT.
- Test requirements grow stricter, and additional checks (performance benchmarks, stress replays) are required.
- Approval requirements expand to include business, risk, and compliance stakeholders depending on impact.

The result is a "narrow neck" near production: many ideas enter the pipeline, but relatively few, well-tested, well-reviewed changes exit into the live market.

Designing for predictability.

Finally, the pipeline itself should be predictable. Teams should understand:

- Typical lead times from code completion to production deployment, given current controls.
- Which types of changes can move more quickly (for example, non-functional monitoring improvements) and which must move slowly (for example, strategy logic, risk limits, regulatory reporting).
- How to package a set of changes into a release that is small enough to reason about, but large enough to be worth the overhead of approvals and testing.

This predictability lets trading and risk teams plan around releases, schedule cutovers at appropriate market times (as discussed later in the chapter), and maintain clear expectations about how quickly the organization can respond to issues or opportunities.

A production-grade CI/CD pipeline for trading systems is not just a convenience for developers; it is a central risk-control mechanism. By combining automated builds and layered tests with formal change tickets, peer review, sign-off matrices, and strict segregation of duties, the pipeline ensures that every alteration to your trading stack is:

- Technically sound, having passed appropriate automated checks.
- Organizationally legitimate, having been reviewed and approved by the right people.
- Operationally traceable, with a clear lineage from market behaviour back to code, configuration, and decisions.

In the next sections, we will build on this foundation by exploring how configuration management, feature flags, and rollout strategies let you adjust behaviour in production while still honouring the same principles of control and auditability.

7.2 Config Management, Feature Flags, and Safe Defaults

In the previous section we built a disciplined path for getting new code into production: version-controlled changes, automated tests, and gated deployments with clear approvals. That pipeline answers the question, *"How does code change safely?"*

In live trading, however, most day-to-day adjustments should not require new code at all. Traders want to nudge aggressiveness, risk officers want to tighten limits on certain symbols, and operations wants to reroute flow away from a problematic venue. Doing all of this through fresh builds and releases would be slow and unnecessarily risky.

This section explains how to design your systems so that:

- Strategy behaviour is largely controlled through configuration rather than code.
- Feature flags allow you to ship capabilities in a dormant state, and then selectively turn them on or off.
- Conservative, "fail-safe" defaults protect you whenever configuration is missing, inconsistent, or stressed.

Together, these practices let you move quickly *within* a safe envelope, while still respecting the governance and audit discipline established earlier.

Why Externalize Behaviour into Configuration?

Think of your trading engine as a machine with two kinds of levers:

- **Structural levers**: the core algorithms, data structures, and system design. Changing these usually means changing code.
- **Tuning levers**: parameters, limits, and choices that adjust how the strategy behaves within its existing structure.

Most operational decisions concern tuning, not structure:

- Lower participation in an illiquid small-cap name for the afternoon.
- Temporarily disable trading on a venue that is misbehaving.
- Increase minimum order size on a futures contract ahead of a roll event.

If these tuning levers are compiled into the code, changing them requires a new build and a full release cycle. That is slow and can blur the line between "business-as-usual" adjustments and genuine code changes.

Configuration as a first-class control surface. The alternative is to design your system so that:

- The *logic* of the strategy is in code.
- The *behaviour* of the strategy under given conditions is almost entirely controlled by external configuration.

"External" here means:

- Stored outside the binary (for example in files, a configuration service, or a database).
- Versioned and auditable just like code.
- Changeable under a clear, lighter-weight governance process than full code deployment, but still with dual control for high-risk items.

Proper configuration management gives traders, risk, and operations a powerful control surface, while your CI/CD pipeline continues to govern actual software changes.

What Belongs in Code vs. What Belongs in Config

Deciding what to externalize is partly art, partly discipline. A practical way to think about it is: "Is this something we might reasonably want to change while the market is open, without re-deploying the application?"

Typical candidates for configuration. Common items that should usually live in configuration include:

- **Per-instrument and per-venue limits**: maximum order size, maximum daily notional, max open orders, max participation rate.
- **Trading eligibility flags**: whether a particular symbol, venue, or client is enabled for a given strategy.
- **Aggressiveness and scheduling parameters**: desired urgency levels, participation caps, schedule curves by time-of-day.
- **Routing preferences**: venue ranking, whether to use certain order types (for example midpoint, dark, or auction orders).
- **Risk thresholds**: warning and hard-stop levels for P&L drawdown, inventory limits, or volatility filters.

What usually stays in code. Conversely, items that typically *do not* belong in configuration include:

- The fundamental strategy logic (how you estimate fair value, how you derive target inventory).
- The structure of your order book model or simulation engine.
- Concurrency and performance-related designs such as threading models or data structures.

These are structural choices that, when changed, deserve the full rigor of the CI/CD pipeline and extensive testing.

Benefits of this separation. By being deliberate about this boundary you:

- Reduce the frequency of code releases needed to manage normal trading operations.

- Allow different teams (trading, risk, operations) to have controlled influence over behaviour without writing code.
- Make your system easier to reason about: code describes what the system *can* do; configuration controls what it *actually* does today.

Designing Safe and Clear Configuration Schemas

Once you accept that configuration is a primary control, you must treat it with the same care as code. A vague, poorly structured configuration is a breeding ground for subtle errors.

Structured, typed parameters. Configuration should be organised and typed, not just a bag of free-form values. Even if you use simple formats such as text files or key-value stores, you should conceptually define:

- **Data types**: integer, decimal, text, boolean, list, etc.
- **Expected ranges**: for example, participation rate between 0 and 0.2; maximum order size greater than zero but less than a risk-defined ceiling.
- **Units**: explicitly specify whether a number is in shares, lots, currency units, basis points, seconds, or percentage-of-volume.

Although you may not write code here in the text, the actual system should validate that configuration values respect these types and ranges before trading with them.

Hierarchical configuration: from global to instrument. Trading systems usually need different settings at multiple levels. A useful pattern is a hierarchy such as:

- **Global defaults**: baseline limits and parameters applicable to everything unless overridden.
- **Asset-class or region-level**: equities vs. futures vs. FX; North America vs. Europe.

- **Venue-level**: specific exchanges or MTFs; perhaps with different throttles or eligible order types.
- **Strategy or client-level**: different clients may have different risk appetites and constraints.
- **Instrument-level**: individual symbols or contracts needing bespoke treatment.

When a strategy needs a configuration value, it should resolve it by walking down this hierarchy. For example, the max participation rate for a specific equity on a particular venue might be:

- 10% by global default,
- overridden to 5% for equities in emerging markets,
- overridden again to 3% for a specific illiquid symbol.

Clear rules for how overrides are applied make behaviour predictable and easier to audit.

Human-readable and machine-checkable. Configuration has two audiences:

- Humans, who need to understand and review it.
- Machines, which must enforce it correctly and safely.

Good configuration design therefore aims for:

- Simple, descriptive names (for example, `max_daily_notional_usd` rather than a cryptic code).
- Grouping related parameters together (for example, all volatility-related settings in one section).
- Commentary fields or description fields that explain the business meaning of each key parameter.

This makes configuration reviews—which are effectively risk reviews—much more effective.

From Configuration to Feature Flags

Configuration controls *how much* or *how* a given capability is used. Feature flags control *whether* a capability is active at all, for whom, and when.

What is a feature flag? A feature flag is a controlled switch in your system that can turn a behaviour on or off without changing code. Crucially:

- The underlying code is present and deployed.
- The flag decides whether that code path is exercised for a given request.

In trading, common examples include:

- A new strategy version that you want to run only for a test client.
- A new order type (for example an auction-only instruction) that you want to enable only on one venue.
- A new hedging module that you want to enable for one instrument at first.

Decoupling deployment from activation. Recall from the CI/CD section that deploying code into production is a controlled, sometimes infrequent event. With feature flags, you can:

- Deploy new code well ahead of when you expect to actually use it.
- Test that it behaves correctly in non-trading modes (for example shadow mode or simulation) while it is still turned off for real orders.
- Switch it on for a small slice of flow at a chosen time, without another deployment.

This decoupling solves an important problem: you may prefer to deploy large chunks of infrastructure during quiet windows (for example weekends), but only activate risky functionality later, in a stepped and observable way.

Dimensions of flag control. Feature flags are more powerful when you can condition them on multiple dimensions, such as:

- **Environment**: enabled in test and UAT, disabled in production.
- **Venue or market**: enabled on one exchange, disabled elsewhere.
- **Client or account**: enabled for one pilot client, disabled for others.
- **Time window**: enabled between particular times or dates.
- **Percentage of flow**: enabled for a random subset of orders, allowing canary rollouts.

You will see later in the chapter how these capabilities support staged rollouts and volume ramping; here the point is that flags make behaviour highly selective and reversible.

Safe Defaults: Assume "Off" Unless Explicitly Enabled

When you accumulate many configuration parameters and flags, an important question arises: *what happens if something is missing, wrong, or contradictory?* Your answer to that question is your default behaviour.

The principle of conservative defaults. In trading, default behaviour should be *conservative*:

- If an instrument has no explicit configuration, it should not trade.
- If a risk limit is missing, the system should assume it is zero or very small, not infinite.
- If a feature flag's configuration is unclear or broken, the feature should be considered disabled.

This is often summarised as "trading must be explicitly enabled, not the other way around." It may feel restrictive, but it turns configuration mistakes into lost trading opportunities, not into uncontrolled risk.

Fail-safe evaluation of configuration. To make conservative defaults real rather than aspirational:

- When the system starts up, it should validate that all required configuration is present and well-formed.
- Any failure to parse, missing key, or out-of-range value should cause either:
  - A clear refusal to start trading, or
  - An immediate clamp to a safe mode, such as disabling affected instruments or routes.
- During operation, if configuration cannot be loaded or updated (for example due to connectivity issues), the system should *not* silently revert to permissive values.

Think of configuration as a contract: either it is present and valid, or the system admits it cannot honour it and steps back.

Guardrails and circuit breakers. Safe defaults interact with dynamic guardrails such as:

- Per-symbol volume or notional caps.
- Firm-wide exposure limits.
- Latency or error-rate thresholds that trigger automatic pauses.

Even if configuration appears correct, live trading can move into unknown territory (for example sudden volatility spikes). Circuit breakers should detect when behaviour or metrics exceed expected bounds and temporarily override configuration by clamping down on activity. Again, if in doubt, the system should favour reducing or halting flow.

Governance for Configuration and Flags

Configuration and feature flags give you flexibility, but they also become potential vectors for mistakes or abuse. Their governance should be deliberate, though generally lighter than code changes.

Aligning configuration changes with change tickets. Earlier we required that all code changes be tied to a change ticket. The same should be true for material configuration changes, especially those that:

- Enable or disable trading for a client, venue, or symbol.
- Adjust key risk limits or throttles.
- Turn on a new strategy version or major feature flag in production.

The change ticket should:

- Describe which configuration keys or flags will change.
- Specify the before/after values.
- Provide an impact assessment and rollback plan (for example immediate reversion to previous values).

Dual control and role separation. Segregation of duties applies to configuration as much as code:

- The person proposing a configuration change (for example a trader) should not be the same person who approves it.
- High-risk changes (for example to a firm-wide max notional limit) should require explicit sign-off from risk or compliance.
- Only a controlled group (for example operations or production support) should have the technical ability to push configuration into the live system.

Many firms implement a "four-eyes" principle for configuration affecting trading: one person suggests and prepares changes; another reviews and executes them.

Logs and periodic reviews. Because configuration and flags may change more frequently than code, their history can become messy unless you manage it carefully. Good practice includes:

- Logging every configuration change with timestamp, user identity, and associated ticket.
- Keeping previous versions (for example in a version control system) so that rollbacks are straightforward.
- Scheduling regular reviews, where risk and trading teams inspect currently active configurations and flags to:
  - Retire one-off overrides that are no longer needed.
  - Confirm that temporary relaxations have been reverted.
  - Check for drift from stated risk appetite.

These reviews act as hygiene for a configuration landscape that would otherwise accrete exceptions and workarounds over time.

Putting It All Together

We can now see how configuration management, feature flags, and safe defaults extend the CI/CD foundation from the previous section:

- The CI/CD pipeline governs how new *capabilities* (code) are created, tested, and deployed.
- Configuration and feature flags govern how those capabilities are actually *used* in production on a day-to-day basis.
- Safe defaults and circuit breakers ensure that when configuration fails, the system errs on the side of reducing risk rather than increasing it.

A well-designed trading platform therefore has two complementary layers of control:

- A slow, highly governed path for code changes, where you accept some friction because the stakes are high and changes are relatively infrequent.

- A faster, but still controlled, path for configuration and feature-flag changes, where business teams can adjust behaviour within a clearly defined safety envelope.

In the next sections, we will see how these tools support structured release planning, staged rollouts, and session-aware cutovers: deciding not only *what* to deploy and *how* to configure it, but also *when* and *how fast* to expose new behaviour to live order flow.

7.3 Release Planning, Go/No-Go, and Backout Plans

The previous sections established the building blocks of safe change: a CI/CD pipeline that produces tested artifacts, and configuration and feature-flag mechanisms that let you steer behaviour in production. This section addresses a more strategic question: *how do you package and schedule those changes so that each release is a manageable, well-understood unit of risk?*

In most trading organisations, the notion of a "release" is broader than any single code commit. A release is the set of changes—code, configuration, data structures, operational procedures—that will be introduced into production together, under a single decision and a single backout plan. Well-run firms treat releases not as bundles of features, but as *bundles of risk* that must be consciously accepted.

We will move step by step:

- From individual changes to coherent releases.
- From vague intentions to explicit release charters.
- From informal confidence to structured go/no-go criteria.
- From wishful thinking about "rollback" to concrete, rehearsed backout plans.

From Changes to Releases: Defining the Unit of Risk

A change in a trading system can be as small as renaming a field or as large as introducing a new algorithm. If every such change were deployed independently, the operational overhead and coordination costs would be unbearable. Conversely, if all changes are always bundled together, you may not be able to understand which change caused which effect.

The release as a planning envelope. Think of a release as a planning envelope that groups together:

- A specific set of code artifacts (binaries, containers) produced by your CI/CD pipeline.
- A defined set of configuration and feature-flag changes that will be applied in close temporal proximity.
- The tests and checks that have been run on that specific combination.
- A clear decision point (go/no-go), after which those changes are considered "live."

Within this envelope, you should be able to answer: *What is new? Why are we doing it? How do we know it is safe enough? How do we undo it if needed?*

Choosing release granularity. Release granularity is a balancing act:

- **Too small**: If every trivial change has its own release, you drown in ceremony, and teams may be tempted to bypass the process.
- **Too large**: If dozens of unrelated changes are bundled, troubleshooting becomes difficult: it is hard to know which change is responsible for a problem.

A good rule of thumb is that a release should correspond to a coherent business outcome or risk theme. For example:

- "New version of the intraday VWAP strategy for European equities, with updated participation logic."
- "Introduction of a new dark-pool routing path for selected clients."
- "Refactoring of risk gateway, no intentional change to risk limits, but major code change to performance."

Each of these examples has a clear purpose and a distinct set of stakeholders who care about the outcome.

Release Charters: Making Intent Explicit

Once you decide on the scope of a release, the next step is to document it in a concise, structured way. This is the role of a release charter.

Elements of a release charter. A good release charter typically includes:

- **Objective**: What business problem or opportunity does this release address? For instance, "Improve fill quality on opening auctions" or "Reduce gateway latency by 10%."
- **Scope**: Which systems, venues, instruments, and clients are in scope? Which are explicitly out of scope?
- **Change set**: High-level description of what is changing:
  - Strategy versions and modules.
  - Risk checks or limit logic.
  - Connectivity components and external dependencies.
  - Configuration and feature flags that will be modified.
- **Risk assessment**: Qualitative assessment (for example low/medium/high) of:
  - Impact if something goes wrong (P&L, client, regulatory).
  - Complexity of change (small parameter tweak vs architectural shift).

  - Novelty (have we done something similar before?).

- **Test evidence**: Summary of what has been done to reduce uncertainty:
  - Automated test coverage (unit, integration, replay, simulation).
  - Manual tests or desk-level validation in test/UAT environments.
  - Any shadow runs or parallel simulations already completed.
- **Success criteria**: How will we know the release is successful in the first hours and days? Which metrics will we watch?
- **Backout plan summary**: High-level description of how we will revert if needed (more detail later).

Why charters matter. Release charters are often perceived as bureaucracy, but they serve three crucial functions:

- They align expectations: trading, risk, technology, and compliance see the same summary and can challenge assumptions before the release, not during a crisis.
- They provide context: months later, when someone investigates a period of odd behaviour, the charter explains what the system was trying to achieve at that time.
- They anchor the go/no-go discussion: decision-makers are not voting on a vague "upgrade," but on a clearly articulated proposal.

Go/No-Go Criteria: From Confidence to Conditions

With a charter in place, the question shifts from "Do we feel ready?" to "Have we met the conditions we agreed would be necessary for this release to proceed?" This is the purpose of go/no-go criteria.

Objective checks. Objective checks are measurable conditions that must be satisfied. Examples include:

- **Test pass rates**: All required automated test suites must have passed on the specific release candidate artifact.
- **Performance thresholds**: Latency in replay or performance tests must not exceed a defined ceiling, or must show a specified improvement.
- **Dry-run validations**: In a non-production environment, the system must have run for a minimum time (for example one full session) without critical errors.
- **Operational readiness**: Monitoring dashboards and alerts for new components must be in place and tested.

Objective checks reduce the room for argument: either they are met or they are not.

Subjective checks. Some aspects cannot be fully captured in metrics and require human judgement. These subjective checks include:

- **Stakeholder readiness**: Do the trading desks understand the change and its implications? Are they comfortable with the planned rollout?
- **Support coverage**: Are appropriate technology and operations staff on hand (and aware) during and after the release window?
- **External context**: Are there unusual market conditions, regulatory events, or client sensitivities suggesting we should postpone?

Subjective checks are best expressed as explicit questions on a checklist, with named owners who must answer "yes" or "no," not as vague impressions.

Building the go/no-go checklist. A go/no go checklist is typically prepared as part of the release charter and revisited shortly before the release window. It should:

- Clearly separate *must-have* conditions (blocking issues) from *nice-to-have* conditions.

- Assign each line item to an owner (for example "head of desk," "risk lead," "release manager").
- Include a section for "deviations and justifications," where any unfulfilled criteria must be explicitly recorded and accepted.

At decision time, the incident commander or release manager walks through the checklist with the relevant stakeholders and records the go/no-go decision, together with any conditions (for example "go, but with volume capped at 5% until further review").

Backout Planning: Designing Reversibility Up Front

Even with excellent testing and careful planning, some releases will behave badly in production. The difference between a stressful but contained incident and a true crisis often lies in how quickly and safely you can undo the change.

Backout is not an afterthought. Too often, backout plans are added as a sentence at the end of a document: "If something goes wrong, we will roll back." In practice, rollback can be slow, complicated, or even impossible if not designed in.

A robust backout plan answers three concrete questions:

- **What state are we returning to?** (which version, configuration, and flags).
- **How do we technically perform the reversal?** (commands, steps, dependencies).
- **Who does what, and how long should it take?**

Types of backout mechanisms. Depending on the nature of the change, different backout mechanisms are available. Common types include:

- **Binary rollback**: Revert to the previous application version by redeploying the prior artifact. This works well when:

  - Data formats and schemas have not changed in incompatible ways, or
  - Both versions understand the same data representations.

- **Feature-flag disablement**: If the new behaviour is guarded by a feature flag, you can turn it off without deploying anything. This is the fastest and often safest option, especially for strategy changes.

- **Configuration rollback**: Revert to previous configuration values (for example risk limits, routing preferences) stored in a versioned config repository. This assumes proper version history and tooling for quick reversion.

- **Traffic diversion**: Route flow away from the affected component or venue, for example:
  - Switch clients back to an older stable strategy.
  - Temporarily route orders through a different gateway or broker.

- **Partial backout**: Sometimes you cannot fully revert (for example database schema upgrades), but you can disable the most risky aspects, such as specific order types or clients, while keeping the infrastructure change.

Each mechanism has trade-offs in speed, safety, and completeness of reversal.

Backout triggers and thresholds. A backout plan must not only describe *how* to reverse, but also *when* to reverse. Rather than relying on ad-hoc debate in the heat of the moment, define, in advance:

- Quantitative thresholds, such as:
  - Error or reject rates exceeding a specified level.
  - Latency exceeding a certain percentile threshold.
  - Slippage or P&L deviation from expected benchmarks beyond a tolerance.

- Qualitative triggers, such as:

  - Consistent confusion from traders about system behaviour.
  - Client complaints or unexpected trade reports.
  - Alarms from middle office or regulatory reporting for anomalous records.

Your backout plan can then state, for example: "If reject rates double relative to baseline in the first 15 minutes, release is rolled back to previous version without further discussion."

Rehearsed Reversibility: Practising Backout Before You Need It

Just as you would not fly an aircraft without ever practising emergency procedures, you should not rely on a backout plan that has never been executed. Rehearsal ensures that the steps are complete, the tooling works, and the people involved understand their roles.

Dry-run backouts in lower environments. Before a major release:

- Perform a full deploy-and-backout cycle in a non-production environment that is as realistic as possible (including data and connectivity).
- Time how long backout actually takes, and compare it to your expectations and to the risk of leaving the faulty release in place.
- Observe where manual steps are complicated or error-prone, and simplify or automate them.

These rehearsals often uncover missing permissions, undocumented dependencies, or gaps in runbooks that would have been painful in production.

Controlled backout drills in production-like flows. In some organisations, it is also valuable to schedule occasional controlled drills, where:

- A small, non-critical flow is deliberately switched to a new version and then back again, purely as a test of operational readiness.

- The exercise is announced and monitored, with clear exit criteria.

This builds muscle memory and confidence that, when an emergency comes, the team can act quickly without improvising.

Ownership and Communication During Releases

Even the best technical plans can fail if roles and communication channels are unclear when pressure rises.

Release roles. For each release, you should explicitly assign:

- **Incident commander / release manager**: The person who coordinates the release, chairs the go/no-go meeting, and has final say (within agreed policies) on whether to proceed or back out.
- **Technical executors**: Engineers responsible for carrying out deployment and, if needed, backout steps.
- **Business owner**: Typically someone from the trading or product side who is accountable for the commercial rationale of the release.
- **Risk and compliance contacts**: Individuals who confirm that the release aligns with risk limits and regulatory obligations.

These roles should be named in the release charter, and their availability during the release window confirmed.

Communication plans. Communication plans answer:

- Who needs to be informed before the release? (for example trading desks, risk, operations).
- Through what channels? (for example email, chat, change-management tool notifications).
- What updates are required during and after the release? (for example "deployment started," "deployment complete," "issue detected, backout initiated," "backout complete," etc.).

Clear communication reduces confusion and prevents individuals from independently taking uncoordinated actions that may worsen the situation (for example traders manually disabling strategies while engineers are mid-backout).

Runbooks and accessibility. Finally, all the release and backout procedures should be captured in runbooks:

- Written in plain language, with step-by-step instructions.
- Stored in a central, easily accessible location resilient to outages.
- Reviewed and updated after every significant release or incident to incorporate lessons learned.

In an emergency, no one should waste time hunting for instructions.

Release planning is where the technical disciplines of CI/CD and configuration management meet the operational realities of trading and risk. By:

- Defining releases as coherent units of risk rather than arbitrary bundles of code.
- Documenting intent and scope in release charters.
- Establishing objective and subjective go/no-go criteria.
- Designing, specifying, and rehearsing backout plans in advance.
- Clarifying roles, responsibilities, and communication patterns.

you turn each deployment from a hopeful leap into a controlled, reversible step.

In the following sections we will extend these ideas to the *shape* of deployment itself: instead of flipping everything at once, we will consider shadow modes, canary cohorts, and staged volume ramping, using feature flags and configuration to gradually expose new behaviour to live order flow under tight guardrails.

7.4 Staged Rollouts, Canaries, and Volume Ramping

Up to this point we have focused on *what* changes enter production (through CI/CD and configuration) and *whether* they should go live at all (through release planning and go/no-go criteria). We now turn to a more granular question: once a change is approved, *how do you let it touch real order flow*?

In trading systems, the difference between a minor incident and a major loss often comes down to how much flow a new version handles, and how quickly. Turning on a new strategy for 100% of volume in one shot is rarely justified. Instead, you want a controlled progression:

- First, run the new version in *shadow mode*, where it makes hypothetical decisions but does not actually trade.
- Next, expose it to a small, carefully chosen slice of live flow as a *canary*.
- Then, if the early signs are good, *ramp* the volume step by step, with clear guardrails that freeze or roll back when metrics degrade.

This section develops these ideas in a structured way and shows how they align with the governance mechanisms introduced earlier.

Shadow Mode: Learning Without Risking Capital

Shadow mode is the gentlest way to introduce new strategy logic into your production environment. The idea is simple: the new version runs alongside the current one, sees the same market data and internal signals, and produces hypothetical orders or quotes, but those outputs are *not* sent to the exchange.

Parallel decision-making. In shadow mode, for each opportunity the system might:

- Let the existing, stable version continue to make the real trading decision.

- Ask the new version what it *would* have done under the same conditions.
- Log both sets of decisions with timestamps, market context, and internal state.

Over time, you build a rich dataset allowing you to compare the old and new behaviour under genuinely live conditions, not just in backtests.

What to compare. Useful comparisons between live and shadow behaviour include:

- **Direction and aggressiveness**: Does the new version try to buy when the old one sells, or quote tighter/wider than the current version?
- **Position paths**: Would the new version accumulate risk faster or in different instruments?
- **Order dynamics**: Does it generate many more cancels, replaces, or child orders?

You can also simulate approximate P&L by combining the new version's hypothetical orders with the actual trade prints observed in the market, yielding a "what-if" performance trace.

Acceptance thresholds in shadow. Before moving beyond shadow mode, define clear acceptance thresholds, such as:

- The new version's simulated P&L must not be materially worse than the current version over a representative period.
- Key risk metrics (peak inventory, drawdown, exposure by sector) must remain within agreed ranges.
- Operational metrics (decision latency, hypothetical order rate) must be acceptable.

Shadow mode does not remove all uncertainty—live execution feedback is still missing—but it filters out versions that are clearly misaligned with expectations.

Canaries: Letting a Small Cohort Go First

Once a strategy passes shadow-mode acceptance thresholds, the next step is to let it handle a *small* subset of live flow. This is the canary rollout, inspired by the old practice of bringing a canary into a mine to detect dangerous conditions early.

Basic structure of a canary rollout. In a canary rollout:

- Both old and new versions are present in production.
- A minority fraction of orders are routed to the new version.
- The majority continue to be handled by the stable version.

The aim is to expose the new logic to real fills, slippage, market impact, and venue behaviours, but to limit the damage if something goes wrong.

Choosing the canary slice. There are many ways to choose the canary cohort. Common slicing strategies include:

- By client or account: Select one or a few clients (ideally informed and consenting) whose flow will be traded by the new version. This is useful for agency flow, where different clients may have different tolerance for experimentation.
- By symbol or instrument: Start with a set of instruments that are important enough to be representative but not so critical that any issue would be catastrophic. You might prefer:

- Mid-liquidity names rather than the most illiquid or the most systemically important.
- A diverse mix across sectors or maturities to avoid narrow overfitting.

- By venue: Route a portion of flow to specific venues using the new logic, while keeping others under the existing logic. This is attractive where venue behaviours differ sharply.

- By random sampling: Direct a random subset (for example 1%) of eligible orders to the new version. Randomisation can reduce selection bias in evaluating performance.

You can also combine dimensions, for example a few selected clients on specific venues.

Sizing the canary. A canary should be:

- **Large enough** to generate meaningful data within a reasonable time frame.
- **Small enough** that if performance is poor, the firm-wide impact is manageable.

For some firms, 1–5% of eligible flow is an appropriate starting point. The precise figure depends on liquidity, risk appetite, and the nature of the change.

Monitoring canary health. During the canary phase, you should monitor:

- Execution quality metrics (fill rates, slippage vs benchmark, effective spreads) for canary vs control.
- Operational metrics (error rates, rejects, timeouts) specifically for canary orders.
- Client- or trader-level feedback if the change affects front-end behaviour.

The key is isolation: your monitoring must distinguish canary performance from that of the main population, otherwise early warning signals may be diluted.

Venue- and Symbol-Based Slicing in Practice

The choice of slicing dimension has practical consequences. Here we explore venues and symbols more concretely, because they link directly to market microstructure.

Venue-based slicing. Venue-based slicing is natural for:

- **Routing logic changes**: For example, a new smart order router path or a different mix of dark vs lit venues.
- **Venue-specific order types**: For example, introducing a new midpoint or auction order available only on one exchange.

Advantages:

- Operational separation: If a venue-specific change malfunctions, you can quickly disable or redirect that venue without touching others.
- Clean comparisons: Benchmarks can be computed per venue, and changes in performance can be clearly attributed.

Risks:

- Liquidity fragmentation: If the chosen venue has atypical liquidity profiles, canary results may not generalise.
- Concentration: If too much flow to that venue is handled by the new version, issues may have an outsized impact.

Symbol-based slicing. Symbol-based slicing is suitable for:

- Strategy logic that depends strongly on instrument characteristics (for example volatility, tick size).
- Changes to intraday scheduling or participation that may behave differently for liquid vs illiquid names.

A balanced symbol cohort might:

- Include a few large, liquid names to test behaviour under high throughput.
- Include some mid- and low-liquidity names to test resilience and limit management.
- Exclude the very riskiest or most sensitive instruments in the earliest stages.

You should be explicit in the release charter about how symbols are selected and what population they are intended to represent.

Volume Ramping: From Small Slice to Full Deployment

Once the canary period shows acceptable behaviour, you can start to increase the share of flow handled by the new version. This is volume ramping: a progressive increase in traffic allocated to the new logic over time.

Why ramp instead of jumping to 100%. Even if early results look good, there are strong reasons not to jump directly from a small canary to full deployment:

- Some issues only appear under higher load (latency spikes, queueing, resource exhaustion).
- Market conditions may change; you want to see the new version under various regimes.
- The organisation needs time to build confidence and operational familiarity with the new behaviour.

Designing ramp curves. A ramp curve is a pre-planned sequence defining what fraction of eligible flow the new version will take at each stage. For example:

- Stage 1: 1% of flow for at least one full trading session.
- Stage 2: 5% of flow for two–three sessions.
- Stage 3: 20% of flow for a week.
- Stage 4: 50% and then 100%, subject to stability.

Each stage transition is conditional on guardrails (discussed next). The exact numbers and timings depend on:

- Volume and liquidity of the relevant markets.
- Criticality of the strategy (client-facing vs internal hedging).
- Firm's risk appetite and past experience with similar releases.

The crucial point is that the ramp is designed *before* deployment, not improvised in reaction to events.

Implementing ramps with feature flags and config. Feature flags and configuration (from the previous section) are the natural tools for implementing ramps. For example:

- A feature flag defines which clients, symbols, or venues are eligible for the new version.
- A configuration parameter sets the target percentage of eligible flow to route to the new version.

The orchestration system adjusts these parameters according to the planned ramp curve, subject to guardrails.

Guardrails: Automatic Throttles and Halt Conditions

Staged rollouts and ramps only help if you can detect when things start to go wrong and react quickly. Guardrails are pre-defined rules that watch key metrics and automatically slow, freeze, or reverse the rollout when those metrics breach thresholds.

Key categories of guardrail metrics. Typical guardrails monitor:

- **Execution quality**: Slippage vs benchmarks (VWAP, arrival price), fill rates, effective spread. If the new version underperforms the baseline by more than a tolerance, ramping stops.
- **Risk and inventory**: Position limits, concentration by symbol or sector, intraday drawdown. Unexpected patterns may indicate faulty logic or miscalibration.
- **Operational health**: Error and reject rates, timeouts, throughput capacity, system latency.
- **Client and desk feedback**: Qualitative reports from traders and clients noticing odd behaviour, especially for agency flows.

Guardrails can be implemented as alerting rules or as hard-enforced limits that directly affect routing decisions.

Types of automatic responses. When a guardrail detects an issue, responses might include:

- **Pause ramp:** Freeze the current ramp stage and halt any further increase in allocation until a human review occurs.
- **Step down:** Automatically drop back to the previous ramp stage (for example from 20% back to 5%) while keeping the new version in limited use.
- **Full rollback to stable version:** For severe breaches, route all traffic back to the old version and optionally disable the new version entirely (often via feature flags).

These responses should be documented in the release plan so that everyone understands what will happen when triggers fire.

Balancing sensitivity and noise. If guardrails are too tight, ordinary market noise will trigger frequent pauses and rollbacks, making it impossible to complete rollouts. If they are too lax, they will not prevent meaningful damage. Calibrating thresholds requires:

- Studying historical variability in metrics to understand normal ranges.
- Considering different regimes (calm vs volatile markets).
- Starting conservatively and relaxing thresholds as confidence builds.

Visualising a Staged Rollout

After introducing canary slices and ramp curves, it is useful to visualise the rollout over time, along with guardrail thresholds. Figure shows a stylised example.

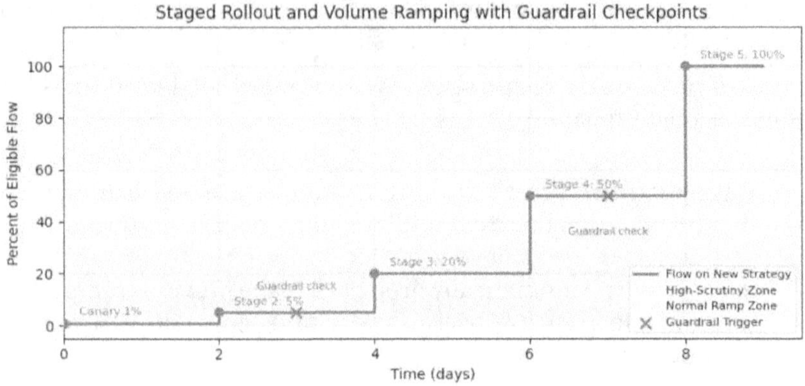

This simple step chart makes several ideas concrete:

- The release does not jump from 0% to 100%; it progresses through planned stages.
- Each stage has a minimum dwell time (here shown as days), giving room to observe behaviour.
- Guardrail checks can occur at each transition or even mid-stage, potentially pausing or reversing the ramp.

Choosing a Rollout Posture: Aggressive vs Conservative

Not all firms and not all strategies should follow the same rollout tempo. Your posture should reflect:

- The criticality of the strategy (core revenue vs experimental line).
- The sensitivity of clients and regulators to missteps.
- The maturity of your testing and monitoring infrastructure.

Aggressive posture. An aggressive rollout posture might:

- Use short dwell times at each ramp stage.

- Move quickly to high percentages of flow once basic metrics look acceptable.
- Be appropriate for internal-only, low-risk strategies or for environments with excellent observability and rapid backout.

Conservative posture. A conservative posture might:

- Keep canary slices small for longer periods, across various market conditions.
- Require explicit human sign-off at each stage transition.
- Be appropriate for client-facing algorithms, regulated algo strategies, or firms with lower tolerance for operational surprises.

In all cases, the important thing is that the posture is *chosen consciously*, documented in the release plan, and shared with stakeholders, rather than being the accidental outcome of ad hoc decisions.

Staged rollouts, canary cohorts, and volume ramping translate abstract ideas about "controlled risk" into concrete operational practices. By:

- Starting in shadow mode to validate logic without risking capital.
- Moving to small, well-chosen canary slices of real flow.
- Designing pre-planned ramp curves for volume increases.
- Enforcing guardrails that automatically pause, slow, or reverse the rollout when metrics degrade.

you create a gentler, more observable path from backtest to full production.

These practices sit on top of the earlier layers in this chapter: CI/CD ensures that each version is built and tested consistently; configuration and feature flags give you levers to direct and limit exposure; release planning and go/no-go criteria frame each rollout as a deliberate risk decision. The next sections will refine the timing dimension further, showing how to align these rollouts with trading sessions, auctions, and calendar events to minimise market impact and operational risk.

7.5 Session-Aware Cutovers and Calendar Planning

The previous sections have focused on *how* to change your systems: CI/CD pipelines, configuration and feature flags, structured releases, and staged rollouts. We now turn to a deceptively simple but critical question: *when* should you execute those changes?

In trading, timing is not just a matter of convenience. Market sessions, auctions, and macroeconomic events create periods of vastly different liquidity and risk. A cutover that is harmless at 02:00 New York time might be disastrous at the opening auction or during a major economic release. Session-aware cutovers and calendar planning are about aligning your deployment activities with market microstructure so that you minimise impact on clients and on the firm's risk profile.

Why Timing Matters: Microstructure and Operational Risk

Electronic markets are not homogeneous over the day or over the calendar. Liquidity, volatility, and order flow intensity vary with:

- Exchange trading sessions (pre-open, continuous trading, closing auction).
- Overlapping hours across regions.
- Scheduled events (economic announcements, index rebalances, expiries).
- Seasonal and calendar effects (holidays, quarter-ends).

From a cutover perspective, these patterns matter because:

- Any technical issue during a high-liquidity, high-attention period is more likely to affect many orders and be noticed by clients and regulators.
- Behavioural comparisons (old vs new strategy) are harder to interpret on days with unusual conditions.

- Operations and support coverage may themselves vary by time-of-day and date.

Session-aware planning acknowledges that not all minutes are created equal. A 5-minute disruption at 10:00 in the continuous session is not equivalent to a 5-minute disruption during a quiet overnight period.

Market Sessions: Pre-Open, Continuous, and Auctions

To reason about good and bad windows for cutovers, we begin with a simplified view of a typical trading day on a central limit order book.

Pre-open and opening auction. Many exchanges operate a pre-open period, during which orders can be entered and cancelled but no continuous matching occurs. The pre-open culminates in an opening auction, setting the first official price for the day.

Key characteristics:

- Order books are building, and indicative opening prices may jump as new orders arrive.
- Liquidity concentrates at the opening print; many benchmarked strategies care deeply about that price.
- Technical issues here can lead to missed opens, mispriced inventory, and unhappy clients.

For most strategy or connectivity changes, the opening auction window is *the last place* you want to discover problems.

Continuous trading. During the continuous session:

- Orders interact in real-time; spreads, depth, and volatility vary with news and time-of-day.
- Volume typically follows a U-shape: higher at open and close, lower mid-day.
- Many intraday strategies re-optimise positions, hedge, and rebalance.

This is where most of your P&L is made or lost. Not all parts of the continuous session are equal: late morning or early afternoon in local time, away from typical news releases, is often a relatively calm period.

Closing auction. The closing auction, like the opening auction, concentrates liquidity and attention:

- Index funds and benchmarked portfolios execute large volumes at the close.
- Many performance metrics and valuations are based on closing prices.
- Any misbehaviour (missed closings, misrouted auction orders) is highly visible.

Cutovers close to the closing auction are generally high risk and should be avoided unless absolutely necessary and specifically planned.

Choosing Cutover Windows Within a Session

With this structure in mind, you can sketch a first set of guidelines for intraday cutovers.

Prefer low-intensity, mid-session windows. For many changes, a practical rule is:

- Avoid the first and last 30–60 minutes of the continuous session.
- Avoid the pre-open and immediate post-open period.
- Avoid periods around scheduled macroeconomic announcements for instruments sensitive to that data.

Instead, target mid-session windows when:

- Liquidity is adequate but not extreme.
- The trading desk and support teams are fully staffed and not overloaded.

- There is time left in the session to observe behaviour and, if needed, back out before the close.

Match the window to the change type. Not all changes are equal:

- **Low-risk operational changes** (for example new monitoring dashboards, minor non-trading UI tweaks) can sometimes be done during the session with minimal concern.
- **Connectivity and gateway changes** should generally be done outside active trading hours, or during the quietest parts of the session, because missteps can cut off entire venues or clients.
- **Strategy logic or routing changes** are best cut over when the market is open but calm, so you can see real trades and still have room to revert.
- **Risk parameter changes** (limits, throttles) may be done intraday but warrant special attention to current positions and flows.

The release charter should explicitly propose a target window and rationale based on these considerations.

Cross-Venue and Cross-Region Considerations

Global trading adds another dimension: multiple venues across time zones may be trading the same instrument or closely related products.

Staggered vs simultaneous cutovers. When a change affects multiple venues or regions, you must decide whether to:

- **Stagger** cutovers (for example Asia, then Europe, then the Americas), using earlier regions as a kind of canary for later ones.
- **Cut over simultaneously** across venues, for strategies that depend on cross-market consistency.

Staggering can reduce risk and improve learning, but may introduce temporary inconsistencies across markets. For example:

- A cross-asset hedging strategy might run the new version in Europe while the Americas leg still runs the old one, creating odd interactions.

When cross-market relationships are tight (for example index arbitrage), you may need coordinated cutovers across regions, or else design the rollout at the level of the entire multi-venue strategy.

Time zone and support coverage. Cutovers should respect not only market hours but also:

- The availability of the relevant support teams. A "quiet" time in one region may coincide with minimal staffing.
- The need for coordination across desks; for example, a change in Europe might affect positions and hedge flows managed later in the U.S. session.

Calendar planning here is as much about people as it is about systems.

Freeze Windows: When *Not* to Change

A freeze window is a period during which changes to production systems are prohibited or severely restricted. The purpose is to avoid introducing new risk during times when:

- The market is already fragile or highly stressed.
- The firm's tolerance for additional uncertainty is low.

Typical freeze scenarios. Common examples include:

- **End-of-quarter and year-end**: When reporting, valuations, and regulatory filings depend on stable systems.
- **Index rebalances and major expiries**: When predictable but large flows concentrate in specific windows.
- **Firm-specific events**: Product launches, client migrations, or known high-volume days.

- **Regulatory deadlines**: When new rules go live and systems are under scrutiny.

Defining the scope of a freeze. A freeze does not have to mean "no change whatsoever." It can be scoped, for example:

- Only high-risk changes (strategy logic, connectivity, risk-engine changes) are frozen.
- Only production environments are frozen; test/UAT environments remain open for development.
- Emergency fixes for critical bugs are allowed, but must follow a heightened approval process.

The key is clarity: everyone should understand what the freeze covers, for how long, and which exceptions (if any) are allowed.

Maintenance Windows and Out-of-Hours Work

Some changes are inherently disruptive: database upgrades, operating system patches, major network reconfigurations. These are often best scheduled during well-defined maintenance windows, typically outside core trading hours.

Advantages of dedicated maintenance windows. Maintenance windows:

- Provide a block of time when traders and clients expect some functionality to be limited or offline.
- Allow infrastructure teams to concentrate on heavy tasks without juggling intraday issues.
- Reduce the risk that a partial, mid-session upgrade leaves systems in a confusing in-between state.

Risks of out-of-hours changes. However, out-of-hours cutovers have their own challenges:

- Fewer staff may be present, especially from business and risk functions.
- Some markets trade nearly 24 hours (for example certain futures, FX), so "off-hours" may still carry non-trivial risk.
- If something goes wrong late at night, you may only discover full impact when markets reopen.

To mitigate this, maintenance windows should be:

- Planned with explicit rollback deadlines (for example "if not fully stable one hour before the open, revert to previous version").
- Staffed with a balanced mix of technology, trading, and risk representatives on-call.

Deployment Calendars: Making the Plan Visible

Once you consider sessions, freezes, and maintenance windows together, it becomes clear that ad-hoc scheduling is inadequate. You need a deployment calendar: a shared, forward-looking view of planned changes and constraints.

What a deployment calendar contains. A comprehensive deployment calendar typically includes:

- **Planned release windows**: Dates and times when significant strategy or system changes are expected.
- **Freeze periods**: Clearly marked blocks when changes are restricted, including their scope.
- **Maintenance windows**: Regular slots (for example weekly or monthly) reserved for infrastructure work.
- **External events**: Major macroeconomic releases, index rebalances, expiries, and known market events relevant to your book.
- **Internal events**: Client migrations, product launches, or platform consolidations.

This calendar should be accessible to trading, technology, risk, operations, and compliance.

Aligning releases to the calendar. When planning a release, you should:

- Check the calendar for conflicts with freeze periods or high-risk external events.
- Select a cutover window that:
  - Respects market sessions (for example mid-day in the relevant region).
  - Leaves enough time before and after for observation and potential rollback.
- Reserve the chosen window so other teams do not accidentally schedule conflicting changes (for example two major releases at once).

Over time, this practice reduces surprises and accumulates institutional knowledge about when different kinds of changes are best scheduled.

Operational Details Often Overlooked

In practice, many incidents trace back not to a flawed algorithm, but to small oversights in timing and preparation. A few recurring themes deserve explicit attention.

Open positions and outstanding orders. Before a cutover, you must consider:

- What open positions does the strategy hold, and how will the new version interpret and manage them?
- Are there outstanding orders (for example resting passive orders, working algo slices) that might be affected by the change?

For some types of cutovers, best practice is to:

- Flatten or reduce positions to a tolerable level before making the change.
- Cancel or hand off outstanding orders to a stable component during the transition.

Ignoring this can lead to inconsistent state, where the new version inherits positions or orders that do not align with its view of the world.

Session restarts and state persistence. Many trading systems reset or perform housekeeping at session boundaries (open, close). When planning cutovers:

- Test in advance how the system behaves around restarts, both scheduled (for example daily) and unscheduled.
- Ensure that persistent state (positions, risk limits, sequence numbers) is correctly carried over or reinitialised.

A release just before a planned restart is risky if you have not validated restart behaviour with the new version.

Coordination with middle office and reporting. Changes can also affect:

- Trade capture and allocation systems.
- Regulatory reporting (for example new tags or changes in how orders are categorised).

It is not enough to cut over the front-end trading logic; you must ensure that:

- Downstream systems are ready for any new fields or behaviours.
- Reporting teams are aware of when behaviour changes, so they can interpret any shifts in data patterns.

Deployment calendars should therefore be shared with middle office and reporting functions, not just front-office and technology.

Socialising the Calendar and Enforcing Discipline

A deployment calendar and session-aware rules only help if they are understood and followed.

Governance around the calendar. Firms often establish:

- A change or release committee that reviews and approves the deployment calendar, especially for high-impact releases.
- Rules requiring that significant releases be listed on the calendar a minimum time in advance, unless emergent risk demands a hotfix.
- Escalation paths for approving exceptions during freeze windows.

This embeds calendar discipline into governance rather than leaving it as a voluntary courtesy.

Making timing part of the release charter. Earlier we introduced release charters. A natural extension is to require each charter to specify:

- The intended cutover window (date, time, and market session).
- The justification for that window, given the nature of the change and relevant market events.
- Any dependencies on maintenance windows or other releases.

Approvers then see timing as part of the risk decision, not as an afterthought.

Session-aware cutovers and calendar planning bring a time dimension to the risk controls developed earlier in this chapter. By:

- Understanding market microstructure across pre-open, continuous trading, and auctions.
- Choosing cutover windows that avoid the most fragile or highest-impact periods.

- Coordinating changes across venues and regions with an eye on both markets and staffing.
- Establishing freeze windows, maintenance windows, and a shared deployment calendar.
- Paying attention to open positions, outstanding orders, and downstream systems.

you reduce the chance that a technically sound release will become an operational incident simply because it was deployed at the wrong time.

In the final section of this chapter, we will complete the control loop by examining post-deployment validation and governance: how to confirm that a cutover has behaved as intended, and how to feed those observations back into model risk management, regulatory reporting, and future change planning.

7.6 Post-Deployment Validation and Governance

By this point in the chapter we have treated a deployment as a carefully planned, session-aware event: code is delivered through a controlled CI/CD pipeline, configuration and feature flags shape behaviour, releases are staged through canaries and ramps, and cutovers are aligned with market microstructure and calendars.

This final section answers two questions:

- What happens *immediately after* a cutover, when the new version first meets real flow?
- How do those observations feed into the broader governance framework: regulatory reporting, surveillance, and model risk management?

Post-deployment validation is not a loose "keep an eye on it." It is a structured, time-boxed process that connects technical health, trading outcomes, and regulatory obligations, and then loops back into how you approve and design future changes.

Immediate Post-Cutover Validation: Structured Checkouts

Every significant deployment or ramp stage should be followed by an explicit validation period, often called a *post-cutover checkout*. The goal is to confirm, as quickly as possible, whether the system behaves within the bounds anticipated in the release plan.

Time-boxed validation windows. Rather than an open-ended "wait and see," define:

- A specific duration (for example the first 30–60 minutes after cutover, or the first continuous session).
- One or more checkpoints within that window (for example at 10, 30, and 60 minutes).
- Who is responsible for evaluating each checkpoint (technology, trading, risk, operations).

At each checkpoint, you compare observed behaviour against pre-defined expectations and guardrails, and decide to continue, pause, or back out.

Golden-signal dashboards for technical health. From a systems perspective, you should already have dashboards showing generic "golden signals":

- **Latency**: End-to-end response times for quotes and orders, broken down by component where possible.
- **Error rates**: Application errors, rejects, timeouts, and disconnects.
- **Throughput**: Messages per second, CPU and memory utilisation, queue depths.

Immediately after deployment:

- Compare these metrics with recent baselines for the same time-of-day and market conditions.

- Look for structural shifts: are tails heavier, average latencies higher, new failure modes appearing?

If basic technical health is not satisfactory, there is little point in examining finer-grained trading performance; stability comes first.

Trading-specific KPIs. Once technical health looks acceptable, you turn to trading behaviour. Examples of relevant KPIs include:

- **Fill rates** for different order types and venues.
- **Slippage** versus benchmarks such as arrival price, VWAP, or primary closes.
- **Rejection codes** and patterns (for example venue-level rejects, risk-gateway rejections).
- **Inventory and exposure paths**: how quickly positions build up or unwind compared with expectations.

These metrics must be segmented so you can isolate:

- Orders handled by the new version versus the legacy version.
- Specific canary cohorts (by client, symbol, venue) where the new behaviour is active.

The question is not simply "are we OK?" but "is the new behaviour consistent with our shadow tests, simulations, and release assumptions?"

Pre-defined decision rules. To avoid emotional decision-making during the validation window, the release plan should include decision rules such as:

- "If error rate doubles relative to baseline for 10 consecutive minutes, initiate backout."
- "If slippage for the canary cohort exceeds control by more than X basis points over N fills, pause the ramp and investigate."
- "If any unexplained risk-limit breach or forced reduction occurs, freeze new allocations."

At each checkpoint, the incident commander or release manager walks through these rules with the relevant stakeholders and records the decision: continue as planned, hold at current exposure, or back out.

Front-to-Back Reconciliations: Proving Books & Records Integrity

Even if trading performance and system metrics look healthy, a cutover can still introduce silent errors in how trades are captured and represented in internal systems. Post-deployment validation must therefore include *front-to-back* reconciliations.

What needs to reconcile. At a high level, every executed or attempted order should have a consistent representation across:

- Front-office systems (OMS/EMS, strategy engines).
- Middle office (trade capture, allocations, confirmations).
- Back office (ledgers, general accounting).

After a change that affects order structures, fields, or flows, you should:

- Select representative samples of trades (across venues, order types, and clients) generated by the new release.
- Trace each sample through the chain of systems, checking that quantities, prices, timestamps, and identifiers match.

Common failure modes. Post-cutover reconciliations often reveal issues such as:

- Missing or mis-mapped fields (for example a new tag not propagated to downstream systems).
- Incorrect instrument or account mappings after symbol changes or platform migrations.
- Aggregation errors where child orders or executions are double-counted or lost.

These can have serious consequences even if trading itself is profitable: inaccurate client confirms, misstated P&L, or inconsistent positions between risk and accounting.

Automated vs manual reconciliations. Ideally, you have automated reconciliation tools that:

- Compare trade feeds across systems in near-real time.
- Raise alerts when mismatches cross defined thresholds.

For a new release, however, you should also plan specific manual or semi-manual checks:

- Middle-office staff inspecting new order types or fields expressly modified by the release.
- Cross-checks of daily summaries (for example total volume, gross notional) between front office and back office.

These deliberate, focused reconciliations complement ongoing automated controls.

Regulatory Reporting and Surveillance Impacts

Changes in trading systems often affect not only internal behaviour but also what gets reported to regulators and how surveillance systems interpret activity. Post-deployment validation must therefore explicitly link to compliance functions.

Regulatory reporting flows. Depending on jurisdiction and business model, your firm may be subject to regimes such as:

- Transaction or order reporting (for example consolidated audit trails, transaction reports).
- Position reporting for large holdings or short positions.
- Algorithmic trading notifications and testing attestations.

A release involving new order types, venues, client classifications, or strategy flags may require changes in:

- Which events are reported (for example new categories of cancellations or amendments).
- How events are enriched (for example algo identifiers, client type, waiver codes).
- How records are grouped or linked (for example parent-child hierarchies).

Post-cutover checks should confirm that:

- Records produced by the new version contain all regulatory-mandated fields.
- Mappings from internal fields to regulatory formats are correct.
- No unexpected increase in rejected regulatory submissions occurs.

Surveillance and conduct monitoring. Internal or external surveillance systems watch for patterns such as layering, spoofing, wash trades, or other forms of market abuse. A new strategy version or routing policy can affect:

- The pattern and timing of orders and cancellations.
- The use of specific order types that surveillance rules treat as sensitive.
- The distribution of trading across venues and instruments.

After deployment, compliance teams should monitor:

- Whether the new behaviour triggers existing alerts more frequently, and if so, why.
- Whether surveillance scenarios still interpret new order flows correctly (for example new tags or fields do not confuse rule logic).

This is especially important for algorithmic strategies, where regulators expect firms to understand and control the interaction between their algos and market-abuse detection systems.

Model Risk Management and Algorithmic Governance

So far, we have treated post-deployment validation as an operational exercise. For many trading strategies—particularly model-driven or algorithmic ones—there is an additional governance layer: model risk management and algorithmic governance.

Strategy versions as governed models. A modern algorithmic trading strategy is a model in the governance sense:

- It takes inputs (market data, client instructions, risk limits).
- It applies logic or statistical models to produce outputs (orders, quotes).
- Its behaviour can materially affect the firm's risk profile and regulatory exposure.

Model risk management frameworks typically require:

- An inventory of models, including each strategy and its variants.
- Documentation of model purpose, design assumptions, and limitations.
- Independent validation and periodic review, separate from the development team.

Each production deployment or major configuration change to a strategy version should therefore update the model inventory and, where appropriate, trigger revalidation or review.

Linking deployments to model approvals. Practically, this means:

- The release charter records which model version(s) are being deployed or re-parameterised.
- The change ticket references the relevant model approval or validation documents.

- Post-deployment performance is explicitly compared to pre-deployment validation results.

If material discrepancies emerge—either better or worse—this may indicate that:

- The model was mis-specified or overfit to historical regimes.
- The production implementation diverges from the validated design.
- Market structure has shifted, warranting a fresh validation.

Model risk and algo governance committees should receive concise summaries of such findings.

Performance, fairness, and stability over time. Beyond the immediate post-cutover window, governance looks at:

- **Performance**: Are strategies meeting their stated objectives (for example benchmark tracking, cost reduction) without hidden risk build-up?
- **Fairness and client treatment**: For agency flows, are different clients treated consistently and in line with mandates?
- **Stability**: Do strategies remain robust across regimes, or do they need frequent emergency interventions?

Periodic reviews (for example quarterly) tie long-run performance back to deployment history, configuration changes, and any policy exceptions granted along the way.

Closed-Loop Governance: From Deployment Back to Planning

To see how all these elements connect, it is helpful to view deployments not as isolated events but as stages in a continuous governance cycle.

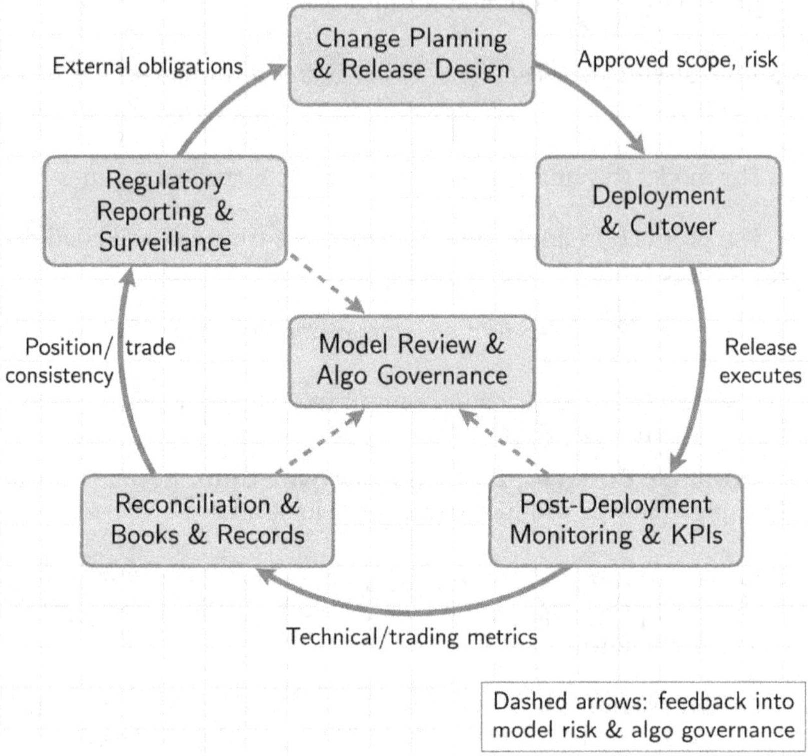

In this loop:

- **Change planning & release design** use past incidents, performance, and regulatory findings to set scope, tests, and backout strategies.
- **Deployment & cutover** execute the planned changes in session- and calendar-aware windows.
- **Post-deployment monitoring** checks technical health and trading KPIs.
- **Reconciliation & books & records** ensure that internal rep-

resentations of trades and positions remain accurate and consistent.

- **Regulatory reporting & surveillance** confirm that external obligations are met and that behaviour remains within acceptable conduct standards.
- **Model review & algo governance** integrate lessons from monitoring, reconciliations, and regulatory interactions to update model inventories, validations, and policies.

Feedback from each stage can change the others: for example, a reconciliation issue may prompt changes to deployment checklists, while a surveillance finding may trigger tighter controls on certain strategy changes.

Reporting to Boards, Committees, and Audit

Finally, governance implies not only doing the right things, but also *proving* to senior stakeholders that you are doing them consistently.

Regular governance reporting. Boards, risk committees, and internal audit typically expect:

- Summaries of significant releases over a period (for example quarterly), including scope and risk classification.
- Statistics on incidents, rollbacks, and near-misses, with root causes and remediation actions.
- Metrics on model inventory changes: new models deployed, models retired, major re-calibrations.
- Evidence that regulatory reporting completeness and accuracy are monitored and that breaches are promptly addressed.

These are not real-time dashboards, but higher-level narratives that show whether the organisation's change processes are effective.

Traceability and audit trails. To support such reporting, your tooling and documentation must make it easy to:

- Trace from any production order or incident back to the specific release, configuration, and strategy version.
- Retrieve the release charter, go/no-go checklist, and post-deployment validation results for that release.
- Demonstrate compliance with change policies (for example required approvals, segregation of duties).

Well-structured records turn regulatory and audit requests from emergencies into routine queries.

Post-deployment validation and governance close the loop that began with CI/CD and release planning. They ensure that:

- New releases are not only deployed, but also objectively verified against technical and trading expectations.
- Books & records, regulatory reporting, and surveillance remain accurate and aligned with evolving system behaviour.
- Algorithmic strategies are treated as governed models, with clear versioning, approvals, and periodic review.
- Lessons from real-world behaviour feed back into how you plan, design, and approve future changes.

In a well-run trading organisation, every production change is therefore traceable, testable, explainable, and reviewable—not just as a technical event, but as part of an integrated risk and governance framework that spans markets, clients, and regulators.

www.ingramcontent.com/pod-product-compliance
Lightning Source LLC
LaVergne TN
LVHW010916300926
849194LV00025B/244
* 9 7 9 8 8 9 6 6 5 2 2 7 4 *